BETRAYAL IN HIGH PLACES

BETRAYAL IN HIGH PLACES

James MacKay

TASMAN ARCHIVES (NZ)

BY THE SAME AUTHOR

HMAS *Quilpie* [Action Thriller] Fiction

Rossiter's Farm [Boys Yarn: Comedy] Fiction

Fire of Samurai [Action Thriller] Fiction

Legacy of War [Action Thriller] Fiction

The Allied Japanese Conspiracy [Historical] Non-fiction

Published by
Tasman Archives (NZ). NSMC Auckland 10, New Zealand.

ISBN 1-897666-46-2

Grateful acknowledgement is made for the photographs supplied from the
Lillian Baker Collection on War, Revolution and Peace, the Hoover Institution,
Stanford University, USA

Wholly produced by
Gillingham Printers Pty Ltd of Adelaide, South Australia 5032

Contents

Preface vii

New Zealand Army and Police Department
    corroborating testimony xiii

Letters from the Prime Minister
    of New Zealand .... xiv, xv

Chapter 1   Voyage to Captivity 1

Chapter 2   Good Treatment and Benevolence? 13

Chapter 3   Prisoner of War 24

Chapter 4   Liberation 83

Chapter 5   Appointment with Destiny 89

Chapter 6   Investigations Commence 103

Chapter 7   The Tokyo Experience 1947-1950 118

Chapter 8   A Litany of War Crimes 1949 179

Chapter 9   Disillusionment 195

Chapter 10 Authenticated War Crimes Documentation 222

    Appendix: The Japanese Killing Fields 257

    Epilogue 260

    Biography: James Gowing Godwin
        1923-1995 261

    Alphabetical Index 265

Preface

I WISH to confirm the authenticity and true background of this book. First, let it be said it was only by diligent research, eyewitness accounts and recorded documentation that finally, such research was prepared in manuscript form.

Since 1951, I have been engaged in tabulating the horrors of war on a part-time basis and specialising in the Asia-Pacific War, 1941-45. Following my retirement from the Merchant Service I collated all of my notes and found sufficient material to warrant the preparation of a manuscript for publication. Nonetheless and before submitting the text, I found it appropriate to update the progression of history as it applied to events from the post-war years.

This was a daunting task that I did not originally anticipate. Many of my inquiries were stone-walled by officialdom who could have helped, but didn't. In some quarters my representations and persona were decidedly unwelcome, perhaps and because, I was getting too close to the truth.

My investigations – originally historical, became unavoidably political as I sensed, aye perceived, collusion and betrayal of everything our former Service Personnel fought to defend. Fortunately, I had a powerful but discreet ally in the person of the late Rt Hon Sir Robert Muldoon, Prime Minister of New Zealand, 1975-84. In his usual frank manner he offered advice on political matters and was particularly helpful in opinioning his view of the Japanese. Sir Robert was a World War II ex-serviceman.

Eventually I completed the first manuscript and submitted it to New Zealand based publishers. Without exception and for a variety of reasons it was rejected. Undeterred, I submitted the manuscript to publishers in Great Britain. There I was successful. In due course the work was published and remains available globally.

The title of my first book aptly conveys its content. *The Allied Japanese Conspiracy: Vol 1*, encapsulates the wartime barbarism of the Japanese as well as revealing the collusion that transpired – in the immediate post-war years, between Washington and Tokyo. I believe for this latter reason and no other, that the book was rejected by the publishing countries named. It was politically unacceptable.

Subsequently and quite astonishingly, further material came into my possession that I can only describe as incredible. It supports all the allegations and references identified in the first published book and removes beyond doubt the suggestion of conjecture and hypothesis.

I refer to material (in its original form) that was spirited out of the Meiji Building in Tokyo in 1950. Operating from this building which was part of SCAP, Supreme Command Allied Powers, were various Allied Liaison Missions, each charged with conducting investigations into Japanese war atrocities. They operated within the Legal Section of General Douglas MacArthur's Supreme Commander Allied Powers (SCAP) organisation.

This Legal Section, incorporating an investigations department, an apprehension department, numerous legal advisors and substantive administration facilities, was on the seventh and eighth floors of the Meiji Building that overlooked the Imperial Palace. Close by but situated in the old tower block of the Goodwood Park Hotel, was an extension of SCAP, accommodating the United Kingdom War Crimes Liaison Mission that was equally extensive. General MacArthur's Headquarters in the Dai-Ichi Building was a short two blocks away.

All buildings within the Jurisdiction of SCAP (General MacArthur), were guarded constantly by white-helmeted military police attached to the United States Occupation Forces.

At this point I feel obliged to address a generally held misconception. In late March, 1948, a cable was despatched from British Headquarters at Singapore to its counterpart in Tokyo. It informed that Britain's Asian and Pacific war crimes investigations and prosecutions was to be wound down. Furtherto, the Tokyo Mission was ordered to drop all charges it might currently be prosecuting, release all Japanese suspects being held in Tokyo's Sugamo Prison – some 55 men and prepare to close down the Tokyo British Mission.

Astounded by the suddenness of the Singapore directive, a message was sent across from the Meiji Building to the British Headquarters in the Goodwood Park Hotel, protesting the order and citing the fact that a Japanese Army private, now in close custody, had made a complete confession to charges of multiple murder and emphasising that voluntary confessions of this nature were rare. It explained how months of meticulous investigative work was involved in locating the suspect, and requested authority to proceed with the prosecution of this war criminal.

The following day – late afternoon, a reply was received via Singapore. The directive was concise and said, 'The prisoner must be set free immediately. All war crimes trials are to cease.' As a consequence of this order, all British arrested war criminals awaiting trial in Sugamo Prison and including the army private were immediately released.

The United Kingdom War Crimes Liaison Mission ceased functioning as such and closed down its operations within two months. Official communiques from SCAP at the same time announced to the world, 'The bulk of Japanese War Crimes has now been successfully completed with regard to investigations and prosecutions.' This was an ambiguous and totally untrue statement that is challenged in the following submission.

If, as the general public were led to believe, war crimes investigations and prosecutions were discontinued as from March, 1948, how then was it possible or for that matter feasible, for war crimes investigations and prosecutions to continue until 10 February 1950?

This is the misconception earlier referred to. Has history been deliberately misrepresented? And if so, for what ulterior motive? As this book progresses, clear and irrefutable proof will be exampled that not 'all' investigations and prosecutions ceased. But why the lie?

Still operating from the Meiji Building and under tight security, Allied Liaison Missions continued their work in tracking down Japanese war criminals – there were thousands to be interrogated. In support of this submission remains the fact – previously unknown, that Allied Investigating Officers continued to apprehend suspects – as they were found, for interrogation and where assumed guilty, prosecution.

The basis of this submission rests upon the simple premise of truthful and indisputable evidence. What, one might dare to ask, is this evidence? The evidence is the documentation and war crimes files spirited out of SCAP's jurisdiction in 1950. All of the material clandestinely removed from the Meiji Building was highly classified and sensitive to the political will ruling the day, and that was the last few days of February, 1950. Not 1948.

The documentation – still in remarkably good condition, bears witness to the fact that even in 1949, war crimes investigations were continuing until abruptly halted in 1950 and at the express orders of General Charles Andrew Willoughby, Chief of Allied Intelligence, second in command to General Douglas MacArthur and a member of the United States Armed Forces.

This documented evidence – particularly the recorded lists of names of Japanese war criminals released on the orders of General MacArthur, is most damning. Worse, is the indisputable fact that hundreds of Japanese war criminals, keenly sought after for monstrous deeds, escaped just retribution and apprehension on the orders of MacArthur.

Because of security considerations, these original files have been severally photocopied – an extremely lengthy process, and distributed to anonymous repositories. The originals have been sighted and perused by legal and judicial officers and sworn statements as to their veracity have been signed and countersigned in three separate affidavits. The original War Crimes Files and Documentation have been retained for posterity and secreted somewhere in Australia.

In a book of this nature it is not easy to know where to begin. Such is the impact of what will be revealed. However, and as a tribute to the late Army Captain, James Gowing Godwin, whose foresight enabled the compiling of the following chronicles, it would be appropriate to acknowledge the care with which James Godwin took to ensure that beyond his lifetime, the historical papers that he removed from under General MacArthur's jusidiction at Tokyo, survived.

It should be mentioned that James Godwin suffered for his country as a wartime prisoner of the Japanese and endured hellish cruelty. In his later writings as an appendium to his wartime diary, he expressed his indignation and concern, aye disgust at the blatant interference he encountered as an Allied Intelligence Officer – more particularly in 1949-50.

Power politics, James Godwin alleged, and in the interests of highly placed Japanese, impeded several criminal investigations. In others, orders were inexplicably received from the Dai-Ichi Building – General MacArthur's SCAP Headquarters, to release certain most-wanted war criminals who would surely have received life sentences or an appointment with the hangman, so notorious were their war crimes.

When abruptly ordered to cease all investigations in mid-February, 1950, James Godwin felt a sense of betrayal. Further orders to permanently dispose of all incriminating War Crimes Files – never mind that more than half of the known war atrocities remained to be prosecuted, or that their perpetrators – with the connivance of police and government officials, continued to evade apprehension. With an uncharacteristic decision, but understandable, James Godwin disposed of his files, not into the receptacles provided, but into his briefcase as opportunity allowed.

Nearly half a century later, the true murderous character of many wartime Japanese is once more exposed to unhindered scrutiny, but this time to the world in general. No longer may conspirators or mere mortals in high places issue orders and decrees of exoneration. Justice long subverted and truth wilfully suppressed, has with the attrition of time and circumstance won through. Thanks to James Gowing Godwin, a true patriot.

47/16B

Police Department,
WELLINGTON. C.1

2nd May, 1946.

MEMORANDUM FOR:-

The Adjutant-General, **Brigadier L.C. Stewart:**
Army Headquarters,
WELLINGTON.

PROSECUTION OF WAR CRIMES: FAR EAST: Lieut. James Gowing GODWIN
Your reference D.339/1/139/A

_____

In reply to your memorandum of 15th April concerning above,
a sworn statement has been obtained from Lieut. GODWIN and is forwarded
herewith, in duplicate, together with the copy of his notes which I
received with your memorandum.

Lieut. GODWIN declined to give information concerning his
detention in Camps in Japan and named several officers who he believed
had kept notes and had covered all he could state in their reports.
He said that he has already been interviewed by not only British and
New Zealand Army Intelligence Officers, but by American Army Intelligence
Officers.

Lieut. GODWIN's statement in the main is generally descriptive of ill-treatment by unknown Japanese, but there are instances of
definite allegations against a Japanese Naval Interpreter Named TAKI
and a Petty Officer named YAMA SAKA.

GODWIN expect to again leave the Dominion with a detachment
of the "J" Force.

(Sgd) J. CUMMINGS

Commissioner of Police.

Incl.

Sworn statement (affidavit) attached to Godwin's testimony with
regard to the sinking of the MV Behar in the Indian Ocean and
the brutal ill-treatment of passengers and crew by the Japanese.
[Refer File 47/16A]

Prime Minister
Wellington
New Zealand

15 July 1981

Mr James MacKay
71 Beachaven Road
AUCKLAND 10

Dear James,

I trust the information supplied with regard to the
Japanese, correlates with your own lengthy research.

As you affirm, much was concealed by the Allies in
the early post war years and it does credit to your
enduring perserverance to methodically record for historical
posterity, the fulfilment of such patient investigation.

I look forward to reading the book upon its completion.

With best regards,

R. D. Muldoon

R. D. Muldoon
Prime Minister

[Recipients comment]

Sir Robert Muldoon was NZ Prime Minister for nine years. He was a Returned
Serviceman (World War 11) and was a rare New Zealander by being forthright
and outspoken as well as a patriotic fellow-countryman. Even during his terms
as Prime Minister he never failed to answer my correspondence, or occasionally
speak with me. It was this esteemed Prime Minister who conveyed the opinion
of the then Attorney General that Article 14 of the San Francisco Peace Treaty
was flawed based as it was on the perceived illegal repudiation of human and
civil rights and the inalienable freedom of citizens to sue an aggressor
country for compensation for wrong doing. International Law, Sir Robert state
should not have been used to entrench a challengable 'Clause' whose main purpo
was to pervert the cause of justice and manipulate the very foundation of law.
He did caution the resources and organization required to challenge Article 14

J.M.

PRIME MINISTER

7 March 1995

Mr James MacKay
181 Manuka Road
Glenfield
AUCKLAND

Dear Mr MacKay

Thank you for your letters of 30 January and 9 February, and for the copy that you sent me of your letter to my colleague, the Hon Warren Cooper.

You asked for my interpretation of the statement that you highlighted in your second letter. My answer to you must remain the same as that of my Prime Ministerial predecessors: New Zealand is bound by the terms of the San Francisco Peace Treaty. This is a matter of international law. The decisions taken in the aftermath of World War II were made in the light of <u>what then seemed the best solution</u>. As a co-signatory of the San Francisco Peace Treaty, the New Zealand Government cannot re-litigate the issues after the event.

I am glad however that we live in a society where people can feel free to research and publish a book such as the one you have written, and where opposing views can be expressed strongly in public and without recourse to violence. Such values seem to me to be fundamental to our way of life.

Yours sincerely

Rt Hon J B Bolger
Prime Minister

[Recipient's comment]

The underlined statement of the Prime Minister is an admission that Article 14 — which was the subject of my letter to him, was based on an agreement of expediency. The Prime Minister was careful to avoid asserting that Article 14 (by itself) was legally sustainable. Instead he adopted a safer course by quoting International Law as being the Treaty's safeguard. He adroitly avoided the contentious issue of Article 14 other than to concede that quote **'what then seemed the best solution'**.

[Writer's comment]: A <u>best solution</u> is a vague excuse that cannot imply observance or the strict application of the rule of law.

J.M.

PARLIAMENT BUILDINGS WELLINGTON NEW ZEALAND

1

Voyage to Captivity

DAWN broke crystal clear on the morning of 9 March 1944, as the MV *Behar*, a cargo-passenger ship of 8,000 tons glided through the calm waters of the Indian Ocean. Averaging fifteen knots and on course for Ceylon from Fremantle, Western Australia, it was positioned 340 miles north-west of the Cocos Islands.

From the north a gentle spice-laden breeze immersed the thoughts of passengers and crew alike with visions of enticing shore-leave at Colombo before the ship continued on its way to Bombay. There were twelve passengers and sixty-eight crew on board – the latter mostly Lascars. The ship's officers – of whom there were eleven, were of British stock. As well, two seventeen-year-old apprentices (officer cadets) made up the balance of the crew.

At seven-bells – 7.30 am, the crew and some off-duty officers – engineering and navigation, partook of an early breakfast while passengers leisurely prepared themselves for breakfast in the officers' dining saloon at eight-bells – 8.00 am. All twelve passenger cabins were situated beneath the lifeboat deck and were comfortably appointed. To add to the passengers' comfort and service, each cabin was provided with a wireless speaker connected to the radio office at the rear of the ship's bridge. By means of a simple volume control fitted to each speaker, music or world news – usually from the BBC or Radio Australia, could be turned on or off at will. Some passengers dallied over their early morning toiletries while listening to the latest war news – which was encouraging. Others, blissfully certain that Japan was being hammered by the Allies, and dressed in light tropical clothing, were strolling in carefree manner along either the port or star-board passenger deck, working up an appetite for breakfast.

The *Behar* was a particularly fine ship and following its maiden voyage from England to Wellington, New Zealand, and being a part-refrigerated vessel, it loaded beef, pork and lamb along with a large tonnage in its chiller holds of butter, cheese and other dairy products. This valuable food shipment was destined for a beleaguered Britain.

On 13 February 1944, Lieutenant (A) S.C. Parker, Sub-Lieutenant (A)* R. Benge and Fleet Air-Arm Lieutenant (NZ)* J.G. Godwin, embarked aboard the MV *Behar* at Taranaki wharf, Wellington. All three officers were posted to war-service in England. At the last minute and prior to departing from Wellington for Sydney, Flight Sergeant (NZ) Allen Barr joined the ship as a fourth serviceman passenger. The other eight passengers were civilians who were merely travelling to Sydney.

After safely arriving at Sydney, the *Behar's* civilian passengers disembarked excepting Dr Lai Yung Li who acted unofficially as the ship's doctor. The *Behar* remained for four days at Pyrmont wharf within Sydney's inner harbour and took on board further frozen foodstuffs while its servicemen passengers availed them-selves of the opportunity to take in the sights of Sydney. Sydney's hospitality – according to the notes in Lieutenant Godwin's diary, was outstanding, though he did lament the shortage of beer – prevalent in Sydney at the time.

The MV *Behar* sailed from Sydney on 22 February 1944 and arrived at Melbourne on the 25th. For the next four days the holds of the ship were topped up with more frozen and chilled food-stuffs while once again the four allied servicemen took in the sights of the sprawling city, made all the more enjoyable with an ample supply of beer.

Their last night ashore was spent at Scotts Hotel in convivial company and where they enjoyed an excellent dinner. The following morning and prior to sailing, four more passengers

*(A) Australian
*(NZ) New Zealand

Fleet Air-Arm Lieutenant James Gowing Godwin

embarked. They were Mrs Shaw, Mrs Pascovey, Mr MacGregor and a merchant captain by the name of Percy Green of Butterfield & Swyre, a shipping company based in Calcutta and Bombay.

The ship sailed from Melbourne on the afternoon of 29 February 1944, and made an uneventful passage to Fremantle where a brief stop was made (at anchor) to enable a small naval party to embark. Their task during the intended voyage to Bombay via Ceylon was to man the four-inch stern gun in the event of an enemy attack.

From the date the ship left Melbourne, most of the passengers idled away the daylight hours in various pursuits. There was the ever present attraction of reading – on cold or stormy days, either in their cabins or the passengers' lounge, and in more pleasant weather, deck badminton, deck quoits, sleeping or just lazing around. In the evenings, cards, dominoes, playing the gramophone or piano, or just listening to the shortwave service of the BBC filled in the hours.

The only bad mark against the ship, but more properly the ship-owners, was the food. In Lieutenant Godwin's diary, it was described as the poorest victualling ever encountered. The Lascar stewards were also cited for being careless in the matter of food presentation and cleanliness.

The Captain of the *Behar* was named Symmons, the Chief Officer, Phillips; the Second Officer, Taylor; the Third Officer, Tate and the Radio Officer, Rowlinson. Because of the nature of their duties, the engineering officers seldom mingled with the passengers. Usually they were garbed in oil-smeared overalls when noticed, and spent a large amount of their time watching over the ship's brand new engines. Of the four passengers who embarked at Melbourne, the two women were en-route to Bombay to join their husbands. Mr MacGregor was on his way to buy a coffee plantation in Kenya for his only son who was serving in the RAAF. Mr MacGregor had originally lived at Nairobi, Kenya, with his wife and family until 1940 before deciding to re-settle in Australia.

Captain Green, a portly gent of varying disposition, was

returning to Bombay after spending three months leave in Australia. His company, Butterfield and Swyre, operated several 5000 ton cargo ships between Africa, Persia and Bombay, sometimes going as far away – in peacetime, as Australia and New Zealand. In the words of Lieutenant Godwin and quoted from his diary, 'I spent many late evenings with Captain Green on board ship drinking beer and the occasional whisky whilst shooting the breeze – yarning.'

On the morning of 9 March, and after an unusually good breakfast of bacon and eggs – a rare treat, some of the passengers went out on deck to play an early round of deck-quoits. The time was about 0845 hours. At 0930 the weather changed to a monsoon downpour – not uncommon in these latitudes but usually only briefly. Most of the passengers retired to the lounge to read, smoke or talk. At approximately 0950 the passengers were startled by an almighty bang coupled with a slight vibration of the ship. Everyone jumped to their feet and rushed towards the exit. A huge explosion followed which shook the ship from bow to stern.

The first thoughts of many were that the ship had been torpedoed. Further explosions filled the air while the ship vibrated constantly. Chief Officer Phillips appeared in haste and shouted an order not to seek safety on deck as shrapnel was flying everywhere.

The passengers remained crowded in the passageway amidst broken glass and the panic-stricken reaction of Lascar stewards. The chief officer attempted to restore calm as the explosions suddenly ceased. Cooly he ordered everyone to don life jackets and proceed to lifeboat stations where the Lascar crew were frantically engaged in the lowering of port and starboard boats.

What followed is easy to imagine. There was a concerted rush up rather steep stairs to the boat-deck. Emerging onto the boat-deck, the first fact noticed was that the rain and overcast had lifted. Away to the east, blue skies and sunlight beamed down between large breaks in the clouds. But chillingly, and much closer, was the forbidding presence of a large heavy cruiser.

Some passengers initially thought it was a Japanese battleship.

By this time the *Behar's* captain had stopped the ship with its stern and the four-inch gun facing the cruiser, the distance between the two vessels being about 1500 yards. Smoke from the forward section of the *Behar* drifted lazily around the ship, sometimes obscuring the cruiser from view. The *Behar* was afire forward and was starting to list to starboard – even though the shelling had been directed at its port side.

Convinced that the Japanese cruiser would not fire any more eight-inch shells at the disabled ship which was clearly doomed, passengers dashed below to snatch personal effects and clothing from their cabins. Equally as fast the passengers returned to the boat-deck only to find that the boats had been lowered, though the crew – already in the boats, had not slipped the grips.

Then the shelling recommenced. At point-blank range every shell struck the stricken *Behar* with destructive force. Amazingly, a couple of shells passed right through the ship's structure and sped on out to sea. They must have been armour piercing shells. Lieutenant Godwin managed to get a grip of one of the fall ropes and slithered down until his descent was terminated by a mass of dark-skinned bodies who were wailing their fright as shells screamed past above their heads before slamming with explosive force into the ship's battered hull.

The rest of the passengers including the ship's captain leapt from the boat-deck before splashing into the sea forty feet below. Shells continued to hit the *Behar*, one of them creating a huge explosion in the engine room. Chunks of the ship, wooden splinters and steel shrapnel began to speed around or ricochet in all directions as the doomed ship dipped its bow into the blue-green waters. That it was sinking was obvious, but still the cruiser kept firing.

Fortunately the crew had slipped the grips of both lifeboats but did nothing else. The boats remained stationary in the water and perilously in the line of fire. One or both of them could easily sustain a direct hit. Against every instinct of self-preservation, the captain and chief officer Phillips splashed and swam their way towards the lifeboat on the starboard side, oblivious to the shrapnel zinging into the water around them. Eventually they both succeeded in clambering into the boat, and none too soon.

By now the *Behar's* two forward hatches had slipped beneath the sea as its stern began to rear out of the water menacingly. 'Give way,' roared Captain Symmons to the terrified and paralysed Lascars. The lifeboat was almost touching the *Behar's* hull.

In response the Lascars wailed even louder, but not one picked up an oar. Cursing his frustration, Captain Symmons jerked his head meaningfully at Chief Officer Phillips. Each seized an oar and between them in the middle of a heap of terrified Lascars, began to row the cumbersome boat to possible if not tenuous safety providing the ship's downward suction did not drag the boat into its seething vortex.

Suddenly the shelling stopped. Then, faintly at first, but distinctly audible came the sound of a put-putting engine. From around the *Behar's* climbing stern, the port lifeboat appeared. It was packed with wide-eyed Lascars and some missing passengers along with three engineer officers. Swiftly lines were thrown and secured to the starboard lifeboat and without pausing, the almost motionless starboard boat was underway.

Quickly scanning the surrounding water, the second officer who was steering the motorised boat, veered slightly towards the sinking ship. There were two people in the water. One was Captain Green, the other, Mr MacGregor. European arms stretched out eagerly to pull the two men inboard as the first boat reached them. Sadly, the Lascars remained immobile and petrified. With everyone accounted for, though some were badly wounded by shrapnel, the motorised boat with the starboard boat in tow, chugged away from the *Behar* with most of the mid-ship section and bridge already engulfed by the inrushing sea.

In the succinct words of Lieutenant Godwin, quoted from his diary, 'Most of the Indians (Lascars) were useless bastards. The women passengers had more courage.' Lieutenant Godwin followed this comment by writing. 'Even after treating some Indian ribs to a few hefty kicks as an encouragement to man the oars, all I got was louder wails. What a useless pack of bastards.'

As it turned out, the *Behar's* stern gun received priority consideration from the Japanese cruiser. Two near misses effectively put it out of action through the expedient of killing three of the naval gunnery squad and severely wounding the remainder. As a consequence not one shell was fired from the *Behar's* flimsy defence.

As if to speed the *Behar* to the depths of the ocean, the cruiser's twin starboard turrets recommenced shelling what was left of the rapidly-sinking ship. Only its two after-hatches, mast and poop remained above water, and they were all angled at forty-five degrees. When the end came it was swift. As if to escape what was now obviously target practice, the doomed ship lurched even higher before rapidly sliding beneath the sea.

Feelings were mixed among the survivors. Some thought that the cruiser might come very much closer and machine-gun the lifeboats. Dark rumours abounded that the Japanese resorted to this barbaric practice. Others thought that as it was a very large warship and quite probably with an admiral on board, their massacre would be out of the question. Credence was given in quick snatches of conversation, that because the lifeboats and survivors represented no adversarial threat, that the cruiser might just steam away. Hopes were crushed following the cessation of target practice shelling. The cruiser stopped its slow circling and steered towards the lifeboats.

The weather had again become brilliantly fine and the smoke from the sunken *Behar* had cleared. Further to the north-east and about three miles away, two more Japanese warships were noticed. Clearly they too were heavy cruisers. Despite their grim situation and not knowing what lay ahead, curiosity extracted the opinion that the *Behar* must have run smack into the middle of a Japanese cruiser task force.

At 1100 hours, the heavy cruiser had approached to within 100 yards before drifting in a slow circle. From the lifeboats the cruiser looked huge and awesome. It was noticed with misgiving that all the cruiser's light armament was aimed in the direction of the lifeboats. Japanese seamen lined the cruiser's starboard rail, with here and there, groups dressed in green who stood out amongst the mass of white uniforms.

The motor of the port lifeboat had been cut and the line to the starboard boat cast off as the intention of the cruiser to close with the boats became apparent. Abruptly a voice speaking broken English sounded forth from a loud-hailer. 'You have been defeated. Do not be concerned. You will receive good treatment. Please to come aboard. Hurry, hurry or we will leave you.'

An intense discussion developed between the two lifeboats' occupants. To accept the invitation would mean becoming prisoners of war. Was that wise? Another line of thought – perhaps persuaded by considerable light armament aimed unerringly at the lifeboats, and supported by the two captains, was that it was most unlikely the Japanese would leave the survivors to be rescued and live to tell of the Japanese cruiser force in the area. Reluctantly it was agreed to accept captivity.

Between loud exhortations to accept good treatment and to hurry, the motor of the port lifeboat was restarted, a line once again secured to the second boat and ignoring the wails of the Lascars, the two boats were steered towards the waiting cruiser. A natural trepidation at what the future might hold, overwhelmed the minds of all excepting the Lascars. They too had heard stories of Japanese atrocities and didn't believe the promise of good treatment. Still uttering despairing wails – which was quite unnerving to the rest of the survivors, they shielded their eyes from the impersonal gaze of hundreds of Japanese seamen, convinced that their hour had come.

The port lifeboat was the first to nudge alongside the cruiser's after-deck, and with its motor stopped was made fast to ropes dangling beside two rope ladders conveniently positioned. Lieutenant Godwin was in the second boat that waited while the survivors from the first clambered in ungainly fashion up the unfamiliar rope ladders. His heart sank as he watched what followed. As each survivor reached the cruiser's railing they were assisted inboard in quite a rough manner and immediately and thoroughly searched.

Rings, watches, wallets, handkerchiefs, money, lighters and cigarettes, everything and anything of value or for personal use was seized. The survivors were then lined up and had their hands bound behind their backs, with a piece of rope leading from their tied wrists that was looped around their necks and retied to their wrists but only after their arms had been yanked upwards. Eyes bulged and breathing became laboured as the weight of trussed arms forced the looped rope around each survivor's neck to cut off air to the windpipe. Only by raising their arms further up their backs – an agonising procedure, could breathing be assisted.

Then it was the second boat's turn. 'We should have taken our chances,' muttered MacGregor. 'This is not good treatment,' he added. Lieutenant Godwin nodded his agreement to both comments. Naively he too had believed the Japanese promise of good treatment on the premise that beggars could not be choosers and in context to their present situation. Determined to thwart the Japanese he slipped his wristwatch into the sea after cautiously removing it. His wallet went the same way before turning to MacGregor urging him to do the same.

'What the hell are you asking me to do?' MacGregor grated as the Lascars began to fearfully climb the two rope ladders. 'My watch is a solid gold Omega and worth a good 400 quid*.'

Godwin shrugged. 'Can't you see what's going on, Mac? The Nips are seizing everything.' He glanced up at the cruiser's deck. 'Better to slip it into Davey Jones' locker than let those yellow bastards take it from you,' he added softly.

Mumbling his reluctant frustration, MacGregor unclipped the treasured watch from around his wrist and slipped it into the sea. 'I was awarded that watch from the Kenya Council for services rendered,' he rasped in a gulping sigh. 'Bugger the Japs!' he muttered vehemently.

Steeling himself Godwin stepped gingerly across empty lifeboat seats with the thought 'every man for himself'. As he

*Australian pounds ($800)

awaited his turn to climb one of the rope ladders his mind quickly raced across the sudden and dramatic events of the morning. There had been no time to make a proper count of survivors or to in any way care for the wounded. Fate indeed had dealt a cruel blow. Loud shouts and a babble of tongues made it clear to Godwin to leave the lifeboat and climb the ladder. Stepping past a securing line attaching the lifeboat to the cruiser he glanced down briefly at what he first thought was a swift tidal current. The thought was dispelled upon the realisation that the warship was probably slightly underway.

A little unsteadily at first but with resigned competence Godwin climbed the rope ladder with a growing determination that once level with the railings he would use his physical strength to assist himself inboard. At fifteen stone and an inch above six feet tall he had no doubt about his ability to avoid the clutching hands of his erstwhile rescuers.

Reaching the railings and with one swift glance a cruel sight met his eyes. Passengers, officers and crew alike, stood some-what hunch-backed in two rows. Their arms were pinioned in a truss-like manner behind their backs causing many to continually gasp for breath in wheezing intakes as the weight of their arms tied to the looped rope around their necks effectively made it a semi-strangulating noose.

Unmindful of clutching hands Godwin clambered over the railing, balanced and stood erect. A Japanese NCO – at least a foot shorter in height, barked an order. 'You will hands up pleese.'

Understanding the pidgin-English, Godwin complied – but not quick enough. A stinging slap to his face from the ill-tempered NCO made him see red. Throwing caution to the wind Godwin retaliated. In one swift movement he slapped the NCO back with angry vigour, the sight of the *Behar's* cowed and suffering victims adding impetus to his well directed counter-blow.

The NCO lost his balance and stumbled backwards. Startled yells and a babble of voices was swiftly followed by a rain of blows from rifle butts by angry marine guards. Strong as he was,

Godwin could not continue to endure such punishment. A vicious thwack to the head from a rifle butt dazed him, causing a loss of balance. Half-conscious he was roughly searched between clenched fist punches before having his hands forcibly tied behind his back. Then the dreaded rope was looped around his neck and slipped under his bound wrists. With a savage jerk his pinioned arms were raised almost level with his shoulder-blades before the rope from his neck was tightened and secured by knotting.

Immediately Godwin's breathing became laboured – as was intended. With kicks and blows rained on him by the still angry marines, he was forced to stumble toward the first row of prisoners and stand at the end of the line while the last of the lifeboat survivors came aboard. MacGregor was treated none too gently and suffered thuggery because he had the temerity to protest.

Even the remaining Lascars who had become docile and submissive, were handled roughly and punched without cause or more probably, because they had nothing of value on them. Incredibly and despite the fact that all the survivors had been unarmed, the Japanese took no chances. An officer stood by with a drawn sword and holstered revolver. He was clearly in charge of the twelve-man marine detail who were armed with rifles and fixed bayonets.

Standing motionless and in distress, the hot tropic sun and searing deck added to the prisoners' discomfiture. Thirst, a prelude to the many tortures to follow, was exacerbated by copious sweating and slow dehydration. All the metal fittings and deck seemed to radiate unbearable heat. If this was the good treatment promised, then, if worse was to come, it would be unbearable.

2

Good Treatment and Benevolence?

THE first act of benevolence was memorable if only for its sadism. After the last of the survivors of the *Behar* were taken on board the cruiser, a heavy machinegun was trained onto the lifeboats. At a signal from the sword-wielding officer it opened fire. Sustained and traversing bursts of fire raked the two lifeboats, reducing them to splintered matchwood. Satisfied, the officer ordered the firing to stop and signalled the demolished boats' securing lines to the cruiser to be cast off.

Turning his attention to the trussed prisoners he ordered them separated. Lascars in one group, ship's officers and the wounded naval ratings in another, and for a third group to be formed comprising the *Behar's* passengers. While this was being arranged with much pushing and blows, the officer heeded the request for water from many parched lips. Swiftly giving instructions to two unarmed ratings he turned his attention to the prisoners once more and spoke to them through the interpreter who had earlier shouted a promise through a loud-hailer of good treatment.

'You are now prisoners of Nippon. The Imperial Nipponese Forces are victorious in battle and will rid the Indian Ocean and Pacific of all Europeans. Because you have surrendered you are now number ten citizens. You will be treated well providing you obey the orders of your new masters. Water is being brought to you to cool you down.' Advisedly, the phrase 'to drink' was avoided.

The two ratings returned carrying a six-gallon container of sparkling water – an otherwise open-topped rice dixie. Enjoying and relishing the moment along with others in the know, the officer waited until the container of water was placed on the afterdeck. Then, beckoning to the survivors he gestured permission for them to shuffle forward to the enticing water. Awkwardly, because of the way they were bound, the prisoners moved forward, some of them asking for cups to be provided. The interpreter responded after listening to a few words from the officer.

'You will go down on your knees like animals do. No assistance will be given.' By this time hundreds of the cruiser's crew lined every vantage point to watch the charade and especially the humiliation of the Europeans. Protesting disgust and bitterness at such sadistic treatment, but anxious to slake their thirsts, the cruel advice was followed. Jostling for space those who were first – mostly Lascars, knelt before the dixie of water and with lowered heads thrust forward, drank greedily.

Spluttering shouts of dismay filled the air as shoulders and heads drew back from the dixie of water. Prisoners waiting their turn stood nonplussed with incomprehension. Gales of laughter and glee swept through the assembled Japanese seamen. The officer who had schemed the sadistic entertainment wore a smirk of satisfaction while sheathing his sword. The enticing liquid in the dixie was seawater.

Though some prisoners remained tempted, it would be madness to drink the saltwater. Resignedly, they shuffled back to their respective groups. The few who had gulped down some seawater would quickly suffer increased thirst as the tropical sun beat down relentlessly. Far to the east the silhouettes of two more Japanese heavy cruisers could be seen. All three warships were steering a north-westerly course – clearly seeking other allied ships to destroy. Thoughts about their dire predicament must have filled the minds of all the prisoners. To those who would survive captivity, March 9, 1944 would be indelibly etched forever.

For the next three hours and for no accountable reason, the three groups of prisoners were forced to sit motionless on the baking hot deck. The coolness of the constant breeze generated by the cruiser's brisk forward motion helped alleviate the intensity of the sun's relentless rays. No talking was allowed by the ever-present guards who strolled around the groups of prisoners with bayonets still fixed to their rifles.

The cruiser's personnel had largely dispersed now that the prisoners were no longer the object of curiosity and life seemingly had returned to normal aboard the warship – except for the prisoners. During this segregation of the three groups and for three long hours, sweating of bodies and dehydration took an exhausting toll. Those prisoners who wore scant clothing suffered worst. But every prisoner endured the agonies of sunburn on exposed arms and legs and on their faces and to the backs of their necks.

To compound this unnecessary torture, the wrists of many were bound too tight which stopped the circulation of blood to the hands. This made the pain in their arms practically unbearable along with the agony endured as weakened arms dragged down the rope encircling the prisoners' necks. Breathing became more laboured as a consequence. The NCO who had originally assaulted Lieutenant Godwin occasionally strutted about wielding a samurai sword. Each time he passed behind Godwin he either struck him a clenched fist blow to the head, or delivered a cruel thwack to his back with the flat of the murderous looking sword. He was a vengeful bastard as Godwin was later to write in his diary.

At the end of three hours sitting under the baking sun, a detail of unarmed Japanese went around the prisoners removing their shoes or whatever footwear worn. Then the ropes around their necks were removed before being ordered to stand. Following a barked order from the NCO, the Lascars were led away first. The *Behar's* officers remained standing in their weakened and thirst-ravaged condition, cracked lips and crimson-hued faces testifying their ordeal of intense sunburn.

The women had all their bonds removed – unlike the rest of the passengers. The wounded, most of whom were suffering from shell-blast or shrapnel inflicted injuries, pleaded for medical aid to alleviate their suffering. Stony-faced guards with slitted slant eyes merely babbled orders for silence. Clearly number ten citizens were to be treated as of no account.

A further half-hour went by before the sadistic NCO returned. Speaking rapidly and in staccato Nipponese he delivered orders to the once again alert guards. This was a noticeable mannerism of all junior personnel in the Japanese Armed Forces, they slavishly followed orders and respected authority as though they were robots. The NCO apparently was held in high respect or fear. Prodded by the tips of bayonets or impelled with the assistance of rifle butts, passengers and officers of the *Behar* were shepherded in rough manner across and along the cruiser's blistering hot deck, their bare feet stinging and burning with unbelievable intensity.

It seemed that every movement inflicted and ordered upon the prisoners was a preconceived and deliberate determination by the Japanese to inflict hateful punishment to their fair-skinned victims. A mind-set of pitiless and demeaning humiliation viciously imposed.

Lieutenant Godwin vividly recalls 'the iron ladder ordeal'. Pushed and shoved like cattle and with their arms still trussed awkwardly – and far too tight, the passengers were separated from the *Behar's* ship's officers and led to a steep iron ladder. Accompanied by shouts and much shoving they were ordered to descend. Trussed as they were it was a formidable task to negotiate each step of the steep ladder without the aid of the handrails. To stumble or lose one's balance meant a fall to the steel deck below. Inevitably and to the delight of the attendant Japanese, none of the passenger-prisoners made it to the bottom of the ladder safely. Most of them lost their balance halfway down and finished up in a sprawled heap on the deck below. Severely bruised and with their sunburned limbs scraped and lacerated they were nonetheless kicked and stood over by other Japanese until managing to stagger to their feet.

For some special reason Lieutenant Godwin was held back to last. The reason quickly became obvious. At fifteen stone and in the prime of life and standing head and shoulders over the accompanying Japanese, he was targeted for special attention. Besides, was it not he who had struck their NCO? Urging Godwin forward they waited until he had taken two descending steps from the fifteen to be traversed before deliberately pushing his body forward. Because of his trussed arms, Godwin was unable to flail the air or grab hold of the handrails. He fell to the deck below with a resounding thump that knocked the wind out of him, jarring every bone in his body and causing stabs of pain to lance through him. Amidst gleeful laughter from the Japanese and while still dazed from his heavy fall he was kicked and stamped upon by other Japanese tormentors below. Drawing on an inner strength, Godwin staggered to his feet and glared around him defiantly. At least it would tell the Japanese, he hoped, that he was not intimidated by such brutal treatment.

Though still suffering from a numbing kick to his testicles, Godwin put on a brave face – if only to disappoint his tormentors as he was led along a narrow passageway to join the rest of the passengers. Then his heart sank. Jostling with uncertainty – albeit with Japanese seamen shouting in his ears, they were being ordered to descend another iron ladder to a further deck below. Having experienced the trauma and pain of negotiating the first ladder, they were reluctant to repeat the exercise.

Shouts turned to blows as the passengers milled around, staring fearfully at the steep ladder. Cunningly, the Japanese encouraged the women to descend the ladder first. Their arms and hands were free and would assist their faltering steps downwards with the aid of the handrails. When both women had reached the deck below the Japanese began shouting impatiently for the rest of the passengers to follow. As Godwin expected, he was held back to last. Clearly it was hoped to break his spirit with a repeat exercise in sadism.

But this time Godwin prepared himself for the certain shove he could not avoid. When his turn came he stepped forward and taking care to keep his balance, ensured that each foot followed the other in quick unison. Thus and step by step, keeping his feet together as much as possible he descended the ladder. Below him several Japanese waited in a close semi-circle, their slitted eyes expressionless but with countenances revealing eager anticipation. The push from behind when it came was not unexpected. Instantly reacting, Godwin tensed his knees and sprang forward, the intention being – if at all possible, to land with his bare feet onto the deck below. His movement was swift and unexpected. Two of the several Japanese waiting below were not quick enough. With a crunching thud Godwin's 15 stone – feet first, landed on top of them.

Howls of rage and fury rose from the throats of Godwin's tormentors as he extricated himself from limp arms and legs. The two lightly built seamen had broken his fall but suffered grievously as Godwin's bodyweight flattened them. Both prostrate men were moaning softly as their compatriots endeavoured to even the score. Once more erect, Godwin endured a bout of thuggery second to none. Boots, fists and knee kicking came thick and fast as well as from all directions. It was lucky indeed that the armed guards had not accompanied the passengers, Godwin thought. It might have been rifle butts and bayonet jabs instead. The thuggery continued unabated and to a point where Godwin could stand no more. He was swaying on his feet when a Japanese officer appeared at the top of the ladder. A swift command from this doubtful saviour stopped the vicious assault and battery.

There followed a quick interrogation by the officer who when being answered, glanced directly at Godwin's bloodied face and bound hands before descending the ladder. By his insignia he was a Lieutenant-Commander whose authority appeared absolute. Poking a foot at one of the prostrate seamen he snapped an order to Godwin's assailants who were standing rigidly at attention. There was no compassion in the officer's expression as he turned to face the tall well-built European prisoner. 'You could be shot for this,' he hissed as the limp forms of the two felled seamen were carried away.

Godwin managed a weak shrug, glad that the Japanese officer could speak English. 'I was pushed from the third top step, sir. I could not help myself from falling,' he replied through swollen lips. Not a little concerned at the thought of being shot he added, 'I did not attack anyone. How could I? My hands are bound.'

The officer sucked through his teeth. 'Ah so! But the men say that you fell on two men deliberately. Is that correct?'

Godwin stood his ground. To admit that he did could well mean his being shot. 'With my hands tied behind my back all I could think of was falling safely. But then I shouldn't have been pushed in the first place surely, sir.'

The officer stared intently at Godwin's battered eyes with just a tinge of admiration reflecting from his own. 'I believe you,' he conceded. Then with a twisted smile he added, 'It seems you have been punished enough.' He glanced in the direction of Godwin's bound hands before adding, 'Either you are a fool or very brave.' Turning on his heel the officer ascended the ladder to talk to a group of seamen standing at attention around the top of the ladder. Snapping orders before face-slapping two seamen he disappeared from view.

Godwin's respite was brief. The seamen hurried down the ladder intent upon carrying out the officer's orders. Pushed, shoved and elbowed, he was propelled along yet another narrow passageway before being led into a confined and disused store-room measuring thirty feet by twenty. The room was well below sea level with an uneven steel deck. Packed into this room were all the survivors of the *Behar*.

It seemed strange that though the survivors were led in different groups from the main deck and via separate port and starboard entrances, they ended up in the same room together deep within the cruiser. It had been unbearably hot on deck but the oppressive heat below decks and without proper ventilation was just as bad. As Godwin was shoved into the room lances of heat coursed through the soles of his feet from the deck's metal plating. This incredible heat radiated itself into the confined space within which the survivors were crammed.

Sweat was pouring from bodies exacerbating the cloying humidity. Steel bulkheads glistened with moisture gathered from the combined perspiration of the overheated prisoners. A constant rumbling from beneath the deck suggested that the room was situated above the engine room, more probably than not, the boiler room.

Even the light clothing of the four guards present exuded copious moisture. Godwin took in the scene at a glance. Two guards stood by the open doorway with rifles and fixed bayonets. Two more carrying makeshift wooden clubs were walking between the seated rows of prisoners ensuring that legs were crossed properly – Bhudda style, and that backs were erect. Infringements were met with blows from clubs and shouts of anger from the two club-wielding guards. The buttocks of all the prisoners were absorbing unbearable heat from the steel-plated deck, but movement of their postures to temporarily relieve the acute discomforture was met with a tirade of shouted abuse and blows from clubs.

The Lascars sat in close-formed rows facing the starboard bulkhead. Behind them and in similar fashion, the remnants of the *Behar's* gun-crew sat likewise. Next to them sat the *Behar's* officers. The last row comprised the passengers and the Chinese doctor. All talk between the prisoners was strictly forbidden and punished with cruel blows. Naturally no one talked – not even whispered. Nonetheless punishment was carried out with vigour against those whose heads drooped or backs bent. The opportunity for such cruel sadism was often as not, administered at the mere whim of the guards. They really didn't need a pretext.

A mighty thwack from a rifle butt to Godwin's head made him stagger forward. A jab from a bayonet that pierced the skin of his left buttock added to his pain and shock. Roughly, he was propelled to a place at the end of the passenger's row and amidst babbling shouts sat down on the blistering hot deck next to Mr MacGregor. Sensibly, Godwin crossed his legs and sat erect. His head ached with the blow from the rifle butt and he knew that he was bleeding from the measured bayonet thrust to his posterior.

Like all the other prisoners he stared fixedly at the starboard bulkhead. Then began seven hours of inhuman torture. Twice the guards were changed during this long ordeal of sitting motion-less. The replacement guards were if anything, worse. Fired with a zeal to punish the enemy – particularly the Europeans, blows from wooden clubs were delivered with frightening regularity. Admittedly the Lascars were submissive and obedient, but then, so were the whites. But despite this blanket obedience, it was clear that the Europeans were being singled out for special ill-treatment. To Godwin's tortured mind, this was not war, it was genocidal hatred.

Thirst, a human desire at first, became a demanding obsession as bodies craved for water. Dehydration, the stinging after-effects of severe sunburn, the shrapnel wounds – especially of the naval gun crew, heat exhaustion and the lingering pain inflicted by wooden clubs, all these things were too much to bear. Mr MacGregor who was sixty-three, was the object of contin-uous sadism. By now not caring much whether he lived or died and with his advancing years a wearying handicap, his head began to droop more frequently and his back to slump.

With perverse cruelty the guards continued to club MacGregor until mercifully he slumped backwards unconscious. Furious at MacGregor's incapacity to endure punishment, the guards vented their wrath on other passenger prisoners, particularly Godwin who by now was black and blue and with eyes so swollen, one was closed up completely.

The good treatment promised by the Japanese prior to capture was just one big lie Godwin thought as he continued to stare at the starboard bulkhead. All feeling in his trussed arms and hands had gone. Dazedly he wondered if his tightly bound wrists had ulti-mately coagulated the blood in his hands. Might he now lose them by necessary amputation? He hoped desperately that the blood circulation had not been completely cut off.

Thirst, unsatiated and excruciatingly demanding, was such that he no longer perspired. Thoughts of the *Behar* and its creature comforts now consigned to the depths of the ocean, were inter-rupted by the arrival of an NCO. Staccato barked commands

heralded blessed relief. Moving swiftly behind the rows of prisoners and stooping down, the guards cut the prisoners' bonds. For
a few moments Godwin felt no relief, a mind-set that created the
fear he had permanently lost the use of his hands.

Slowly at first, then more positively, exquisite tingles of pain
spread through his hands. Traces of feeling began to overcome
numbness, but try as he might, Godwin could not make his arms
respond to the urge to slope forward and rest on his lap. It seemed
as though they were paralysed.

Moving between the rows of seated Lascars, guards completed
removing their bonds before kicking and shoving them to their feet.
Then in single file they were led from the room. Next came the turn
of the wounded naval ratings and the *Behar's* navigation and engineering officers. They too were led out in single file. One of the
naval ratings, a youngster barely twenty, actually had a piece of
shrapnel protruding from his abdomen. A large patch of coagulating
blood interspersed with signs of fresh bleeding, indicating to even
the most callous that he was seriously wounded, made no difference
to the pitiless guards. Clubbing the wounded rating about the head
and shoulders, they hastened his departure from the room.

Until ordered to stand, Godwin sat motionless. Thoughts of the
Geneva Convention crossed his mind at the sight of such mindless brutality. The slanted and slitted eyes of his captors making
him wonder bemusedly if perhaps they might have originated
from a different planet. Their actions were not human nor were
they civilised. In numerous ways they acted like robots, but with
an insatiable lust for inflicting maximum pain and humiliation
and, he soliloquised to himself, they had the brazenness to call
themselves The Sons of Heaven.

MacGregor though sitting up, was clearly a sick man. One of
his ears had enlarged and turned purple – the result of a vicious
blow from a club to his head. His neck and upper arms showed
obvious signs of club marks. Deep-seated contusions – an angry
purple in colour, serrated his neck and arms, the crotch of his
white shorts were stained a faint yellow, a consequence of invol-
untary urination precipitated by the beatings endured and his

lapse into unconsciousness.

Godwin gritted his teeth while mentally vowing that if he survived, such brutality that he had witnessed and endured, would have a day of reckoning.

He cautiously flicked a quick glance at the guards with his one good eye. They were standing in a group jabbering with the NCO, occasionally directing malevolent glances at the intimidated prisoners. What new form of sadism Godwin thought, were they scheming?

The answer came in accustomed Japanese form. With gestures, blows and a few well-aimed kicks, the exhausted prisoners were forced to their feet. The two women looked at the end of their tether as once more standing upright they leaned against each other for support. MacGregor had to be assisted to his feet, fatigue and heat exhaustion weakening the capacity to help himself. Godwin stood nearby helplessly, still unable to move his arms sufficiently. Though his hands felt warm and moveable they remained strangely weak. The best he could offer was an encouraging smile – that hurt, from his battered face. A guard noticed the smile and reacted quickly. With all the vigour his short stature would allow he swung an open palm upwards catching Godwin completely off-guard.

Reeling back from the stinging face slap Godwin glared out from his one good eye and down at the puny guard. He appeared no bigger than an average fourteen-year-old European boy. But what the guard lacked in size was compensated with a surfeit of malice and cruelty. Godwin suppressed his renewed anger and instead stared woodenly at the deck-head anxious not to undergo a further bout of thuggery. His face felt swollen and his cheekbones ached. Blood from freshly opened cracked lips trickled into his parched mouth. Sighing inwardly he dwelt on how much more brutality he could endure from the hateful little yellow men.

3

Prisoner of War

THE preceding chapters were taken from the handwritten diary of Lieutenant (Fleet Air Arm) James Gowing Godwin. The author has attempted to narrate the feelings and experiences of Lieutenant Godwin as impartially and factually as possible. One cannot help but be moved by the suffering endured or remain impervious to the moment as each brutality is recounted. Clearly the serving ranks of the Japanese Armed Forces were convinced that the war for them had already been won and that there would be no accountability.

Because the following chronicles encapsulate the intrigues and wheeling and dealing that prevailed in post-war Japan, necessity compels a condensed resume of Lieutenant Godwin's experiences as a prisoner of war. His diary – well written, cogently articulates the evil intentions harboured by the Japanese in their war of expansionist aggression. Having been at the receiving end of appalling brutality, Godwin had no hesitation in characterising their unscrupulous mentality.

'The Japanese are a dangerous lot,' Godwin wrote. 'They cannot be trusted. They make promises with no intention of observing them. Inherent to their nature is the propensity for deceit, deviousness, cunning, intransigence and false politeness. As Europeans we find it difficult to accept or interpret such combinations of duplicity and to ignore these characteristics is to do so at our own peril. Japan will not be satisfied until either it conquers or owns the world. That is its goal. That is its ambition.'

Godwin's diary goes on to record the following trauma of captivity. 'I was made to take my place at the end of the line before we marched out of the stinking hot hell-hole that had been our torture-chamber for well over seven hours. My left buttock ached with pain following the use of my legs. The bayonet jab I had suffered earlier must have been deeper than I had first thought.'

'Extreme thirst, a most trying frailty, screamed within us for relief. I could think of nothing else but cool water. Led by a guard complete with rifle and fixed bayonet, we shambled along passageways and up and down steel ladders that sloped steeply. The handrails were a boon to our weakened state as we followed the guard like submissive lambs. Every now and then a rifle butt was jabbed into the small of my back accompanied by shouts to move faster. It was my bad luck to be at the end of the line because immediately behind me was the other armed guard. I prayed that he would not use the bayonet-end of his rifle. Once was enough.'

'Eventually we arrived on the after main-deck and were led towards a crude row of makeshift toilets. They seemed put together for use by dwarfs. We were halted and made to wait in compulsory silence as the two women and three other prisoners used the WCs. At this point and while waiting my turn an evil bastard broke away from a group of watching Japanese seamen and kicked me good and hard in my left buttock. Not only did my bayonet wound begin to bleed again, but spasms of pain coursed through my body. "You brave bastard," I muttered.'

Shouts of anger from the two armed guards close by followed by the unslinging of their rifles seemed to suggest that this cowardly attack was frowned upon and would not be allowed to be repeated. Godwin was quickly disabused of this notion. His muttering was considered the more serious offence and was suit-ably punished. Thwack! A rifle butt wielded with moderate force hit him on the back of the head. Godwin staggered forward seeing a myriad of stars. The cruel and unexpected blow not only dazed him but caused a partial loss of balance. Drunkenly he strove to remain on his feet as arcs of pain lanced through his body.

Responding to Godwin's reaction with glee, ripples of laughter came from a score of delighted seamen who appeared to relish the sight of this big European being punished by a fellow Nipponese. Godwin for his part took no notice of the merriment that his torment caused. Instead, he managed to stand upright once more though with the blackest ambition. He savoured the thought of strangling with his bare hands the guard who had delivered the cowardly blow. But then, as reason returned, the presence of the other guard deterred him. He too was armed with a rifle and fixed bayonet.

Sighing with inward relief Godwin managed to stoop his large muscular frame past a small opening in the makeshift canvas screen that covered and ensured the privacy of the WCs which were nothing more than used five-gallon paint containers. Sitting on the sharp edged rounded tops was extremely awkward, more so for Godwin as he tried to avoid his bayonet wound from coming into contact with the metal edge. But oh the blessed relief to be able to relieve himself. Irritable shouts from the waiting guards to hurry up dispelled the sheer pleasure of being alone no matter how briefly.

Having finished his primitive toilet and once more standing at the end of the line of prisoners, Godwin followed the footsteps of others in front of him and proceeded to weave a most confusing return to the inner bowels of the cruiser. This time three steep ladders were traversed before finally the leading guard halted at the end of an oppressively hot passageway. Barking orders and pointing his rifle menacingly he indicated to the prisoners to enter a searingly hot room similar in size to the one where they had first been imprisoned. The ship's captured officers and two youthful cadets were already there but stared at our entrance blankly. They had been forbidden to talk. Hunger and desperate thirst afflicted all of us as the passengers sat down alongside the seated officers and on a very overheated steel deck.

The same rumbling thud of ship's engines could be heard from beneath the deck, only this time somewhat louder. Noticeable was the absence of the two armed guards. Once the passengers were seated beside the ship's officers, they disappeared. With mouths parched and tongues swollen, no one had the inclination to even whisper. Thoughts centred on water, cool, cool water. Two unarmed Japanese seamen stood languidly by the entrance to the room. They were watchful but not hostile. There was no sign of wooden clubs which was a heartfelt relief to everyone. The Lascars presumably had been returned to their original imprisonment room or perhaps? Disposed of. This was not idle conjecture as the Japanese were capable of any atrocity.

The clatter of metal cannisters from the passageway aroused an instant hope for water, perhaps food too? Nostrils keened the hot air seeking a whiff of food, while ears strained hoping to hear the lap of water. Like salvation at the twelfth hour, two catering orderlies stepped into the room carrying dixies of water, rice and soya patties. In a small container a small pile of blue enamel bowls and chopsticks completed the pending feast.

As if on cue, a junior lieutenant entered the room. Like automatons the four Japanese snapped to rigid attention. Godwin observed the slavish discipline of the seamen in the presence of an officer. His thoughts fleetingly turned to the lieutenant commander who had suggested he might be shot. There too at the base and at the top of a steel ladder, a number of seamen had also stood at rigid attention in the presence of that officer – even when face-slapped by him.

Glancing around the room and at the prisoners, the lieutenant spoke in clipped imprecise English. 'You will to eat now. Pleese, no talking. You will to stand in line. You will to drink water first. Bowls of food will be given. Pleese then to return to your places for eating. No talking.' He glanced once more around the room before adding, 'Lights to go out in half of an hour.'

Pleased and gratified sighs of relief swept the room as the lieutenant made a quick exit. Perhaps the stifling heat in such closed quarters was too much for him. Shuffling and staggering to their feet officers and passengers alike including the Chinese doctor formed the semblance of a line. The *Behar's* captain ensured that the two women and the two young cadets stood at the front of the line. One of the Japanese orderlies dipped an enamel bowl into the container of water before passing it to Mrs Pascovey. The other orderly served a reasonable ration of boiled rice and a soya pattie into another bowl and passed it to Mrs Pascovey who had already half-consumed her bowl of water. This procedure was followed with the rest of the passengers and officers until everyone was attended to. Then, the dixies containing the food, a few leftover bowls and chopsticks, were taken away by the departing orderlies. However, the container, still half-full of water was left in the room intentionally. Were the Japanese human afer all? Godwin wondered as he returned to his place on the uncomfortably hot deck. After seating himself he luxuriated in the sensation of water trickling down his throat. The feeling was exquisite.

The two unarmed Japanese guards were as relaxed as the prisoners and chatted amiably between themselves as they lounged by the room's entrance until four more ratings arrived with short planks, canvas and an empty five-gallon paint drum. For the next fifteen minutes constant activity could be heard from the passageway intermingled with the sound of sawing and hammer-blows. The two amiable guards frequently exchanged chatter with the work detail and for the most part were now standing in the passageway watching proceedings.

Without close supervision and helped by the distraction of the work party, the prisoners exchanged furtive but whispered conversation. They were all appalled at their earlier treatment, especially the women who were still in a state of shock. The wounded naval ratings aroused the most concern and compassion. They had endured the same punishments as the others but displayed a very special kind of fortitude and stoicism, enduring the pain of their untreated wounds in silence, which in any event was forced.

At great personal risk Dr Lai Yung Li surreptitiously examined the wounded ratings with a fixed expression of helplessness. In a properly equipped surgery he would be able to remove the splinters and suture the open wounds. With the aid of local anaesthetic the task would be painless and with the aid of antiseptics and adequate bandaging, the young ratings would quickly recover.

The pity of it all was the certainty that the cruiser would have a well equipped sick-bay and dispensary on board as well as a surgeon-commander and probably two doctor-lieutenants, but perversely and because prisoners were considered number ten citizens, medical treatment was denied. Without such medical treatment – indeed surgery, the rating with the steel splinter deep in his abdomen was sure to eventually die. Complications and ill-treatment would ensure the correctness of his diagnosis.

Returning to his place on the deck the Chinese doctor gave a helpless shrug to those around him. Without the barest of facilities he could do nothing. Mr MacGregor who had chosen to sit beside Godwin whispered, 'I wonder how long we'll be prisoners in this hell-hole? At least the guards are not as vindictive as the other lot that we had to put up with. God Almighty! I never thought I'd end up as a prisoner of war, especially of the Japanese. Christ! They're right bastards.'

Godwin eyed the room's entrance as he whispered back. 'I wish I knew, Mac. But don't let the Nips get you down. They're just picking on you because of your age.' He forced a twisted smile. 'Aren't you glad now that you slipped your watch into the sea?'

'Too damn right,' MacGregor whispered feelingly. 'God!' he exclaimed softly, 'I need more water. This heat's killing me.'

'Hold on,' Godwin whispered. Hissing louder than he would normally dare, he caught the attention of one of the cadets who was filling bowls with water for the women, the wounded and the incapacitated. The cadet who was still not yet eighteen made his way to Godwin's side. 'Mr MacGregor needs more water, lad,' Godwin whispered while reaching across for MacGregor's bowl. 'How much water is left?' he thought to ask. 'About a quarter of the container, sir,' the cadet whispered back.

Godwin nodded. 'After you've brought Mr MacGregor's water, you'd better tell Captain Symmons how much is left. He might decide to ration it as God knows when we'll get any more. The Japs are so unpredictable,' he whispered back with a meaningful stare.

The cadet nodded and moved away gripping MacGregor's

bowl. Godwin sighed with thankfulness that the cadets had not
been singled out for special punishment other than the unavoid-
able brutalities endured by all. Youth was on the cadets' side and
would certainly help to sustain them in the uncertain times ahead.
His brief musing was interrupted by the arrival of a sour-faced
chief petty officer who stamped into the room and immediately
shouted, 'No talkee. No talkee.'

The whispering ceased instantly. Glaring around the room the
NCO rasped in poor English. 'Numer ten citzens lisen. Your lavat
is alonga passage. Go now soon lights sleep. You do same. Lights
on only in passage. Do not try escape. Much punishment will
follow.' His baleful glare changed to a sneer. 'Nippon Number
One. America-Australee Number Ten.' Turning away he snapped
orders to two relief guards armed with wooden clubs. Standing
behind them holding rifles with fixed bayonets stood two more
guards.

Godwin groaned inwardly. It was unlikely the guards with the
wooden clubs would set about clubbing people in a darkened
room. But what about necessary visits to the toilet installed in the
passageway? For a brief time the prisoners had not been
tormented or punished but now, it seemed that the Sons of Satan
had returned. He watched the chief petty officer's quick departure
with foreboding.

One of the club-wielding guards noticed the quarter-full
container of water. In a gesture of pure malice and with his back
turned to the prisoners, he urinated into it. The second guard
followed suit as did likewise the rifle carrying guards. Inward
sighs of despair and a feeling of returned hopelessness filled the
hearts and minds of the prisoners. Only sadists could stoop to
such a despicable act. With the constant heat and quite hot deck,
thirst would quickly return. Barely had the guards stopped
laughing at their own perverted sense of humour than the lights in
the room went out.

All the guards stepped out of the darkened room and into the
lighted passageway. Their muted conversation became casual,
desultory. Occasionally one of them would stand silhouetted at

the room's entrance staring into a darkened void, his ears straining for the slightest whisper of conversation, with a rifle or club at the ready.

Exhausted by the day's traumatic events and marvelling at their survival from the cruiser's eight-inch guns, the prisoners stretched out on the constantly hot deck each vowing individually and silently to avoid going to the makeshift passageway toilet if at all possible. The presence of the four hostile and armed guards could not bear thinking about. For some, thirst had already returned, but with the water deliberately spoiled, their thirst had to be endured. For others who could not easily go to sleep, their minds wondered about the simple matter of time. Was it night? Was it day? All sense of time or the hour eluded them. Eventually sheer fatigue dispelled such thoughts whereupon the healing mantle of sleep took hold.

Godwin slept in fitful dozes. The heat of the deck was such that to lie prone for too long in one position produced a pins and needles sensation that denied an undisturbed sleep. Besides, the hardness of the steel deck with all its discomfort ensured a rest-less night. At first Godwin thought he was dreaming a whispered voice in his ear, then a hand on his shoulder brought him fully awake. 'What's wrong?' he muttered, his one good eye searching to identify the face above him in the darkness.

'It's me, Mrs Shaw,' a trembling voice above him whispered. 'I can't hold on any longer but I'm scared to go to the toilet on my own.' She paused before adding. 'The seriously injured sailor wants to go to the toilet too, James. Will you accompany us? There's safety in numbers isn't there?'

Godwin sat up and peered towards the entrance before replying, 'There's four of them, Mrs Shaw,' he whispered. 'Numbers don't mean much to the Nips. Anyhow, ask Mrs Pascovey if she wants to relieve herself. I'll move across to the wounded rating and wait for you there.'

Two minutes later and with shared apprehension, Mrs Pascovey, Mrs Shaw, the wounded rating and Godwin presented themselves at the room's entrance before calling to the guards. It was Godwin who made their request clear. Pointing to his crotch he asked, 'May we use the toilet please?'

To the left of the guards the passageway ended up against a steel bulkhead. To the right and some forty-five feet distant it ended at the base of a wide steel stairway. There was no sign of a makeshift latrine. One of the guards holding a wooden club appeared to understand. Beckoning to the prisoners he led the way towards the sealed off end of the passageway. He had taken no more than eight paces before stopping at a steel door set into a steel bulkhead. Opening the door he latched it back to reveal a large cupboard that had been emptied of its contents and turned into an ingenious WC. Gesturing impatiently he indicated to the women to step forward and use it first.

Godwin stood back with his gaze averted before staring with alarm at the wounded naval rating who was swaying on his feet. Oppressive heat and a steady loss of blood along with a high temperature had produced a state of semi-consciousness in him. 'I don't feel too bloody good,' he managed to gasp weakly.

'No talkee! No talkee!' a guard holding a rifle shrilled. Gripping his club firmly another guard stepped forward, his slitted eyes and inscrutable expression concealing his sadistic intention. Thwack, thwack! two swift blows from his club and delivered with force on the rating's head and shoulders had the desired effect. The rating slumped to the floor unconscious.

'You bastard!' Godwin hissed. 'The man could be dying!'

Another guard unslung his rifle with a mean look on his face. Clearly punishment was in order because both of the male prisoners had spoken when forbidden to. Dropping to one knee Godwin turned the rating over onto his back, mainly to relieve the pressure of the steel splinter digging further into the wounded man's abdomen. Thwack, thwack, thwack, three swift blows to his shoulders and head from behind and delivered by the club-wielding guard monitoring the latrine, almost felled Godwin. Rising unsteadily to his feet he turned to face the cowardly attacker.

Crunch! a jolting blow to Godwin's head delivered by a rifle butt and from behind, felled him. Collapsing to the deck and with stars and lights straining his optic nerves he remained motionless, stunned if not concussed. It may have been seconds or minutes, Godwin couldn't be sure until noticing the absence of the women. Probably he thought dazedly, it was minutes. he must have been knocked unconscious by the blow from the rifle butt.

He came back to reality with the sensation of being kicked. A jabber of alien voices shouting at him. Rapidly Godwin recovered his senses if only because the kicking hurt. Opening one eye he stared up at his tormentors. Four pitiless and inscrutable faces stared back at him. Another vicious kick to his ribs compelled the urgent effort to regain his feet. Rising unsteadily and hurting all over he managed to stand upright before watchfully glaring down at the short-statured guards. Apart from a blood-stain where the rating had fallen, he too was missing. Godwin's thoughts raced.

He jerked a glance at the makeshift latrine. It was empty. Perhaps he was back in the room? Maybe the women assisted his return to the room's tenuous safety? Or, a more chilling thought crossed Godwin's mind. Had the wounded rating been disposed of?

Another blow from a club wielded with considerable force and accompanied by angry shouts from the guards hastened Godwin's retreat back to the darkened room. Once inside he stumbled towards his place on the deck. Thirst and heat exhaustion were no help to his pain-wracked body. His head ached with splitting spasms of acute discomfort as he wearily slumped onto the ever-hot deck. Before lying prostrate he searched with his one good eye about him. Dimly he could see the badly wounded rating lying motionless between his less wounded mates. Sighing with helplessness Godwin stretched himself out to try to sleep. He knew no more until awakening to a fully lighted room.

Thus ended the first day and night as prisoners of the Japanese. The good treatment promised had been a deliberate lie. Godwin's body ached abominably as he slowly strove to achieve a sitting posture like the others who were already awake. The heat was oppressive and his tongue and mouth felt like sandpaper. Thirst, now a constant companion, became a plaguing obsession. The supply of water seemed very much in the hands of the guards. 'These morons knew our distress and need for water, but delighted in their power to supply or deny,' Godwin later wrote in his diary.

Two hours after awakening, the prisoners were provided with rice and barley balls by two inoffensive catering orderlies. A fresh container of water was also supplied. While the orderlies dispensed the food and water, a petty officer strolled around the room before eventually pausing beside the naval ratings who were helping their seriously wounded comrade to stand on his feet.

To his credit, the petty officer peered at the rating's severe abdominal wound, muttering softly in Japanese to himself. Then, as if to satisfy some inner curiosity, he slowly walked past the line of prisoners, glancing keenly at each one in turn.

Godwin's face came in for particular attention as did Mr MacGregor's contused ear and badly bruised face and upper torso. Turning abruptly on his heel the petty officer stamped out of the room beckoning the four guards to follow him. There followed a plainly audible tirade and what sounded like wooden clubs falling to the deck. From an angle the rifle-bearing guards could be partly seen standing to attention. One of them was wearing a chastened look.

The two orderlies exchanged knowing glances while dispensing the food and water. They could naturally understand what the petty officer was saying. Obviously the petty officer could not speak English but if he had, Godwin would have had no hesitation in reporting the matter of the night guards urinating into an earlier container of fresh water. Among the many sadists on the ship, was it possible that there was at least one Japanese human being? The mere thought gave the prisoners a silent hope as they sat on the deck quietly eating their food.

The orderlies had collected the food dixies and made a swift exit from the overheated room. But like their first visit, the fresh container of water was left behind. The two rifle-bearing guards patrolled the passageway without once pausing and scowling menacingly into the room. The other two guards – now without clubs – remained by the entrance looking somewhat crestfallen. Without weapons of assault they looked totally harmless. Godwin took a chance and whispered to MacGregor, 'That PO must be a decent cove. It's obvious he's given all the guards a good ticking off. I'm glad the clubs have been removed.'

MacGregor nodded. 'But what happens when that PO goes off watch? Will other Sons of Satan return?' he whispered back.

Godwin shrugged. 'Your guess could be right, Mac; in that case we should whisper to the others to go to the toilet now,' he gave a tired smile. 'While we have tamed guards.'

Quickly the suggestion was spread in whispers. Then in ones and twos the prisoners approached the unarmed seamen guarding the entrance for permission to go to the bonjo (latrine). This was grudgingly given and without recourse to verbal abuse, blows or kicks. For the next hour a semblance of sanity reigned. The armed guards patrolling the passageway remained watchfully aloof, but in no way hindered the progression of prisoners to and from the toilets.

Without the aid of clubs the guards ignored the whispered conversations taking place in the room. They could however have kicked and used their fists, but in the stifling heat and without weapons had not the will. Perhaps, Godwin thought, there might be another reason. Were the guards expecting the petty officer to return? This could explain their continuing exemplary conduct. He knew that discipline was strict and unquestioning obedience to orders absolute, but with authority absent? It was a conundrum that exercised his thoughts.

It was just after Captain Symmons had ordered the two cadets – who were detailed to dispense a third of a bowl of water each hour – that a party of four rifle-carrying guards, without fixed bayonets, arrived at the entrance to the room. Godwin's earlier conjecture was proved right. Into the room stepped the 'human' petty officer accompanied by a rating who, judging by the insignia on his uniform tunic, was attached to the cruiser's

Signals Division. Standing before the seated prisoners, the petty officer gestured to the rating to speak.

'Pleese you will listen,' the rating began. 'You will follow the guard detail up to main-deck. There you will have your temperatures taken and health checked. All wounds will be treated. Afterwards you will have shower wash and be disinfected. Afterwards you will be returned to this room and provided lunch. Because of your good behaviour you will continue to receive good treatment.' The signals rating jerked a quick bow before beckoning the prisoners to rise. The two unarmed and morose guards swiftly hurried forward to help the women to their feet before turning to assist Mr MacGregor.

Godwin climbed to his feet unaided, staring hard but not unkindly at the 'human' petty officer. Mentally he vowed that if the cruiser was sunk in battle and the crew captured, he would put in a good word for the petty officer – that is, if they both survived. The voice of the signals rating and the clipped way he spoke English also rang a bell. It sounded very much like the voice that had hailed the lifeboats from the cruiser. Certainly the promise of good treatment sounded the same and had a familiar ring. As for the two former club-wielding guards, Godwin was not impressed. Their sudden solicitude for the prisoners was purely for the petty officer's benefit.

MacGregor stood beside Godwin and whispered, 'If that good treatment promised is to be believed, we can only expect it when this PO is on duty. What do you reckon?'

For a reply Godwin gave an assenting nod. He was quietly studying the correct formalities of naval discipline. There was no shouting or knee-jerk reactions, nor was there any shoving, clubbing, elbowing or kicking. Clearly, the officer in charge dictated the behaviour of those under him. It could either be sadism or chivalry. Feeling perfectly safe – for a welcome change – Godwin took his place at the end of the line, confident he would not be cracked over the head with a rifle butt, or have the wind taken out of him with a blow to the small of the back.

Traversing passageways and steep stairways, the group

suddenly emerged into bright sunlight and just in time to view a Mitsubishi reconnaissance aircraft being catapaulted from the cruiser. Further back and in shielded bays, two similar aircraft waited in reserve or as replacements. Godwin noted everything his one good eye could record. The gun turrets were large and from each protruded twin eight-inch guns – formidable armament. There wasn't the time to assess all of the cruiser's light armament but clearly, it was considerable. Recalling the lifeboats' approach to the warship the previous day, Godwin was satisfied that it had four twin-gun turrets which made eight heavy guns. A cruiser to be reckoned with.

Unexpectedly and while Godwin waited patiently at the end of the line, a thermometer was slipped into his mouth. Two medical orderlies led him by the arm to a first-aid deck dispensary and quickly checked him over. Removing the thermometer, his name and injuries were written down after which he was steered in the direction of a ten-foot square enclosed by sturdy canvas six feet high. Two Japanese seamen were directing a fine but copious spray of seawater into the structure's interior.

This was the shower-wash earlier promised. Godwin relished the thought as he stripped off his light clothing and entered the makeshift shower-room carrying his clothing with him. A rating handed him a small tablet of Palmolive soap – probably captured, as the first delicious stream of water fell on him. The shower lasted five minutes during which he soaped and washed his bloodied underwear and shorts and to a lesser extent his blood-spotted shirt. All the while a pleasant spray of water cleansed his skin. Then it was all over.

Heeding orders to leave the shower, Godwin stepped out and quickly wrung out his light attire. Within a couple of minutes he was clothed and standing beside the deck dispensary. A medical orderly gestured to him to lower his shorts and underwear. There followed several pricking sensations that indicated his buttock bayonet wound was being sutured. It was an uncomfortable experience without a local painkiller but at least his wound would now have a chance to heal. Liberal swabs of antiseptic were applied to the cuts and contusions on his scalp, face and neck. An eye mask was placed over his blackened and swollen right eye before finally he was motioned to rejoin the line of prisoners waiting to return to their hell-hole prison above the engineroom.

Godwin had been astute enough to note the sun's position in the sky. He estimated that, give or take fifteen minutes, it was about 12.30 pm. Resuming his place at the end of the line and feeling refreshed – even his clothing was already half dry under the tropical sun, his spirits lifted even more as two ratings stopped beside him and offered a full mug of water. Drinking thirstily, he swallowed the precious fluid in five gulps. Returning the empty mug to the water detail, he let out a satisfied belch. The only immediate discomfort was the extremely hot deck.

Two guards armed with rifles and fixed bayonets took up position behind Godwin. Suddenly alarmed he peered towards the front of the line of prisoners. There were two more similarly armed guards but standing a little to one side was a most unwelcome and not to be forgotten face. Its owner was none other than the sour-faced chief petty officer of earlier acquaintance who had declared that Nippon was Number One and a few other slanted comments. Godwin's heart sank as the order was given to move off with the sour-faced CPO leading the way. The 'human' PO seemingly, was now off watch. Swallowing his disappointment and trying to dismiss trepidation, he shuffled forward in motion with the prisoners' progress.

On the circuitous route to their prison-room he was clubbed once on the head for being too slow in descending a steep ladder and on several occasions suffered painful jabbing rifle butt thumps to the small of his back for no apparent reason. But it was while traversing an area close to a seamen's mess that undisciplined mayhem erupted. Godwin describes it as follows.

'A crowd of mean-looking bastards spilled out of their messroom. Some were gripping broom-ends and other items useful in an attack. The assault was swift and delivered with bloody-minded malice. Blows were rained on the prisoners with hateful ferocity as they shuffled past. Cries of pain and distress were completely ignored by the chief petty officer. He never looked back once. I suffered countless blows even to having a steel dixie slammed against the side of my head. It was struck with sufficient force to cause me to stagger with dizziness. As quick as the assault started, it was over. Chuckling merrily, the seamen melted back to their mess-room. To add to the injustice I received a blow across the nape of the neck from a rifle butt for staggering out of line. I still suffer from this injury with spasmodic twinges of pain years after this vicious incident.'

The constant blows to the head from rifle butts were not only damaging to the skulls but must have been responsible for many minor fractures and brain damage that in the years ahead – if the prisoners survived – would manifest into debilitating disabilities. But then, it was wartime and the Japanese could do as they pleased.

Once more bruised and battered, the prisoners returned to their prison-room and sat on the baking hot deck in terrified silence and with their backs erect and faces staring at the port-side bulkhead at the behest of the sadistic CPO. To ensure obedience to this order, two guards, armed once again with wooden clubs, prowled between the seated prisoners, occasionally inflicting blows for the slightest infraction. For some sadistic reason one of the guards delighted in striking Mrs Shaw – she invariably yelped with pain that seemed to give this thug a perverse buzz. The CPO had left the room but his cruel orders were being faithfully obeyed.

Mr MacGregor was in bad shape and began to mumble in spite of the order for total silence. Accordingly he was beaten more than most. Godwin who was seated beside him silently cursed his utter inability to prevent the mindless brutality. Then came blessed relief. Two catering orderlies entered the room with dixies of food and a container of precious water. Following them came two medical orderlies supporting the seriously wounded naval rating. He had been operated on and the shell splinter removed from his abdomen. But there seemingly, mercy ended. He was returned to join the rest of the prisoners and to endure their hardship and vicissitudes.

Doctor Lai Yung Li had been separated from the white prisoners during the rough medical treatment on the main deck and was transferred to join the imprisoned Lascars who, happily, were still alive. Some of the Lascars had been sighted by the two young cadets who had been taken to a separate table for questioning. These snippets of information had been relayed between the prisoners in whispers while awaiting their return to the prison-room.

At an order from one of the club-wielding guards, the prisoners rose unsteadily to their feet and formed themselves into a line to be fed. Sufficient has been said to convey a mixture of scant mercy, rigorous punishment, mindless cruelty and vicious brutality. It is time now to follow the mind-numbing experience of captivity that followed.

For seven long days the prisoners were confined to the prison-room. During this time the *Behar*'s officers and Godwin were taken up onto the main deck and closely questioned by interrogating officers who could speak passable English. On the two occasions this occurred little information was elicited other than name, rank and serial number – if applicable. Godwin was closely questioned about the strength and composition of New Zealand's Armed Forces but surprisingly, he was not pressed to provide the location of New Zealand military camps or naval installations. The Japanese knew this already.

On the afternoon of 15 March, the three cruisers in line ahead proceeded up the Sundra Straits. They were met by four Japanese destroyers detailed to escort the larger warships to port. In anticipation of disembarking the prisoners that evening they were brought up on deck and herded into a tight group though forbidden to sit. The Lascars and the Chinese doctor were also brought up from their prison-room and made to stand in another tight-knit group on the opposite side of the cruiser.

The several warships made an imposing sight though somewhat depressing to the eyes of the prisoners. It did appear that the Imperial Japanese Navy was invincible. To port was the coastline of Sumatra, to starboard, Java. At about 5 pm a reconnaissance aircraft was catapaulted from the cruiser, quickly disappearing from view. The name of their cruiser – Godwin was able to find out – was the *Tome*. By the general condition of the ship it was plainly evident by its neglect and barnacle-encrusted sides that it had not been dry-docked or serviced – probably from its commissioning. In many areas it was filthy dirty, only the armament standing out in a state of pristine readiness.

Water, ever a human need, especially to the prisoners subjected to the sun's fierce rays, was denied. With parched mouths and dry lips they waited for an end to their misery aboard the cruiser. At 7.30 pm and finally, the cruiser dropped anchor in Tanjung Priok harbour – the port for Batavia – now renamed Djakarta. Throughout the night and well into the next morning, the prisoners remained guarded by seamen armed with rifles and fixed bayonets. They were allowed to sit but no water or food was provided. Those who wanted to urinate were permitted to release their bodily waste through the ship's railing. Sea snakes, of which there appeared to be plenty, glided across the harbour's still waters, gobbling up excreta expelled by the prisoners.

Twice during the very warm night, tropical downpours occurred. Lasting no more than ten minutes each time, they provided sufficient cooling water to satiate thirst through the expedient of opened mouths and cupped hands. Saturated clothing was savoured with quiet pleasure if only because it provided a cooling effect and diminished the ever constant malaise of prickly-heat, a discomforting scourge.

With the sun once more beating down relentlessly on the heat-exhausted prisoners, and at about midday, a Japanese lieutenant accompanied by six armed guards arrived and proceeded to read out the names of prisoners who were to be transferred to another cruiser. They were as follows.

Captain Symmons, Lieutenant Parker, Lieutenant Benge, Chief Officer Phillips, the *Behar's* Radio Officer, Lieutenant Godwin, Captain Green, Dr Lai Yung Li, Mrs Shaw, Mrs Pascovey, L/S Kershaw, Apprentice Griffiths, Apprentice Williams, A.B. MacLeod (Bosun), F/Sgt Allen Barr and Chief Engineer MacWeir.

Immediately following the announcement of names for transfer, food in the form of riceballs and water was issued. Ravenously hungry and thirsty beyond compare, the meagre rations were quickly disposed of. The water was treated like nectar for the gods as parched mouths and rasping throats savoured the cooling liquid. Godwin notes in his diary that it was his twenty-first year and that on the morrow it would be his twenty-first birthday.

At 1.30pm those selected for transfer were forced into a line and had their hands bound tightly behind their backs. A long rope was then looped around each prisoner's neck and tied to the next prisoner's neck, etc. Then, without delay the prisoners were shepherded from the cruiser, down a gangway and onto a large motor launch. Talking was forbidden as was glancing around the harbour. To ensure that the prisoners saw nothing, a canvas screen was quickly erected to achieve this objective.

The prisoners were heavily guarded and with an officer in charge. After about twenty minutes through a rather choppy sea, the launch came alongside the cruiser *Aoba*, which the prisoners later learned was carrying the admiral in charge of the cruiser force. After cumbersome climbing and with some difficulty, the prisoners ascended a primitive-type gangway at the stern-end of the cruiser. Some amusement was afforded to the cruiser's watching sailors when one of the guards fumbling with his rifle, fell into the sea and had to be fished out with a boat-hook.

The accommodation provided was exactly the same as the previous cruiser, excepting that if anything, the room was even hotter. Rough treatment was immediately dished out as bonds were swiftly untied. Elbowing, kicks and shoves preceded outright thuggery. For what reason none of the prisoners could understand. If it was a hate syndrome, then, that's all it could be. The prisoners were tired of becoming punching bags, but for their own safety dared not protest. Barely had the prisoners been ordered to sit on the deck and face the starboard bulkhead, than an evil-looking petty officer stamped into the room accompanied by two armed guards. He shrilled in poor English:

'Lieutenant Parker! Lieutenant Godwin! You follow quick time. Hully, hully.' Bemused by his selection and that of Parker, Godwin rose to his feet. What devilment was in store he wondered. At this point Godwin recounts in his own words what followed.

'Parker and I were led out of the hell-hole and compelled up ladders and down ladders and along numerous passageways. Talk about a rabbit warren! At times we passed grinning monkeys or sour-faced individuals who looked anxious to do us a mischief. I felt bloody nervous because the armed guard immediately behind kept jostling me with his rifle. Judging by the overpowering heat and the noise we were in close proximity to the engineroom. A small steel-meshed door screened from the top to its centre was unlocked and I was pushed inside.'

'I found myself in nothing more than a cubbyhole – about the same size as a WC closet. There was just enough room to sit on the floor with knees drawn up. I started to protest but the Jap NCO barked "Silence!" The door was slammed and locked in my face. As soon as that bloody door was shut I started to feel the heat, real heat. It was simply terrific. Huge steampipes attached to the small deckhead exuded an intense heat. There was no ventilation. It was like a furnace. I stripped off my meagre clothing while starting to sweat profusely. The deck was unbelievably hot as were the bulkheads. I tried to lie down and rest. The effort very nearly finished me. Almost cooking, I watched as steam rose from the sweat pouring from my body and from the condensation accumulating on the deck. I pleaded through the steel mesh to the armed guard on duty for water. He stood unmoved, inscrutable and impervious to what I was enduring.'

'Repeatedly I called out that my cell was too hot and that I was thirsting for water. He didn't budge. Surely this bastard must have known my distress even if he couldn't understand me.'

'After about an hour a full-bearded first class petty officer (the "jaunty" I think) unlocked the door, handed me a huge bottle of water and entered into a discussion with an officer who had also arrived. After a couple of minutes the officer went away. During their conversation I took copious gulps of water from the bottle. Almost immediately my sweat glands began working again. Motioning for me to follow him, the first class CPO led the way as I clutched my discarded clothes and the precious water bottle. The armed guard also followed, but never closer than three feet behind.'

'After what seemed a dozen passages and several ladders we passed through what was clearly a chain locker – practically on top of the gear used for hauling up the anchors. A solid steel door was opened though it did have many rounded perforations. These were obviously intended for ventilation though most of them were clogged up with grease-laden grime. Once inside the small room and with the door locked behind me, I glanced around with a sort of hopeless interest. Judging by the variety of long-dried paint spills, it must have been a once-used paint locker. At least I had sufficient room to stretch out and sleep and not on the deck either. Two large canvas covered scrubbing boards laid end to end would suffice as a crude bed. From the deckhead a lightbulb that was to burn incessantly night and day gave ample light. The steel deck felt cool as did the bulkheads.'

For a number of days Godwin was kept confined and alone but only for the reason of more intense interrogation. Being a Fleet Air-Arm pilot and attached to HMS *Illustrious*, a British aircraft carrier, the Japanese felt that Godwin could supply much more valuable information. Hence his isolation for ready accessibility. For the next few days Godwin was interrogated at great length, but try as they might, the Japanese could not elicit any more information than they had. Despite Japanese disappointment, Godwin was not clubbed or ill-treated. Food, mainly rice and though frugal, sustained him. A container of water was placed in the paint locker each morning, and a guard was always available to escort him to the WC as required.

After lunch of two small biscuits and some foul-smelling black pickle and on the eighth day of isolation, Godwin was released from his 'private quarters' to join up with Lieutenant Parker who had similarly been confined, but in a proper ship's 'brig'. He too had been constantly interrogated. Almost like an anti-climax, departure from the cruiser was brisk and sudden. Together with all the European prisoners who looked drawn and thin, they were taken ashore by launch and incarcerated in a newly-opened prison camp.

If treatment of prisoners on the cruisers was considered less than civilised, then, in the prison camps, it was plain barbaric and primitive. Guards, from the most humble private, insofar as prisoners were concerned, seemed to be a law unto themselves. At the slightest pretext and upon any imagined excuse, they would administer suitable punishment. Forgetting to bow to a soldier of Nippon was usually punished most severely. Sheer thuggery or a crack over the head with a rifle butt could be expected for this imagined insult.

The camp that the *Behar* prisoners were taken to was situated between the port and Batavia. Food was plentiful to the indigenous natives of Java, but not to prisoners of the Japanese. Intentionally or otherwise, a regime of wilful rationing was imposed. Often as not the rice – quite often cooked the previous day, would be served the following evening and likely as not was on the verge of fermenting. Either the cooks were the worst in the world or were following instructions to make the food as unpalatable as possible, Godwin's diary notes.

'Though we were constantly hungry, the food when supplied, was bloody awful. Typically a dirty looking fire bucket would be brought in to our hut and which would be full of riceballs with a few bits of rotten cucumber or pickle on top. The food smelled like stale beer and was most unappetising. Few of us – despite our hunger, could stomach this trash. Often as not unless our hunger became desperate, the bucket would leave our hut half-full. A side effect to this bad food, was the certainty that those who were really hungry and cast caution to the wind and choice, ended up with severe bouts of diarrhoea.'

Godwin goes on further to relate: 'Each evening at 8.30 the hut doors were opened wide and we were made to stand up in two ranks for about half an hour until an officer made his nightly rounds. Our best efforts in shuttering all ventilation and window-less apertures to repel ravenous mosquitoes was completely undone. In that vital half hour thousands whined their way in to plague us for the rest of the night. We were bitten so often that sleep became near impossible. Later on we found that sleeping during the morning or afternoon – when the mosquitoes were absent, was the clever thing to do.'

'What all of us disliked about the prison camp was the uncouth-ness and occasional brutality of the guards, the absolutely rotten food, no protection from mosquitoes and having to stand up for up to an hour – depending on what Japanese soldiers were guarding us, until an officer made his rounds. The latrines were another problem. Primitive, stinking and without paper or water-flushing, we were forced to use broad-leafed plants or our fingers to wipe an individual's anus. After three weeks we gradually resigned ourselves to sitting out the war as prisoners of the Japanese.'

'On 10 April 1944, an officer and NCO, both armed with pistols, came into the camp and rounded up all the *Behar* survivors, Lascars excepted, whose whereabouts was unknown to us. We were ordered into a large bus which drove out of the camp and onto the main Batavia-Tanjung Priok roadway. I don't know the actual direction but eventually the bus turned in at the entrance to a large private house. With gardens ablaze with flowers and neatly manicured lawns, it brought back nostalgic memories of an almost forgotten civilisation. Alighting from the bus we stood in line as the officer began to read off six names.'

'Captain Symmons, Captain Green, Lieutenant Parker, Lieutenant Benge, Dr Lei Yung Li and Seaman Bosun MacLeod.' Godwin goes on to describe the grouping of those whose names were called and the arrival of two armed guards from the front porch of the house. The rest of the prisoners were ordered back onto the bus which then resumed its journey. The prisoners left behind were last seen being escorted towards the house.

After several changes of direction and a half hour later, the bus turned into the entranceway of another grand house. Alighting from the bus the rest of the prisoners led by the Japanese officer walked towards the house with the NCO bringing up the rear. Puzzlement, even wonderment, filled the thoughts of all the prisoners as they entered the house and filed through a spacious hallway and out to a well-shaded back porch. After being lined up, names and rank – where applicable – were read out, after which the ages of all present were asked. Again Godwin's diary is quoted.

'An ugly gold-toothed European-looking Nip, who I later learned had been a spy in England, told us not to worry. We would be okay. A number of Japanese officers were strolling about in pairs or sat in garden chairs. The instant we were told not to worry, I became uneasy. With formalities over, this bastard who I named Toothy, led the way to small out-houses with stone and brick floors. The chief engineer and first mate were put in the same room, the others myself included, in separate ones. As I further learned, the property belonged to a Dutch planter who had built up a prosperous business but who was now incarcerated in a prison camp. The out-houses were originally built as extra guestrooms.'

'We stayed in these peaceful and civilised surroundings for countless days during which time, and for reasons beyond me, I was interrogated by Nip intelligence officers twice each day. There wasn't a damn thing I could add to earlier questioning aboard the cruiser. For some peculiar reason I seemed to be considered a master-spy which did not help my peace of mind. Spies usually were shot. These persistent bastards seemed to have it fixed in their bird-brains that I flew reconnaissance and intelligence flights, not combat missions. They were particularly interested in the camera gear used to photograph Japanese installations from the air.'

'My return to New Zealand for a spot of leave, now that the war was going favourably, was not believed. I was told it was their belief that I was more probably instructed to return to my country for further intelligence training. It was pointed out to me that junior members of the Imperial Japanese Armed Forces did not

and would not return home until the war had been won. The same
criteria surely applied to the Allied aggressors? It was best I
confessed as continuing kindness and patience extended to me
could not continue to be guaranteed. This garbage was impressed
upon me every day without fail.'

'New Zealand, I was assured, was marked for conquest as was
Australia. Sooner or later Japan would control the destinies of
both countries. They were sparsely populated and would be
colonised by Japanese pioneers, therefore it was useless to resist.
As an inducement I was offered repatriation to Australia and
100,000 guilders if I cooperated and told all I knew. On some
days the interrogations were conducted brusquely accompanied
by threats of being handed over to the Kempei Tai – the Japanese
Military Police and equivalent to the Nazi Gestapo. On other
days cigarettes and blandishments were the order of the day, even
attempts at pseudo camaraderie. I was becoming convinced that
my inquisitors were well-educated, reasonably well-informed
and as unpredictable as an aroused snake.'

'As for my quarters, they had once been comfortably furnished.
But now, spartan would be the more correct word. I had two thin
grass mats to sleep on and two small grass mat pillows. A large
single window had been boarded up and the single set of french
doors covered by a rattan venetian blind. Suspended from the
ceiling hung a large and most welcome mosquito net. The single
electric blub glowed night and day, but this did not bother me. A
wash basin and large jug of water for ablutions was left intact as
was an ornate wall mirror. The latter was a most useful guide in
reflecting my physical condition. Gone were the marks of thuggery inflicted aboard the cruisers. My eyes were both normal and
I was growing the traces of a beard. I could see that I was looking
thin, but nonetheless felt reasonably well. Even the bayonet
wound in my buttock was almost healed.'

'The food was reasonable, but oh how I hungered for bread – an
item never provided during my entire incarceration as a prisoner
of war. Rice was the staple diet and had no appeal, but if I wanted
to survive I had to eat it. I should add during the many interroga-

tions, I was not struck once in anger. At times the Nip officer's patience did wear thin, but on such occasions, threats not blows were delivered.'

'On the afternoon of Saturday 15 April, I was questioned by the Nip officer in charge of the place. He was a major in Army Intelligence. He asked me exactly where I was going if the *Behar* had arrived at Ceylon and why I continued the cock and bull story of rejoining the aircraft carrier *Illustrious*. I remember him sighing with feigned regret as he politely conveyed the news that I would be shot the next day for non-cooperation. It was up to me whether I lived or died. I could tell this crafty bastard nothing of military value but really began to worry. To be sentenced to death at twenty-one was a hell of a thought. That night I slept little. I kept imagining being tied to a pole and blind-folded. A severe thunderstorm that night did not help matters, to my tormented mind, the cracking and booming sounded like a firing squad volley. Sleep eventually overcame me.'

'The next morning – it was still dark – two armed guards roughly shook me awake. I dressed quickly being anxious to avoid blows from rifle-butts, and followed them to a waiting truck. I climbed into the back with the two guards following close behind. There ensued a rather long drive – almost an hour – before finally the truck halted beside some other vehicles in an isolated clearing. Alighting from the truck my hands were bound behind my back as "Toothy' stepped from the truck's cab. He gave an ingratiating smile before asking if I had reconsidered my perilous position.'It was now full daylight and I could take in everything at a glance. My blood froze as my eyes briefly rested on three newly dug graves – waiting for occupants. There were no execution poles to be seen as I licked dry lips. I had the wind-up and a sudden desire to urinate. But all I could do was to shake my head. A party of Nip soldiers stood in a group holding rifles. Without doubt this was the firing squad.'

"Toothy" smiled evilly. "Tell the truth and you will be spared," he softly hissed.

'I stared back at him dumbly. I simply had nothing to say.

"Toothy" swung on his heel and joined three other Nip officers who were chatting away amiably. All three of them were wearing evil-looking samurai swords. From behind another parked truck three dishevelled and battered figures emerged. That they were Allied soldiers there was no doubt. By their tattered uniforms I guessed that two were Dutch and one, Australian. I was damned scared myself but couldn't take my eyes off them as they were led with their hands tightly bound behind their backs, towards the waiting graves.'

'A feeling of nausea swept over me as the three prisoners were forced to kneel at each grave. "Toothy" swung a glance in my direction and rapped an order. I was jabbed in the back with a rifle-butt and forced to walk to within twelve feet of the condemned men. My two guards took up position each side of me. What followed is hateful to relate.'

'The three sword-carrying officers strolled towards the kneeling soldiers unsheathing their samurai swords as they did so. Their faces were expressionless, pitiless, as they approached their intended victims. I was being forced to watch barbaric executions that I had only heard about. I felt sick wondering why I was to be shot while the prisoners in front of me were to be beheaded. Perhaps the Japanese liked cruel variety, part of my brain screamed. But then, a shaft of hope raced across my mind. Where was the fourth grave? Mine?'

'Clinging to a tenuous hope that I might yet be spared, unless my body was dumped into one of the existing graves, I stood weak-kneed in a mesmerised trance. The kneeling prisoners looked around and up at their executioners with defiant expressions as spread-legged, the officers casually inspected the cutting edges of their swords. It was not just the heat of the early morning sun that made me perspire. I was sweating with emotion, fear and anxiety and wondered if the three condemned men felt the same, though by their counte-nances it was difficult to tell.'

'Unexpectedly the three kneeling men stared at me. They would have noticed that I too was bound and a prisoner.'

Two voices called across in Dutch, "Hierbij neem ik afscheid."

Then a solitary voice accompanied by a defiant grin. "Gidday digger."

'Three swords flashed. Three heads were parted from bodies. It was a hell of a drama watching the heads drop out of sight and two bodies keeling forward, blood still pumping from severed necks. The Australian was slumped forward with blood spurting from his headless trunk. Indifferently, the officer who had beheaded him, used the toe of his boot to despatch the body into the grave. Immediately three Nips armed with shovels set about filling in the graves. The Japanese watching the executions looked with admiration at the three officers who had performed the deed. The executions were a text book example of one-stroke efficiency. I couldn't see compassion on any of their inscrutable faces.'

Godwin's notes record the fact that unaccountably he was marched back to the truck and assisted – because of his bound hands, into the back. If the Japanese had wanted to put the fear for his life into him, they succeeded. One of his guards, 'quite good-looking for a Nip' opened a small canvas satchel during the return journey to the house. He passed across a mango to the other guard and bit into one himself. Then, glancing at Godwin, he extracted a small banana from the satchel, peeled it and offered the fruit. Godwin shrugged his thanks indicating with his eyes that he couldn't use his hands. The guard nodded understanding and held the banana to Godwin's mouth. It tasted good and with the guard's thoughtful assistance he ate it to the last piece. If ever there was a conundrum this was it, Godwin was to later write. It was almost like a split-personality. On the one hand the Japanese could be vicious and cruel. On the other, some but not all, could display a rare kindness. An enigma indeed.

Once returned to the house, Godwin was escorted to his room and left in comparative peace for the rest of the day. He had the uninterrupted time to reflect on the morning's events and to dwell on the bravery of the executed soldiers. Not one of them cried out for mercy. He would always remember that. Accompanying his evening meal of rice balls and a passably good curry came none other than 'Toothy'. Displaying his gold teeth in a flashing smile he told Godwin that he came as the bearer of good news. As from the next day he (Godwin) was to be assigned to the garden detail. He would be required to mow lawns, weed gardens, collect rubbish and burn it. The work would be light and healthful and he could eat as many mango or coconuts as he liked from the trees and palms surrounding the house. 'Toothy' went on to say that it was only by his intervention that he (Godwin) was not executed because he ('Toothy') believed that when questioned again, Godwin would be sensible and tell all.

'The lying bastard,' Godwin wrote in his diary. 'This moron deliberately put the fear of Christ into me. I'm not sure if he's playing mind-games and fancies himself as a psychologist. But one thing I'm sure of, this bastard has psychopathic tendencies in a most cunning way.' Strangely and for the rest of Godwin's confinement at the big house, he was not questioned again.

Days turned to weeks in almost unreal tranquillity. Godwin enjoyed the gardening chores and with a plentiful supply of fruit available whenever he wanted it, his weight returned to fifteen stone. One day while gathering up some rotting leaves, a snake not much bigger than a large lizard wriggled along his arm before dropping to the ground. Being from New Zealand where there were no snakes, he recoiled with revulsion. He had felt a prick in the palm of his hand an instant before, but initially guessed that it was a thorn. Now alarmed, Godwin stared at his right hand. There were two tiny puncture marks close-set and visibly swelling. There was a sick-bay of sorts set up in the spacious hallway of the house. Without hesitation he ran towards the house much to the startlement of a nearby guard.

Once inside he dashed toward an ex-Dutch Imperial Javanese guard whose job was house security. 'I've been bitten by a bloody snake,' Godwin croaked. 'Are there antidotes handy?'

'What snake, what snake?' the guard responded, more than anxious to help.

'A little bugger,' Godwin answered. 'Not much bigger than a lizard. I think it was green and black, ah, sort of mottled!'

The Javanese guard smiled, 'There are many of them in Java. Make you sick. Not kill. Where bite?'

Godwin thrust out his right hand. A soft reddish lump beneath the two punctures looked ominous. 'I fix,' smiled the Javanese. In an instant he had gripped Godwin's wrist with one hand and with the other withdrew a bayonet from its scabbard. Without pausing he jabbed the bayonet point into the reddish lump.

'Ouch!' Godwin yelped, taken by surprise at the guard's quick action and the sharp hurt that followed.

'You go to water tap. Do not lift arm. Soon all venom gone,' the helpful guard urged. An irate Japanese guard panted into the hallway, but stopped short on noticing Godwin's bloodied hand. The Javanese guard indicated a wriggling snake with a motion of his hand before pointing to Godwin's limp arm.

'Ah so!' the Nip guard nodded his understanding. Slinging his rifle he led the way to an outside water tap. Godwin followed feeling his right hand throbbing and wondering. Was it the snake-bite or rough surgery? For the next twenty minutes he bathed and squeezed his injured hand until reasonably satisfied the venom had been expelled from his system. He was about to go to his quarters for a lie-down, when looking up he noticed a medical captain approaching. Dr Magata Haruo visited the house twice a week, mainly for the benefit of the large number of Japanese officers billeted. It was his day to call.

'I am told you have been bitten by a snake,' he stated pausing beside Godwin. 'Are you feeling sick?' he enquired.

Godwin shook his head. 'Not really, doctor, but the hand hurts though.' He extended his hand for the doctor's inspection.

'Hmm?' the doctor pursed his lips. 'The veins in your arms are not distended. That's a good sign. Go to the sick-bay in half-an-hour and have your hand-wound stitched. The orderly will be on duty then.'

'What about an antidote?' Godwin asked.

The doctor gave a knowing, professional look. 'By the looks of

it you've squeezed out most of the venom. Perhaps as an after-
effect you might get a headache. I'll instruct the orderly to give
you some aspirin.' Turning away he took a few steps before
pausing and glancing back. 'Snake-bite is not as bad as being
killed in battle. Think yourself lucky at your circumstances,' he
sighed. 'After all it was your people who started the war.'

Godwin took a few seconds to comprehend the doctor's last
remark. It was as unnecessary as it was untrue. The whole world
knew about Pearl Harbour. He choked back an indignant
response and instead, headed for his quarters. Barely had he
entered his room than pandemonium broke loose. A hand-oper-
ated siren began to wail its mournful warning. Godwin takes up
the story:

'A flight of Allied aircraft – a number of them bombers, flew
across the sky some three miles to the east. The house could not
possibly have been a military target, but by the reactions of the
Japanese one would think so. All prisoners were quickly gathered
together and hurried into a nearby rubber plantation. Armed
guards watched us closely, their rifles pointed menacingly. In the
peace and quiet of the rubber-tree plantation it was comforting to
hear the thud of bombs. The air-raid seemed to be concentrated
above the port. I hoped desperately that if the Japanese cruisers
were at anchor, that at least one might be sunk. The faint sound of
gunfire could be heard as the aircraft pressed home their attack.

'After the Allied aircraft had departed, the siren wailed the 'all
clear'. We were escorted to the front of the house and made to
stand waiting for an officer to appear. The roughly made sandals
that earlier I'd been provided with, pinched my feet terribly. It
was a relief to temporarily discard them and savour the cool
freshness of the thick lawn underfoot. It was remarkable how the
slightest favours of nature could mean so much, but then, comfort
as a prisoner of war in the order of things was discouraged.'

'It was none other than "Toothy" who emerged from the front
porch of the house. He was carrying a list and by his jerking walk
and mannerism, I could tell that something was up. Halting in
front of the assembled prisoners he raised the large sheet of rice-

paper to his eyes and began to read out names who he assured us were being transferred to a proper prisoner of war camp. With each name he gave a number and impressing upon us not to forget. Mine was No. 5 and the *Behar's* radio officer, No. 3. While this was happening three trucks stopped just inside the grounds to the house. First, numerous armed guards alighted – all with their rifles sporting fixed bayonets. Then followed the rest of the *Behar's* complement – Lascars included.'

'I was later to learn that the port of Tanjung Priok got a hell of a pasting from the air-raid and a number of ships sunk or damaged. The new arrivals joined our group on the lawn as the trucks swiftly departed. "Toothy" occasionally strode around consulting with a Jap officer and two NCOs who had arrived with the fresh batch of prisoners. Judging by his expression he looked none too pleased and continually glanced at another list supplied to him by the escorting officer. Something was afoot. But I couldn't imagine what. The only conclusion I could reach was that ultimately, all the assembled *Behar* survivors – not just the original few of us, would end up in a prison camp. But where?

'Unexpectedly some Nip officers' batmen walked from the front porch towards us carrying containers of water and quartered coconuts. It was damned thirsty work standing under the hot rays of the sun and the repast was bloody welcome. I was about to grab a piece of coconut when the Javanese guard who had lanced my snakebite hurried from the house towards me. The purposeful look on his face prompted me instead to grab a tin mug and scoop water from a container. Within seconds and in huge gulps I downed two mugfuls knowing that when, or if I returned, there would be no water left.'

'Speaking quickly to an NCO, the guard hurried towards me calling out as he came: "Dr Haruo is waiting for you in sick-bay. Come quick-time!"'

'Nodding understanding I followed the Javanese to the house carrying the sandals in my hand. Once in the hallway I slipped the sandals on before reporting to the sick-bay. Dr Haruo was seated in a small alcove adjacent to the sick-bay, with behind him the semblance of a dispensary. Sighting my approach he waved permission to enter the dispensary. Instead of an orderly suturing my hand he did and remarkably, injected some local anaesthetic. That done, he supplied a few aspirin tablets before ordering me to stand erect and keep still. For no reason that I could understand he began measuring my chest – air in air out, etc before measuring my feet and height. Even my neck was measured as were the length of my arms.'

'Transferring his measurements to notes on a pad he looked up and asked, "Are all your family tall?"'

'Shrugging I answered, "My dad is six feet, but my sisters and mother are just average." Unnecessarily I added, "I'm six feet two." '

'The doctor glanced at the pad and nodded before asking, "What is your staple food at home?" '

'A surge of enthusiasm filled my thoughts at the realisation that I could, in a backhanded way, utterly denigrate the food the Japanese rationed out to their prisoners. Taking a deep breath I launched forth. "Breakfast can be anything from toast and marmalade to rolled oats and cream usually followed by pan-fried potatoes, bacon or sausages and eggs. Lunch quite often is sandwiches with meat fillings and pickle. As for dinner at night it's either a rich meat and vegetable stew, fried fish and chips, or roast lamb, pork or beef. Often in cold weather we have a thick tasty soup first. If we still feel peckish, there's steamed pudding or a milk pudding with stewed fruit and custard if we want it. Ah, cream is always available." Satisfied at my description of a staple diet, I further added: "Of course there's supper before we go to bed. This can be anything, but usually it's cake or toast, tea or cocoa." '

'The doctor scribbled something on his pad while talking. "This is a rich calorie diet. It could explain why Caucasians are so physically large." He looked up askance. "What about rice?" '

' "It goes well with curry," I conceded, "but compared with fresh bread it is not popular." '

'Again the doctor made notes: "Your information confirms a thesis in my research. I'm obliged. You may go." '

Godwin left the sick-bay elated at the opportunity to glorify his country's standard of living in comparison to Japan's poor one. It also plainly conveyed the disgraceful food supplied to the prisoners in comparison and which the doctor would know about.

It was about 4.30 in the afternoon when Godwin rejoined the prisoners on the front lawn. Absolute confusion seemed to reign. From somewhere 'Toothy' had procured a long cane and was using it with great vigour on the shoulders and backs of the prisoners, particularly the Lascars. Four large buses had arrived and were parked at the entranceway – just outside the main gate. Godwin was certain that the air-raid had not precipitated what appeared to be a panic evacuation of the prisoners. Could it, he wondered, have something to do with being transferred to a proper prisoner of war camp? But why the unseemly rush?

A Japanese Army staff car swept into the drive and stopped alongside the front porch. Four senior army officers got out and strode towards the milling prisoners. 'Toothy' and another officer hurried towards the approaching staff officers. There followed several minutes of discussion before the staff officers turned as a group and made their way to the house. Whatever had been said galvanised 'Toothy' into redoubled activity, almost frenzied. Laying about with his bamboo cane and shouting unintelligibly he managed to finally separate the prisoners into numbered groups before herding them with the assistance of the armed guards towards and into the waiting buses.

It was not yet five o'clock when the buses, in convoy, were speeding along the main road towards Batavia. In the bus that Godwin rode, the armed guards detailed as escort, forbade talking. As the miles swept past it was a pleasant change to view the passing scenery. However the journey was marred by the sight of what was clearly a prisoner of war camp. Male European prisoners with shorn heads and clothed in green fatigues stood or walked aimlessly behind a high barbed wire enclosure. Other prisoners – work parties and heavily guarded – could be seen re-entering the camp. Godwin felt sure the prison inmates would be

Americans, Dutch, English and probably Australians. Rapid
twilight was descending as the buses turned into what appeared to
be a large but deserted camp some four miles past the occupied
camp noticed earlier. Godwin was moved to write:

'What a bloody hell-hole this place looked. Generally untidy
and extremely filthy from a sanitation point of view. The buses
stopped in front of a dilapidated building – partially destroyed by
fire – but what froze the blood in my veins was the sight of
several wooden coffins and a line of body bags containing
corpses. Two trucks were parked near the bodies and were
already half-full of filled body-bags. Unarmed Japanese – probably Korean conscripts, were wearing white-gauze face masks
and gloves and under the supervision of a Japanese NCO, were
busy loading the corpses into the two trucks. What a bloody
welcome and thought provoking I considered with a sinking
feeling. Whatever had taken so many lives must have been an
epidemic of major proportions. We were soon to find out.'

'Bundled off the buses, we were lined up in our respective
groups and numbers and marched off to disgraceful-looking
habitation, described as our permanent quarters. Those whose
steps faltered, either in dismay or shock, were viciously clubbed
by unsympathetic guards who seemed impervious to the sight of
such a tragedy. Even at the sight of such multiple death, they
remained pitilessly unmoved. It was near dark when we entered
the long hut assigned to our group. There were no beds.
Everything in the hut had been removed. Even a water barrel by
the door had been emptied and smelt strongly of disinfectant. Our
thoughts and subsequent whispers said it all. Cholera!'

'That night was the worst night I had ever spent in captivity. We
slept or tried to on an earthen floor. Mosquitoes bit the hell out of
us. Thirst became a nightmare if only because the barrel was
empty. But then and despite our craving, even if the barrel had
been full, not one of us would have touched a drop. Cholera
among other things had many carriers, particularly unclean
water, and then, why had the barrel been disinfected?'

'We stayed in this hell-hole for three days and were only fed twice. The water that was brought to us had been boiled, we were assured by a junior Japanese lieutenant who was in command of the camp. The food consisted of over-ripe black-skinned bananas, gooey soggy rice and boiled fish heads. A touch of salt in the rice or added to the fish heads would have helped us to swallow this trash down, but in the view of the Japanese, this would have been spoiling us. Each night we slept on the earthen floor in acute discomfort. There was nothing to lay our head on as all the reed mats had been earlier removed and burnt. Those of us who had consumed some of the rotting bananas, went down with acute diarrhoea. At first, alarm akin to panic beset us. Were we to be the next victims of a cholera plague? The early symptoms were similar.'

'If the Japanese had intended to keep us in this hell-hole of a camp indefinitely, then nature had other ideas. On the third day and just before noon, word reached us that fourteen of the Lascars were seriously ill. They were kept apart from the other prisoners and because of their numbers, occupied a special hut. Our hut was at the end of a row of seven, but apart from savage mosquito bites and dysentry we were surviving tolerably well though getting thinner by the day. After a meagre lunch of boiled rice, nothing more, we sat in front of our hut still ravenously hungry. The skimpy lunch on the third day was only our second meal since arriving at the camp. None of us had the energy to walk around, preferring instead to sit beneath the shade of large fruitless mango trees. It was from this vantage point that we could see Lascars suddenly dropping into crouching positions and defecating. Some who could make it, managed to reach their crude latrines. A few Lascars just simply lay down, defecating as their illness dictated.'

'All of our group became seriously worried. We were witnessing another cholera outbreak and knew that it was not a matter of if, but when the cholera spread, how many of us might succumb? Weakening by the day through lack of food and severely rationed water, we could do nothing but await the inevitable. Desperately concerned, myself, Chief Officer Phillips and Dr Lai Yung Li, formed ourselves into a deputation to convey our fears to the Camp Commandant. Captain Symmons wanted to come along as well but he was too crook with diarrhoea. It was the Chinese doctor who opinioned earlier in the day that judging by his observations and medical experience, he was certain that amoebic dysentry was also afflicting the Lascars which would hasten the fatality rate if combined with cholera. This really put the wind up all of us.'

'Our meeting with the Camp Commandant, Lieutenant Ito, was as fruitless as it was acrimonious. This mongrel told us that brave Japanese soldiers who were guarding the Lascars were not complaining, but as number ten citizens (us), he was not surprised at our cowardice in facing possible death. He went on to add that as we had started the war and oppressed Asian people, we should suffer the consequence. I was rash enough to mention that the brave Japanese soldiers slept in proper beds, had mosquito nets and much better food. The commandant got bloody excited by my comparison and biffed me across the face for my temerity. The upshot of this useless meeting was that we were herded into our hut for the rest of the afternoon. At least Dr Lai Yung Li frightened the commandant when he said:

"You have another cholera plague and more than probably an outbreak of amoebic dysentery on your hands. I should know the signs as I am a medical doctor." He sighed for effect. "Even the brave Japanese soldiers may die." '

'At about four o'clock in the afternoon and by simply watching from windowless apertures, dramatic developments took place. Two trucks and an army staff car screeched to a stop in front of the commandant's house. A dozen or so Korean conscripts jumped from the back of the two trucks and protected by white-gauze face masks and wearing gloves hurried towards the Lascars' quarters. Some were carrying containers of disinfectant, others, body bags. Two army officers dashed into the house.'

'They've got the bloody wind-up,' commented McLeod, the *Behar's* bosun, who was taking everything in at his watching post. An hour earlier a Japanese guard had been observed acting strangely. Instead of strutting around with haughty indifference and among some sick Lascars prone on the ground, he was somewhat stooped and with one free hand was occasionally clutching at his stomach. Dr Lai Yung Li whose attention was called to the fact nodded knowingly and offered his opinion that the guard was suffering the unmistakeable signs of dysentry – probably amoebic he had volunteered indifferently.'

'Everything that happened subsequently, was astonishing by its swiftness. Just before sunset four buses and a further three army trucks arrived at the camp. Guards burst into our hut and screaming, elbowing, shoving and prodding with their rifle butts had us assembled outside and into a bus within five minutes. Everything was done with such speed it was as though we had a train to catch, which unbeknown to us was the actual reason.'

Godwin's diary goes on to record the collective opinion of his group that a second outbreak of cholera at the camp was too much for the Japanese to ignore. If one guard had been noticed suffering abdominal pains, might there have been others unknown? Even by harsh Japanese standards, the camp was too much of a health risk. Even if only for the sake of its soldiers. The bus that Godwin was on led the way into central Batavia before finally stopping at a large railway station in the captured city.

During the hasty departure from the camp and because talking was forbidden, Godwin had time to collect his thoughts. In his opinion it was reckless of the Japanese High Command to reopen a camp that was patently a morgue and still a danger to health. Disinfectant alone could not hope to eradicate such a manifest health problem. The camp and its dilapidated buildings should have been torched. Apart from isolated instances, the general attitude of the Japanese Armed Forces to sickness or wounds was one of indifference and appalling neglect. His thoughts were interrupted by a shrill demand from a guard for all prisoners to leave the bus. Godwin describes what followed.

'We were led onto one of the station's platforms where a train was ready and waiting. Whilst arrangements for seating were being finalised, an officer with a reasonably civil disposition told

us some news that really exhilarated us. He said we were going to
Sourabaya, eastern Java, where we would be staying for two or
three days before being repatriated to Darwin by ship in exchange
for wounded and captured Japanese. This really sounded
wonderful and gave us a lot to talk about after we finally boarded
the train and took our seats in a third class carriage. After being
counted by an NCO, a large urn of weak but sweetened tea was
placed beside two friendly former Imperial Dutch Javanese
guards. A couple of chipped china mugs were also supplied. Then
to our surprise and as the train pulled out of the station, the civilly
disposed Japanese officer returned bearing two full packets of
American cigarettes and a box of matches and invited those of us
who wanted to, to smoke.'

    'Before leaving our carriage for his own, the officer who we
named, "the good guy", handed over some occupation money to
the senior guard with some words and gestures that clearly indicated our group as being in for something special. Throughout
the night and well into the next morning we had a period of
liberty damn near like an excursion picnic. We were able to talk
freely, crack jokes and make light of our past tribulations and
vicissitudes. The chief and most exciting topic of conversation
was our pending repatriation to Australia. The two friendly
Javanese guards gave us the run of the carriage and ensured that
our tea urn was refilled twice during the night when the train
briefly stopped at two railway stations. Bamboo baskets of food
were also obtained, either an assortment of fresh fruit, or delicious tasting chicken curry swamped in reddish and nourishing
juices and accompanied with perfectly cooked rice. Though the
curry was hot to our sensitive palates we wolfed it down using
small crude wooden spoons.'

    'Our guards ate the same food and drank the same tea, obliv-
ious to the fact that their discarded rifles were within easy reach
of the prisoners, but then, why would anyone want to escape?
Were we not being repatriated back to Australia? Only a fool
would think such thoughts. At about four o'clock in the morning
and while the train was rattling on through the night, the "good

guy" officer paid us a brief visit. By then and at that hour most everyone was dozing. He spoke quietly with the guards and passed across some more occupation money before leaving as silently considerate as he came.'

Godwin took pains to example any instance of genuine humanity or civilised conduct by his captors and in a brief reflection goes on to say, 'We did come across the odd Jap who had no heart in what they were ordered to do. Sadly, the good guys were outnumbered 100-to-1 by the baddies. To try to understand the Japanese psyche in human terms was damn near impossible. However it could be said that the cult of samurai played a large part in formulating the Japanese mind-set and with all the evils inherent. A good example would be the consequences of a too rigid discipline exampled as follows and which one of our friendly Javanese guards personally confirmed.'

'Amiably chatting away with the two guards in our carriage, I touched upon the matter of executions of allied servicemen and civilians by the Japanese. Both guards shook their heads in genuine disapproval at the practice. Pressing them further I learned that a crime or captivity transgression – even of a minor nature, was sufficient justification for the taking of a life. But chillingly, death was quite often ordered at the whim of whoever was in charge. Arbitrary executions were more the rule than the exception. I told the guards of a triple execution I had been forced to witness and who the victims were. Both agreed that it was more than likely that the victims had escaped from a work-party or prison camp. As an example and as a deterrent to other prisoners, their executions would be ordered – usually by beheading.'

'I cannot speak too highly of our two Javanese guards and the "good guy" Japanese officer who I learned was in permanent charge of 200 Javanese guards who had been conscripted into the Japanese Armed Forces. It was with a tinge of genuine regret and as the train pulled into a suburban station of Sourabaya that the two kindly guards mentioned the certainty of our transfer into the custody of waiting Japanese guards. It was 11 am as the train finally hissed and creaked to a stop alongside a platform strangely bare of civilians but with numerous Japanese soldiers – all carrying rifles with fixed bayonets. Most of us shook hands with our carriage guards before alighting from the train, repatriation to Australia uppermost in our thoughts.'

'Then hell returned. Shoved, kicked and generally abused, we were formed into two lines before being marched from the station and into the backs of waiting trucks. Most of the Japanese guards thought that some of us were allied pilots recently shot down and subsequent to an air-raid on 18 May. Their attitudes were rather ugly because of this misconception. None of us knew that Sourabaya had been bombed. It was only later that we learned a large floating dock in the port had been sabotaged and sunk by pro-Allied Javanese workers at the port. We were subsequently told that many of them had paid a terrible price after being arrested on suspicion by the Japanese Kempetai. Some had been shot, others died during torture, many had been beheaded and not a few had been crammed into bamboo pig-baskets and thrown to sharks in the sea. To divert suspicion, the floating dock had been sunk during a heavy air-raid, but this did not fool the Japanese. Divers were sent down to inspect the hulk for bomb damage. Their ensuing reports confirmed that there was no bomb damage other than a machinery-room had been sabotaged and all ballast-cocks and valves irreparably damaged.'

Godwin returns to the departure from the railway station with mixed feelings. 'We were forbidden to talk during the bumpy ride to our new prison camp, but thoughts of eventual repatriation sustained us. The only disquieting factor was the presence of so many heavily armed Japanese guards. If we were going to be eventually released, why the draconian security? Once arrived at the camp and with our groups still kept apart, we were assigned a tolerably habitable hut with wooden flooring and rattan-screened windows. Sleeping mats were provided along with mosquito netting, but the latter were useless. They were riddled with holes large and small that later and as experience proved, were no deterrent to these annoying pests of the night.'

'Our guards were a particularly vicious lot and for the next few days delighted in inflicting punishment for the slightest infringement of a camp rule. Not lowering one's head in a dutiful bow even to the most humble Japanese soldier, brought on an ordeal of thuggery and rifle butting. Black eyes and cracked skulls – at least concussion – was an inevitable consequence. I became quite convinced that the Japanese mind-set, albeit swaggering and the constant predilection for over-arming themselves in the midst of weakened and passive prisoners, was a direct pointer to their low self-esteem and massive inferiority complex. This opinion held credence if for no other reason it would explain such inexplicibly cruel conduct.'

'The three days opinioned by the "good guy" Japanese officer on the train stretched to six then to nine until we lost count. Repatriation it seemed, was taking the Japs a hell of a long time to arrange. As one dreary day dragged on into the next, our spirits and hopes gradually diminished. Not helping this soul-destroying situation were the nightly attacks by persistent and ravenous mosquitoes. The food was appalling and almost inedible. Water was strictly supplied and if in the sweltering heat we longed for it, then, too bad, we were simply made to suffer the rigours of thirst. Brutality by the guards had returned with a vengeance. Each time a guard came anywhere near us we would wearily climb to our feet and dutifully bow. Some of the guards would feel cheated by such passive subservience. It denied them a pretext for inflicting punishment, nonetheless a few guards didn't bother with a pretext. With a singlular bloody-mindedness they would continue to approach a prisoner with bowed head and then "Wham!" a stunning thud from a rifle butt to the head either felled the intended victim, or would cause the attacked prisoner to sway and stagger in shock and dizziness. Most of us became paranoiac and close to nervous breakdowns because of these inhuman and unwarranted club or rifle butt assaults.'

'The guards despised us and as a consequence made life a living hell. The Korean conscripts who sometimes guarded us were just as vicious. Ethnically, it was hard to tell the difference between a Jap or Korean. They all looked the same and yes, were as cruel as each other. I lost two stone in this one camp alone and suffered constantly from the runs (diarrhoea). It was a hell of a relief to all of us when we were assembled and told that finally our repatriation to Australia had been arranged. Standing there under the hot blazing sun with thirst parching our mouths was bad enough, but I had recently endured a beating from two guards that had blackened my eyes to a point that I could only squint out of them. Thus and being the recipient of such recent brutality – and showing the signs of it – I began to doubt the renewed repatriation promise.'

'Clearly a neutral power would be involved, but where the hell were its representatives? That the Japanese were lying was not improbable. They were past masters at cunning and deception. These thoughts crossed my mind until the Jap officer addressing us mentioned that all prisoners would be embarking at the port of Sourabaya the following day, 11 June. He then wished us well, adding that he hoped we would convey to the Australian authorities the adequate food and good treatment we had received as prisoners of war.'

'To believe or not to believe, this was the question that exercised my mind both in the latrines and out of them – I was making urgent visits every twenty minutes. For once I kept my thoughts to myself. Why spoil it for the others? If hope and consolation had uplifted their thoughts, then, so be it. They had nothing else going for them. Only the morrow would tell.'

At this juncture Godwin relates the sudden arrival of a Japanese naval NCO. 'An evil-looking mongrel accompanied by four heavily armed guards burst into our hut and read out four names. Mine was one of them. Stepping forward as ordered, our hands were bound behind our backs and we were marched from the hut. I mentioned to this NCO bloke that I was suffering from diarrhoea and was evacuating every twenty minutes – which was as long as I could hold on for. In response the NCO biffed me across the shoulders with a thick bamboo cane that bloody hurt and before shouting an order for silence. Who the hell this bloody bastard was plagued my thoughts as we were led towards a small but solitary wooden hut close to the guards barracks.'

'There followed three hours of incredible inhuman treatment. Once inside the hut which was a kind of scantily supplied store-room, we were made to kneel on top of scores of spread out thumb-tacks and remain motionless. Christ! the pain was agonising. Then we were subjected to a harangue of all the abuses inflicted upon Asia by the imperialist Europeans. We did not deserve to live and would lose the war that we had started. This sort of garbage went on for ten minutes or so accompanied by energetic blows from the thick cane, the favourite place to strike being our bunched and tied hands. Had my hands been free I'd have happily strangled this bastard despite the presence of the grinning guards.'

'Mentally I named this sadistic bastard "The Snake". Never had I come across a moron like him. He was in a class of his own and clearly bore a genocidal hatred of Europeans. We were made to sit cross-legged on the floor and to endure repeated thwacks across our bare thighs from the cane. Occasionally one of the armed guards would crack us over the head with a rifle butt. God, those stunning blows and always from behind, were insufferable and damned jolting. Twice I nearly passed out after two particularly heavy blows to the head. To make matters worse, I defecated a runny mess that completely soiled my shorts. As an extra punishment I was face-slapped and struck with a clenched fist several times.'

'There was no agenda or reason for this continual brutality which carried on from one variety of ill-treatment to another. We were made to stand and suffer kicks – delivered with some force at our posteriors. But the tongue whacking was the worst ordeal. Once again kneeling and with more thumb-tacks sinking deep into our knee-caps we were forced to extend our tongues and await a downward stroke of the cane. Perfect strikes were evidenced by instantly bloodied mouths as our tongues were split open. The Snake got a perverse and sadistic pleasure out of our distress and the blood. He was our tormentor extraordinary and clearly relished the power he held over us.'

'After further beatings and ill-treatment that seemed to go on endlessly and quite literally black and blue all over, we were allowed to speak but only to repeat parrot-fashion, what the Snake told us to say. Here are some of the phrases as I recall. "All prisoners of the brave Nipponese are cowardly scum." "Brave Nipponese soldiers are too honourable to surrender." "The Imperialist British and Americans as well as the Dutch attacked Nippon and started the war." What stuck in the throat was the last phrase I can remember. "The Emperor of Nippon is our master and ruler of the world." Half conscious and with a splitting headache from countless butt-end rifle blows, our tormentors abruptly ceased their sadism. Our hands were untied before just one armed guard returned us to our hut. The Snake and the other three guards headed for the guards barracks yabbering and chuckling between themselves, no doubt looking forward to their evening meal after an exhausting period with the prisoners.'

Godwin was naturally angry at the unwarranted thuggery inflicted upon himself, Lieutenant Parker, the radio officer and the *Behar's* bosun. It was clearly a selective exercise designed to humiliate and cower the four most physical or strongest prisoners from among the *Behar's* officers and passengers. It took two hours for fellow prisoners to extract thumb-tacks from eight kneecaps and to help with what comfort could be offered. With no recourse to first-aid supplies, their efforts mainly centred upon compassion and comforting words. A confusing enigma filling the minds of all the prisoners in the hut was the contradiction in terms concerning their promised repatriation. Godwin summed up this perception and growing doubt succinctly.

'Prisoners awaiting imminent exchange with another Power should not – would not – be brutally ill-treated or visibly marked. What made the Snake act with such reckless disregard? Did he know something that we didn't?'

As if to confound conjecture, doubt and speculation. The next day as promised, the *Behar's* ship's officers, naval ratings, engineering officers, the bosun and two bridge cadets along with the passengers were hurried into the back of waiting trucks and transported to a captured cargo-passenger ship at the port. With a minimum of formality though still under heavy guard, they were embarked and settled into large cabins assigned before 11.30 on the same morning. The transfer from prison camp to ship was astonishing by its very speed and as Godwin was to record, 'It was bloody good to know that we would be leaving the Snake and his thugs behind.'

'The ship had two tiers of passenger accommodation on its upper decks, the lower one being assigned to all of the *Behar's* white personnel. It was clear to us that we had seen the last of the Lascars. It seemed a hard fate for them as though hailing from Goa in India, they were still British subjects and should have been included for repatriation to Australia. Just before noon Lieutenant Parker and myself were transferred from the roomy cabin and relocated in a smaller but fairly comfortable two-berth one on the same deck but on the starboard side. To our delight the cabin sported a wash basin and taps with running water. There were no drinking cups or glasses, but now quite used to making do, we cupped our hands and drank the clear water with great gusto. Satiated and with occasional belches, we sat on a bulkhead settee and discussed our plans upon reaching Darwin.'

'Obeying orders, we remained in our cabins but too excited to think about food, even though it was lunch-time. At about three o'clock we felt the throb of ship's engines. Glancing out the open porthole we could see an opposite wharf and buildings slowly slipping past. At last, we were on our way to freedom and civilised sanity. We could now finally rejoice.'

It was an hour later before the slow throb of the ship's engines ceased. Faintly came the rumble of a windlass and the clatter of chains. The ship had dropped anchor out in the stream. Godwin and Parker discussed the possible reason between themselves as they gingerly massaged the countless and quite painful wounds to their kneecaps. Both agreed that it was most probably because of the threat of Allied submarines lying in wait outside the harbour's

waters. A departure at nightfall would be the most sensible decision, but wait! The Allies would not torpedo a ship carrying
Allied prisoners of war surely? What the hell was going on?

Godwin's diary encapsulates the events that followed and in his
own words: 'A Nip naval NCO burst into our cabin and told us to
report on the ship's main deck aft' Suppressing our new-found
doubts we followed him to the number five hatch where the rest
of the *Behar* prisoners were assembled. Containers of rice and a
watery soup made of fish-heads awaited us. Bowls and civilised
spoons and forks were handed around following which an
extremely fat Japanese with a dirty apron tied around his waist
served us. A ladle of soup was splashed into our bowls along with
a dollop of rice. Then we were told to sit on the canvas covered
hatch and eat.'

'The food was plain but it was freshly cooked and had salt in it.
Hunger returned as our appetites were whetted by the salted food.
The soup though plain was quite nourishing and with the addition
of rice went down passably well. The blazing sun was uncomfortably hot, therefore we were pleased after we had finished our late
lunch to be told that we could exercise under some large awnings
on the lower passenger deck. What delighted us the most was the
complete absence of the hated and usually heavily armed military
guards. In their stead two naval ratings with pistols strapped to
their waists kept watch over us. They were rather quiet types and
left us alone. For a good half-hour we strolled and chatted with
various individuals from the *Behar*. Captains Green and
Symmons, both bearing up well to the hardships of past imprisonment, echoed the same reservations that Parker and myself
entertained with regard to the ship anchoring in the stream. But
then, the absence of Japanese soldiers reinforced the rationale,
even if it was only conjecture, that the ship was indeed Australia -
bound. Perhaps it was waiting for a neutral Power emissary to
come aboard and officially record our numbers for repatriation.
Such a likelihood was a distinct possibility. With such cherished
hopes at the back of our minds, the sun slowly sank westward.'

'At five o'clock a ripple of excitement swept through the *Behar* survivors as word spread that a large launch could be seen approaching the anchored ship. Hopes remained buoyant as the launch came ever closer. Japanese merchant seamen took up position at the head of the gangway which was lowered at an angle of 45° and to within two feet of the water's surface. It was when the launch was within one mile of the ship and just visible through the naked eye that our hopes received a crushing blow. It appeared to be packed with Japanese soldiers with bayonets affixed to their rifles glinting in the setting sun.'

' "The bloody pestiferous mongrels are returning," muttered Parker."

'I was bloody crestfallen as well,' wrote Godwin. 'Such a large number of Japs killed the idea of going to Australia. It would not have been logical. We watched in silence as the launch came alongside the lowered gangway. In a vague sort of way it seemed like we were being taken prisoner again. Dr Lai Yung Li who was standing next to me murmured his thoughts in measured fatalism.'

' "There are too many Japanese soldiers. We are not going to Australia. I feel that this ship is sailing for Japan."

'This was an opinion I didn't want to hear,' Godwin wrote. 'The very suggestion of sailing to Japan was depressing, but I could hardly disregard the Chinese doctor's opinion. Parker rejoined me by the ship's rail. His breathing was strained as he surreptitiously pointed to an NCO who was standing behind three bandaged Japanese army officers. As wounded men it was obvious that they were returning to Japan. There were at least twelve other soldiers who were likewise bandaged. The rest of the soldiers, numbering about thirty, were armed and following each other up the gangway. Then my eyes focused onto the NCO pointed out by Parker. My heart sank. It was none other than the Snake.'

'I stared dumbly at Parker. He at me. We were lost for words. Dr Lai Yung Li gestured to the wounded Japanese and repeated his belief that the ship and us were going to Japan. I reluctantly nodded. Going to Japan was bad enough, but the prospect of having the Snake on board for the precarious passage didn't bear thinking about.'

'Abruptly Nip soldiers swarmed around us. They were like bloody angry wasps. In a trice I along with all the *Behar's* complement, excepting the two women, were handcuffed. We were herded from the deck with shoves and kicks and taken to a large solitary cabin at the end of the main deck and above the stern. I think it was called the poop. Here we were forced to sit on a very dirty deck and in complete silence. Four mean-looking bastards with bayonets fixed to their rifles guarded us. How we could escape and to where, seemed to be beyond the comprehension of the Japanese. If it was a case of playing mind-games, they were winning. We were all becoming bloody depressed and thoroughly fed up with our change in fortunes.'

'We sailed from the anchorage at Sourabaya that evening at 1900 hours on 11 June 1944. The ship coasted westward off the northern shores of Java and in sight of Javanese fishing boats displaying flickering oil-lamps. At about 9 pm blankets were thrown into our cabin-prison – one per person, plus some apologies for pillows. They were as flat as boards and gave off a bad odour – like stale urine. Fortunately our hands were cuffed in front making it possible to spread a blanket and lie down. The rest of the night passed without harassment though we thirsted dreadfully for water. We did however have the blessing of a cool deck and mercifully, sleepy-eyed guards – two of them actually fell asleep.'

'The next morning we had rice and a type of soup for breakfast. We were each supplied with half-pint mugs and told to retain them for the voyage. After wolfing our meagre breakfast we stood in line holding our empty mugs out for water that was being dispensed from two fire-buckets. An NCO who had arrived and was watching proceedings waded in among us and began clouting anyone close because we had not bowed our thanks for the trash supplied. As if this wasn't enough and to our dismay the Snake entered our prison. He was carrying that damned bloody cane again. Without asking questions he waded into us with sadistic fervour. I copped a couple of vicious thwacks – one across the face that made my tongue bleed again. He was an absolute bastard during the whole voyage and was definitely a sadist. He enjoyed inflicting pain and distress.'

'There was no one to complain to nor could we do anything to help ourselves or ward off the blows because of the bloody handcuffs. Occasionally an officer, ship or army, would saunter by during our many punishments, but these bastards were just as bad. They would walk past with complete indifference. It was impossible to refuse to do what the Snake told us to do in regard to our personal discomforture. Any reluctance was corrected with thwacks to head and shoulders and across our shins. God, these leg blows were stinging thwacks that lingered for some time. How I came to hate that bloody cane. For variety the Snake would kick us in the shins if we were slow in obeying his perverted and hate-filled orders. Sometimes and assisted by like-minded guards, the Snake would charge into our prison and lay about with his cane for no reason whatsoever. The guards would assist by hitting us with knotted lengths of rope, lumps of boxwood, the flat of Dutch swords captured in Java and of course with clenched fists. As a consequence of this deliberate and mindless cruelty, we were fast becoming nervous wrecks.'

'Occasionally we were allowed to shower in cold water, but always with a slit-eyed bastard gazing at our private parts. Even showering or going to the WC we had to endure the restrictions of the handcuffs. It was hell. There was one Nip – a cook I think, who spoke reasonable English. He had lived in the United States prior to the war and whispered to me on a rare private occasion, that he was a naturalised American citizen. He lamented the fact that Japan was at war with America and opinioned that Japan could not hope to win. America he said, was too big, too strong, too clever. I remember nodding agreement and gratefully accepting two bars of Nip chocolate. This Nip was a decent guy and deplored the brutality of the guards. I could sense his fear of the Snake, but equally, his loathing.'

'One day dragged on into the next as the ship was steered cautiously north towards Japan with some brief stopovers

enroute and many precautionary deviations. Allied submarine
activity was worrying the Japs stiff. They were sustaining an
unacceptable rate of torpedoings, and what made them really
angry, they had no way to retaliate. Here is a list of the stopovers
made during the voyage.'

'Arrived at the Rhio Islands (south of Singapore) at about 1900
hours, 13.6.44. Sailed 14.6.44 at 1900 hours. Arrived at
Singapore 1400 hours, 15.6.44. Left Singapore in convoy 0700
hours, 17.6.44. Sighted Formosa on morning of 24.6.44.
Formosa last sighted about 1200 hours, 25.6.44. Anchored for
night 25.6.44. Anchored for night 26.6.44. Anchored for night
27.6.44. Arrived at Kobe, Japan, 2000 hours, 28.6.44. As was
expected the Snake went out of his way to make all the prisoners
fearful and miserable. On one particular day and because one of
the ships in the convoy had been torpedoed, we were made to sit
blindfolded from sunrise to sunset and without moving. The calls
of nature and thirst were utterly ignored by the guards, but worse,
the Snake would tread silently into our cabin-prison and then,
wham! wham! thwack! Prisoners would be caught completely
unaware and suffered grievous blows from the hated cane and the
flat of a sword.' After the war Godwin wrote, 'This bastard
vanished into obscurity. He was never prosecuted or punished,
but then, neither were thousands of other Jap war criminals.'

'The ships in the convoy comprised one aircraft carrier that
looked seriously damaged and to the best of my recollection, no
aircraft flew off or landed on this floating hulk. A large heavy
cruiser – the Nips had lots of these, and four rusty destroyers
escorted two valuable tankers and the two remaining cargo ships
as well as ours. It was noticed that once the convoy was north of
Taiwan and closer to the safety of Japan, the Snake's brutality
increased drastically. Anyone who caught his sadistic eye but for
no valid reason, was wacked and thwacked mercilessly. During
his welcome absences we used to whisper to each other – just to
keep our spirits up, that as a boy he had no toys. In less kinder
mood, particularly if suffering from the Snake's recent attention,
he would be described as a son of hell and the Emperor's illegiti-

mate son and much, much more besides.'

'On other occasions and just for variety, the Snake made us repeat parrot-fashion that the Nipponese people were a superior race and that the white race were in general a degenerate hedonistic society of misfits, doomed to be slaves of Nippon – he never used the word Japan or Japanese – and that only by the Emperor's benevolence were we allowed to live. The last day at sea before reaching Japan was probably the worst. We were made to do stretchups – still with the bloody handcuffs on, and in time to this lunatic's orders. In our weakened state – I was still suffering from the after-effects of diarrhoea as were some other prisoners, the physical strain was tremendous. Those who collapsed were beaten with knotted ropes, boots, bayonet scabbards, broomsticks and the ever present cane. The latter had by now split in several places and was inflicting punishment that opened the flesh cruelly. I have no hesitation in saying that not only the Snake but many guards had a vicious streak and an undeniable genocidal hatred of Europeans.'

'Towards evening of the same day and physically and mentally exhausted, the prisoners were at last left in peace. The sheer luxury of being left alone to nurse our bruised, lacerated and exhausted bodies was a hell of a relief. Watchfully guarding us were two rifle-carrying morons who, to break their boredom, would move around our prison-cabin, checking that our handcuffs were secure and just for pleasure, would kick anyone who was slow to raise their hands for inspection. Mr MacGregor who was very sick had no strength left to raise his arms. Taking this as a defiance of orders given by Imperial Nipponese soldiers, he was kicked and clubbed with rifle-butts. Not unexpectedly he keeled over onto his side unconscious. Thinking the blackest thoughts – if only I wasn't handcuffed, I could only sit and watch helplessly.'

'Then, the grand finale descended upon us. The Snake returned with four club-wielding guards. Screaming his rage at the sight of MacGregor lying recumbent, he dashed towards his prostrate body waving the cane with evil intent. Yelling, kicking and thwacking with vicious blows he managed to make MacGregor sit up in a semi-conscious state. Then, for good measure, he lashed the old man a vicious thwack across the back with the cane. Not even the cane could stand such abuse. It broke in half. Foiled, the Snake seized a rifle from the nearest guard and reversing it, struck MacGregor a cruel blow to the back of his head with the butt-end. Without a sound MacGregor slumped sideways. Realising he could inflict no further pain for a while, the Snake turned his sadistic attention to the now trembling prisoners. I wondered how much more I could endure as he and the four other club-wielding guards laid into us.'

'Peering through several open portholes, soldiers and seamen feasted their eyes on thuggery and battery second to none. Not one inscrutable face showed disapproval other than amusement. We were hit, thumped, bashed and clubbed by these psychopaths amidst yells of pain, pleas for mercy and the stench of freshly discharged diarrhoea. Either our tormentors were naturally pitiless or were half-insane. The beating of the two women was particularly cruel and totally uncalled for. I was bashed many times – because of my size I think. Then, just as abruptly, the beatings ceased. I think the stench of urine and excreta became too much for these sadistic bastards. Casting squinted malevolent looks at the terrified prisoners, our torturers departed, the sound of their imbecilic laughter depressing, soul-destroying.'

Godwin later wrote in his diary: 'This was the last beating inflicted upon the prisoners aboard the ship. Whether it was because Mr MacGregor was found to be dead after these murderous bastards had left us, one will never know. The women cried tears of despair when MacGregor's body was carried from the oppressively warm and stinking cabin. Even in death his corpse revealed a mass of cruel marks and many dried bloodstains. At least he was at peace and beyond the Snake's hate-filled malevolence. We expected an officer to check out Mr MacGregor's cruel death, but nothing happened. Life seemingly to the Japanese, was cheap. I vowed that if I ever had the chance I would track the Snake down after the war was over. But as later events proved, the Yanks went soft on these murderous bastards and let too many of them off the hook.'

With the arrival of the convoy in Japanese home waters it was not just a case of steaming into port as Godwin's diary records. He mentions the caution and trouble the Japanese went to in their attempts to avoid Allied submarines that were known to be increasing in numbers and lying in wait off Japan's ports. Torpedo attacks by these submarines were most prevalent at night and where patrolling Japanese aircraft attacks were useless. The Japs were really scared of the ever-increasing submarine attacks and as a counter to reduce the high rate of shipping losses that could not be sustained indefinitely, they resorted to anchoring in sheltered bays and the like at night, he wrote. As a consequence all shipping including convoys only voyaged twelve hours out of every twenty-four in Japanese home waters.

The ship that Godwin and the other prisoners were on, finally docked at Kobe on 28 June 1944. Ahead of them awaited almost fifteen months incarceration as prisoners of war. On the evening of the ship's arrival at Kobe, the prisoners were escorted ashore by a detachment of military police (Kempetai). Still handcuffed, ropes were tied to their necks and in a long humiliating file they were led through several streets to a commandeered tram and rode to a distant railway station. Once aboard a waiting train and at 2300 hours, they commenced a journey to Ofuna, a centre near Tokyo. Wearing thin tropical clothing and accustomed to the heat of the tropics, the prisoners felt the cool night air as being akin to being quite cold.

Thirst as ever afflicted them all. Repeated pleas to stony-faced guards for water was a sheer waste of time, however, and after fifteen hours, the thirsting prisoners were given some dry biscuits to eat and some leftovers of very salty tinned fish. It was damned embarrassing to be led through the streets of Kobe with ropes around our necks and handcuffed, Godwin wrote. Hundreds of impassive slant-eyed Japanese stared at us as though we had come from another planet. A few spat on us or threw stones. If it was an expression of hate it was hard to tell. Their features remained inscrutable. To many of us the densely crowded streets and the alien environment, created the impression in our minds that it was we who were on another planet.

A lasting impression shared by all the prisoners was the sheer density of people and to the point of being as prolific as ants. For the small size of the country it seemed over-populated. Could this partly be the reason for Japan's war of expansion we wondered between ourselves? At least it explained Japan's ability to pour millions of soldiers into its war of aggression and with the obvious capacity to treble its Armed Forces from such a vast human resource. This thought was chilling, Godwin summarised in his diary though he did in typical fashion, add his impressions of the population in general and as follows:

'What a mouldy, dirty, poverty-stricken looking bunch they appeared. If their Armed Forces were reasonably well-fed, the civilians didn't look it. Small of stature and thin, they looked somewhat pitiful in their mended rags. How could the West fear such pitiful creatures? Even in my weakened state I could have mixed it with six of them in unarmed combat. But here I must pause. Even a boy can pull the trigger of a gun. With the Japanese penchant for being heavily armed, even to wearing swords, and their known fanaticism, size really doesn't come into it. Add to this their enormous numbers and blind faith in their Emperor, whichever way you look at it, they represent a formidable force.'

'The salted fish, perforce eaten because of sheer hunger, only exacerbated our thirst as the train rumbled on through quite picturesque scenery. Still the guards would give us no water despite our pleading. Visits to the Benjo (toilet), a stinking hole at the end of the carriage, were an exercise in fortitude. Slightly recessed from the centre aisle and screened by a split bamboo curtain, it had no paper nor water for flushing. For a so-called civilised country, it was a bloody disgrace. Japan had copied most everything from the West, but the basics – like sanitation, had not advanced with the rest of its progress.'

'We finally arrived at Ofuna around 1230 hours on June 29. Some third class Nip sailor met us at the platform where we were compelled to stand around for a whole bloody hour with the guards watching us like hawks. At this point thirst was becoming critical and with gestures, etc we conveyed to the sailor the pressing need for water. This ignoramus couldn't understand our sign language or pretended not to. Shrugging, he looked at his wristwatch before consulting with two of the heavily armed guards. It was bloody pathetic really. As battered, emaciated, thirsty and handcuffed prisoners, why the need for so many rifle-toting guards? What the hell were they scared of? Sure and in general, they were smaller than us, but they had guns!'

'After our long wait on the station platform and being gawked at by teeming throngs of civilians, the guards assembled us in two lines and once again tied ropes around our necks and attached to each other. All of the guards had army kitbags and compelled a number of prisoners to carry them. This was damned cumbersome handcuffed as we were and with our arms sloped in front of us. Then with a gesture the naval Nip led us from the station. As our footwear had been removed before leaving the cursed ship, the narrow twisting cobble-paved streets were as hot as hell under the burning early afternoon sun. Occasionally we were spat upon by civilians, while some, more vengeful than others, thumped and kicked us. The escorting guards merely grinned their pleasure at our humiliation.'

'What with my aching knees – consequent to the thumb-tack ordeal in Java, and having to lug a Nip kitbag awkwardly, I was bordering on the urge to change a few eyes from slanted to black. Fed-up, honest to goodness rage boiled within me. I'd had a gutsful. But, commonsense prevailed. It was better to put up with the hateful reactions of the populace and to endure kicks and thumps, rather than be felled by a rifle-butt. How I had learnt to fear rifle-butts.'

As Godwin's diary relates, the final episode into captivity unfolded as the prisoners trudged for two and a half miles past crowds of Japanese civilians and a gauntlet of spitting and fist-

waving potential antagonists. The soles of the prisoners' feet
ached and seared as the hot pavement added to their thirst for
water and abject misery. Looming into view was the unmistakable contour of a prison camp. A high wooden fence surmounted
with coils of rusty barbed wire. A raised watch-tower beside an
open and waiting gateway. Two guards slowly pacing – also
waiting, and no surprise, with bayonets fixed to their rifles.

Once inside the camp and with the main gates shut behind
them, the prisoners were allowed to put the heavy kitbags down
after which the ropes around their necks were untied and handcuffs removed. For all of them it was a blessed relief to simply let
their arms hang loosely by their sides. There followed a surprisingly accurate roll-call by an English speaking NCO until the
name MacGregor was called. The name was called again
followed by a continuing strained silence. Clearly, the officer in
charge of the prisoners aboard the ship had either forgotten to
erase MacGregor's name or, as was quite probable in view of the
fact that not once did he visit the prisoners during their ordeal on
the ship, the Snake as likely as not, failed to report the death.
Disposing of MacGregor's body would have been simple by the
convenient expedient of slipping the corpse over the side. After
all, the Snake was capable of anything and besides, it was he who
had murdered MacGregor.

Captain Symmons stepped once pace forward and called across
to the NCO that Mr MacGregor had died at sea. Without being
asked he stepped back into line. With the roll-call completed, the
prisoners were separated and marched off to various spartan
looking huts and immediately ordered to shower and place their
clothing in receptacles for delousing. The prisoners must have
delighted in the cold water cascading down their bodies and into
their mouths – especially mouths. Godwin mentions this godsend
especially, because all of the prisoners were at the end of their
tether with thirst.

In the following days and after interrogation, the prisoners
were escorted from the camp in twos and threes for unknown
destinations within Japan. As a group the *Behar* survivors ceased

to exist. There was no opportunity to farewell each other, just an order from the Camp Administration backed up with the arrival of escorting guards. Captivity, forced labour, medical neglect, starvation and brutality, all these vicissitudes awaited in scattered parts of Japan.

In due course Godwin was interrogated after which and with only five minutes notice, he was escorted by two armed guards from the camp, taken to a train and accompanied by his guards, travelled to POW Camp 15D based on the outskirts of Niigata, a seaport on the north-western coast of central Honshu, the largest island in Japan. For the remainder of the war he was forced to perform slave labour – ten hours a day in exhausting toil. Rigorous conditions, constant brutality, a starvation diet consisting of food not fit for pigs, took its toll. On the day that the *Behar* was sunk, Godwin weighed 214 pounds and was aged twenty-one. Eighteen months later and following liberation from a POW camp in Japan, he weighed 85 pounds, a weight loss of 129 pounds. He was still six feet two inches but otherwise he was an emaciated walking skeleton – just skin and bones.

Godwin believed that it was his youthfulness and reserves of vigour that saved his life. Prisoners ten years or more older than himself suffered a grim mortality rate. The ones unfortunate enough to succumb in the older age group lacked the endurance to withstand vicious ill-treatment, malnutrition and forced labour. Many were captured Allied servicemen who suffered recurring bouts of malaria and various tropical and debilitating diseases. The Japanese perversely denied the desperately sick medical attention. In many instances prisoners also died of untreated war wounds. As if to hasten their deaths, their pitifully small food rations were either reduced further, or cut off completely. If this wasn't a policy of deliberate genocide, then what was?

Godwin was later to write – when he was fully recovered after convalescence in New Zealand, that one of the largest Allied cemeteries in the Pacific-Asia area was in Japan itself – to Japan's lasting shame. Not one military battle was fought – other than

Allied air raids, within the Japanese Home Islands and commonly recognised as part of Japan. An invasion was avoided through Japan's surrender, yet many thousands of Allied servicemen and civilians are buried in Japanese soil and as the International War Graves Commission will confirm. Most of these now forgotten victims did not die in combat. They were systematically brutalised and starved to death. Untreated illness and forced labour to the point of collapse also took a terrible toll. Then there were the executions that the Japanese nowadays don't want to talk about and wish the world to forget.

4

Liberation

WHEN peace and sanity was restored to Japan in August 1945, there began a massive operation to repatriate huge numbers of Japanese soldiers back to their homeland from Asia and the Pacific. The Allied Authorities were staggered by their sheer numbers in occupied lands. The largest Japanese Army to surrender in one area was the Kwantung, a force comprising 594,000 men and which included 148 generals. This vast army surrendered to the forces of the Soviet Union following direct orders from Emperor Hirohito.

On a lesser scale but huge in relation to the land occupied, was the 100,000 Japanese Army occupying Rabaul in the south-west Pacific. Other occupied countries and islands too numerous to mention were also garrisoned with an amazing number of soldiers. At war's end, there were 5,500,000 men serving in the Imperial Japanese Army alone. Had a conventional war continued and two atomic bombs not been dropped, Japan might not have surrendered so easily. It did after all, have a huge number of men bearing arms and willing to die for their Emperor. A fight to the death would have cost the Allies an enormous toll and in the process would have guaranteed the mass murders of all those held in captivity by the Japanese. Thus the dropping of the two A-bombs was well justified.

All this information was eventually learned by prisoner of war James Godwin, prison number 1562 soon after being freed from POW Camp 15D, Niigata. It wasn't until 4 September 1945, that Godwin was liberated. It took the Allies some time to locate and liberate prisoners from a number of POW camps. Some were registered, some were not – particularly the slave labour camps.

Battle hardened Allied Occupation Forces – the advance guard, were shocked and angry each time a prisoner of war camp was liberated. The prisoners without exception were grotesquely emaciated, walking skeletons with sunken eyes and all wearing a haunted look. They had been starved and malnourished and forced to work to support Japan's war effort. Many of the prisoners were extremely ill and neither cared whether they lived or died. Despite immediate medical attention and copious supplies of baby food, a number of prisoners died. They were too far gone to save.

In many instances, camp guards with fearsome reputations were either transferred by the Japanese Army immediately after Japan surrendered or simply disappeared. Accountability for their brutal actions cunningly avoided. Against this background of past cruelty and current deception, Fleet Air-Arm Lieutenant James Gowing Godwin was liberated to return to a sane civilized world. On 26 September, he along with many other New Zealand and Australian ex prisoners of war were placed aboard an allied hospital ship and transported south, away from a land of fanatics, misery and death.

After returning to New Zealand, Godwin who was still only twenty-two, made a quite rapid recovery. Standing him in good stead was his comparative youth and strong interest in sport. Solid substantial meals and a kind environment did much to restore his vigour and physical well-being. After five months of hospitalisation and relaxed convalescence his weight increased dramatically. From eighty-five pounds it rose to almost 200, just twenty pounds less than his weight before capture. For a period of time and like most returned prisoners of war, Godwin was disinclined to talk about his harrowing experiences, they were too soul-searing to re-live, too depressing to dwell upon. It was this very silence – maintained by a lot of returned prisoners – that denied future generations the real truth about Japanese barbarity and coincidentally, saved Japan from many sordid disclosures and unforgivable examples of brutal terror. That a country could wage a war of such ferocity and fanaticism and then virtually get

away with it, seemed incomprehensible, but with murdered or
reluctant witnesses, or simply by understandable default, justice
to a large degree took a holiday.

With his well-being and vigour restored, Godwin took stock of
his post-war situation. There were all sorts of rehabilitation
schemes being introduced by the Labour Government of the day
for returned servicemen. Large numbers of them accepted these
'rehab loans' and returned to 'civvy street', but Godwin was not
one of them. He had majored well in all subjects in his earlier
years at school before completing his education at college. It was
the war that prevented his going on to university. Notwith-
standing, he was naturally talented and had sufficient education
to become one of his country's youngest commissioned officers.

But now, and with the world conflict resolved, it was time to
evaluate his future career now that the guns had ceased firing.
Finally, and with his mind made up, Godwin applied to the New
Zealand Naval Authorities for a further posting. Included in the
curriculum vitae he submitted was his wartime diary testifying to
his experience as a prisoner of war. Along with this information
he reminded his service aboard HMS *Illustrious* and his acquired
ability to speak Japanese and recognise Japan's alphabetical
symbols, an achievement gained during his incarceration in
Japan.

He was not to be disappointed. Two weeks after posting his
application he received an official OHMS letter from Wellington.
Several matters were raised, chief among which was a request for
a medical clearance. Godwin was requested to report to the Royal
New Zealand Navy Administrative HQ at Wellington and to
bring his medical clearance with him. He was also to prepare
himself for an examination in the Japanese language as well as
being tested in interpreting Japanese alphabetical characters and
symbols. There was, the letter concluded, every possibility of an
overseas posting subject to his passing the required stipulations.

Godwin duly complied with the requests contained in the letter,
along with producing a medical clearance. He passed the
Japanese language and alphabet course satisfactorily before

being interviewed by a desk-bound Naval Commander for a personal resume about himself. A further two weeks passed before a phone call to his residence from the Naval HQ excited his hopes. He was to report at the HQ the following morning at 9.30.

Unbeknown to Godwin, his war service records, even his diary, had been despatched to the British Admiralty (Intelligence Division). Liking what they read – particularly that Godwin was fluent in both reading and speaking Japanese, a cable was despatched to Wellington from London requesting Godwin's services in Tokyo as a War Crimes investigator. During the cabled exchanges that followed, it was decided to second Fleet Air-Arm Lieutenant James Godwin to the Second Australian War Crimes Section based at Tokyo and under the supreme jurisdiction of General Douglas MacArthur. It was further decided to commission Godwin as an Army Captain: Intelligence.

Godwin was astounded but delighted at the Tokyo appointment and had no difficulty in accepting his new role as a captain in the Australian Army. It must have been a wonderful feeling for him to leave the NZ Naval HQ the following morning with his assignment confirmed and posting to Tokyo via Sydney already arranged. A fortnight's leave was granted before he was required to pick up his tickets at the Huddart Parker building in downtown Wellington and embark aboard the MV *Wanganella*, a fast and comfortable passenger liner plying between Wellington and Sydney.

Godwin was very close to his family, but especially, his two sisters who adored him. Still a bachelor and with fourteen days of precious leave and travel warrants available to him, Godwin made the most of it. He spent a few restful days in the Marlborough Province, staying at the peaceful country town of Blenheim in the company of his family. He visited Nelson, Motueka and Collingwood on the ninth and tenth days and looked up some schoolboy chums. For the next three days he returned and stayed at Blenheim, savouring the peace and quiet of a typical rural NZ countryside and knowing only too well the frenetic and teeming environment that awaited him in Japan. His elder sister, Moyra, and in the absence of his younger sister, went out of her way to do anything for him, not really knowing when he might return from Japan.

On the morning of the 14th day of his fortnight's leave, Godwin was driven by car to the small port of Picton – some twenty-five miles away, accompanied by his parents who were naturally sad to see him go. With fond hugs and farewells said, Godwin embarked aboard the SS *Tamahine*, a Cook Strait passenger ferry that though reliable and always on time at either Wellington or Picton, was even better known for its slight but permanent star-board list. The passage to Wellington in reasonably fine weather took a little under three-and-a-half hours and by 4.30 pm, Godwin had presented himself at the Huddart Parker building to collect his *Wanganella* passenger tickets.

A little after 7.30 in the evening, Godwin had boarded the large passenger ship and amongst numerous people and a babble of voices in the ship's main boarding foyer, he wended a somewhat restricted path to a wide stair-well that led to his single cabin on the next deck above, with a steward carrying his luggage leading the way.

Precisely at 9 pm, the *Wanganella* slipped its moorings and moved at moderate speed up harbour until at a certain point in line with a quarantine station on Somes Island, it steered a few points south-west of Barretts Reef beyond which lay Cook Strait and the major shipping lane to Sydney. Godwin sighed with anticipation as he leaned against the ship's rails. The opportunity to investigate past wrongs by the Japanese, a comforting thought.

Captain James Gowing Godwin, New Zealand Army
(attached to Australian Army Intelligence, 1947)

5

Appointment with Destiny

IT was a particularly hot Tokyo day as Army Intelligence
Captain James Godwin waited patiently in front of a large
reception desk for previously approved security clearance. This
entailed a photo of himself along with pertinent details of his
height, colour of hair and eyes and any other distinguishing characteristics. The thick glossy security pass would he knew, have a
Security Seal embossed along with a supplied security code.

He breathed deeply while casually glancing around the bustling
foyer. He had arrived at Tokyo's port from Sydney by passenger
ship the previous day where he had been met by a down-to-earth
Australian Army Major by the name of Rafferty. With introduc-
tion dispensed with, Rafferty led the way down the ship's
gangway – a broad almost staircase affair, and into a waiting
army pool car. The driver had swiftly deposited Godwin's
luggage into the car's boot before driving to a rather large inn that
had escaped the fire-bombing of Tokyo and which had been taken
over in its entirety by the QM Division of the Australian
Occupation Forces.

Once allocated a room and after being shown where ablutions
etc. were located, Rafferty had mentioned that compared to
Australia, the inn was a dump but was the best available. It
was, he had added, only three blocks from where Godwin
would be working. With a twisted grin he had further remarked
that at least it was bloody better than a Japanese prison camp.
Godwin's thoughts wandered to the big austere multi-storey
building where he had been shown his separate office – immediately next to a large room accommodating the secretarial
pool – mainly nimble-fingered typists. The previous day had

indeed been busy, he mused to himself as a polite voice called, 'Sir, sir?'

Abruptly Godwin's mind returned to the present. A pretty and quite young American girl was holding an Investigating Officer's Warrant and his vital Security Pass. 'These will provide access to all three buildings within the Supreme Allied Command Headquarters,' she advised with an assuring smile. 'Don't lose them, Captain,' she added thoughtfully.

'I'll look after them,' Godwin smiled back. 'It's tough trying to get past those Provosts without official ID.' Tucking the two important and convenient size cards into an inner tunic pocket of his new Australian Army uniform and flashing a smile of thanks he turned and made his way out of the Goodwood Park Hotel, one of the three Command buildings that had been commandeered immediately following the Allied occupation of Japan.

The Meiji building – one of the three Command centres, was situated nearby but across the street. Like the building he'd just left, it was guarded by white-helmeted Provosts (American Military Police). They looked quite snappy in their smart uniforms and all wore holstered forty-five calibre guns. Parked in front of both buildings, Godwin noted, were a couple of MP army jeeps with noticeable whip aerials attached near to their spare wheels at the rear. White helmeted drivers sat languidly behind their steering wheels.

Flashing his newly acquired pass, Godwin entered the building with a spring in his step. He was looking forward to his new duties with a resolution and enthusiasm that overcame inner doubts as to his competence for the job. Flying an aircraft which he was good at – especially off aircraft carriers, was one thing, but investigating war criminals was a totally different endeavour, however, having been a prisoner of war gave him a personal insight into the mind-set of the Japanese. He could not be fooled or hood-winked nor would passive meekness or duplicity cloud his judgement. He had been an unwilling guest of these bastards he thought grimly, and if he had anything to do with it, justice would be fairly served.

Arriving on the seventh-floor via an antiquated elevator, Godwin strode purposefully towards Major Rafferty's office. It was two doors past his own and to reach it he had to pass through the secretarial pool and the chatter of several typewriters. Within the building and on each floor there were numerous offices that accommodated various departments servicing unified Investigative Sections of the Allied Powers. By far the largest presence was American.

Major Rafferty was standing in front of a bank of filing cabinets at the far end of the large office. With a frown puckering his expression he was closely examining two files, one to the other, puzzlement plainly obvious. He looked up at Godwin's approach, his frown turning to a sardonic grin.

'Ah, Godwin,' he greeted. 'How did you get on across the road? Everything okay?'

Godwin removed his cap before replying. 'It went like a breeze, sir, other than having to wait a bit, but yes, I'm now fully armed.' He smiled tapping his tunic pocket. 'I have the keys to the door.'

Rafferty's grin melted to a look of understanding. 'It's those bloody provosts,' he remarked. 'They stopped Colonel Donaldson a fortnight ago. He was ropable. Mislaid his pass and had to return to his digs to get it before allowing him into the building.'

'Jeez! a Colonel?' Godwin breathed. 'Is security that tight, sir?'

Raffety nodded. 'It has to be, captain.' He indicated the open drawer of a filing cabinet. 'There's wheelers and dealers out there and still the odd fanatic. We can't be too careful.' He glanced at the open drawer. 'There's powerful interests who might do anything to get their hands on these dossiers,' he flicked the two files in his hands. 'These for example.'

Godwin nodded before asking a question. 'There's a lot of filing cabinets, sir, which ones are classified?'

'The whole bloody lot,' Rafferty's answer was quick. 'Every file relates to one sort of atrocity or another,' he sighed with a knowing look. 'As you'll be finding out, many of them relate one to the other and to make it damned difficult, some of the war criminals listed have two identities. The worst bastards threw away their pay-books and assumed the identities of private soldiers killed or missing in action.' He shook his head, 'The records section of the bloody Japanese Army covered up for a lot of these mongrels by listing them as transferred or killed in action and this was after Japan surrendered unconditionally.'

Godwin nodded, the advice didn't surprise him in the least. He was well aware of Japanese intransigence and duplicity. 'So where do I start, sir?' he sombrely asked above the chatter, whings and pings of busy typewriters.

'I've left a couple of completed files on your desk. They've been satisfactorily investigated with the help of the War Crimes Registry at Singapore. The two bastards involved were damned hard to find. They were hiding out in their home-towns under assumed names. One of them is locked-up in Sugamo Prison awaiting trial, the other committed seppuku (suicide) just before we had a chance to arrest him. The bastard was tipped off.'

'Tipped off? By whom?' Godwin looked askance.

'The Precinct police for the area,' Rafferty said heavily. 'We can't prove it but we now know that many a slippery mongrel has evaded us with the aid of sympathetic cops. The bigger the fish the more support they get,' He sighed, 'A lot of the police haven't come to terms with losing their war, besides, the accused who murdered and massacred their way across the Pacific and Asia, are considered heroes by many civilians and police alike,' he shrugged, 'Now you see what we're up against.'

Godwin rubbed his chin thoughtfully. 'I didn't know, sir. I'm glad you told me.' He glanced towards his office. 'I'll get stuck in and read up these files right away, unless you want me for something else?'

Rafferty's expression changed to a knowing smile. 'I like your enthusiasm, Godwin. Let's hope that what you encounter, and some of it's bloody awful, doesn't diminish this outlook.' He glanced back at the files in his hand. 'Keep an open mind and good luck.'

Taking this as a dismissal, Godwin turned towards his office, little knowing that ahead of him lay nearly three years of exhausting and frustrating investigative endeavour. He was to learn beyond any doubt, the capacity for suspects to brazenly lie, admit nothing and deny everything. His wits and commonsense would be tested to the full when interrogating past masters at deception and falsehood. But today at least, he would merely be swotting and acquiring the knowledge of investigative proce- dures as well as brushing up on Japanese language skills and interpretation of alphabetical characteristics and symbols that would make him one of the best linguists and interpreters within the War Crimes Investigative Section of SCAP (Supreme Command Allied Powers).

The office assigned to Godwin was he thought, built for a dwarf. Even the desk though broad, was so low it was difficult to place his knees under its varnished but well-scratched top. Some unimportant books placed under its stout wooden legs made a tremendous difference in accommodating his six-foot plus frame. The chair was reasonably okay, but he made a mental note to acquire a small slab of foam rubber to cover some protruding upholstery screws securing the chair's leather lined horse-hair padding – originally intended about fifty years previously to make the seat comfortable. One small window allowed in suffi- cient natural light and fresh air if he so desired. He noticed that a name-plate with his army rank was affixed to the partly opened door. Two filing cabinets and a tier of three empty shelves completed the spartan furnishing of his office. In front of Godwin was the usual desk bric-a-brac as well as a very large blotting pad, pristine in unscribbled readiness as well as two green cardboard folio covers within which reposed the two War Crimes Files that Rafferty had mentioned.

The room-size of the office, Godwin mentally noted, appeared to be about twelve feet by twelve and though the furnishings were minimal, gave the impression of being cramped for space. Bending across and reaching out with his hand he pushed the edge of the door to the closed position. It helped to reduce the constant noise of typewriters. Drawing the two folios towards him he flipped back the cover of the first and began to read.

Godwin hadn't really noted the time when he began to read the resume and full summary of the first file. It was so engrossing, mind-chilling and bizarre that minutes turned to half-hours then hours. He had almost completed reading the official text and was looking forward to perusing several pages of hand-written notes supplied by the investigating officer when a light knock on the door heralded the arrival of a lass from the adjacent secretarial pool; she was holding a saucered cup of tea.

Godwin glanced at his watch and was startled to note that it was 3.30 in the afternoon. 'Crikey! smoko' time already?' he grinned. 'Strewth! How time flies.'

The typist daintily set the hot drink on the desk and replied in an unmistakable American accent. 'Major Rafferty suggested you might like tea, sir.' she smiled coyly. 'All of us girls prefer coffee. Uh, the Major said that you took milk and two lumps of sugar. Is that okay, sir?'

Godwin nodded his appreciation while trying to figure how the Major knew he liked milk and sugar and for that matter tea. But of course, the penny dropped, during breakfast at the inn that morning he had ordered a pot of tea, milk and sugar. Clearly the Major who had shared his table was an observant bloke. 'Er, thanks,' he offered belatedly.

Lingering in Godwin's mind was the compacted information read from the file. The stark clinical realism of murder committed under the guise and defence of military necessity and finally admitted by the defendant, was outrageous in view of the known facts. Three Dutch prisoners of war and two Dutch Mill-Hill Fathers (Clergy), who had been captured and executed inside their Catholic Church, had been entrusted to the care of a Japanese Army NCO strictly ordered to remain at the rear of a Japanese reconnaissance patrol carefully probing the surrounding area for any sign of an armed allied presence.

Native islanders who had been fearfully watching the NCO and two Japanese soldiers from the shelter of a banana plantation had, after the war, stated on oath that the three soldiers – two of whom, one being the NCO, and identified by name, had after closely guarding the prisoners for two hours, forced all five at the point of bayonets to walk to a church on the outskirts of a deserted village. The native witnesses had discreetly followed and witnessed the beheadings of the three bound Dutch civilians in a grave-yard next to the church. The Catholic priests had been taken into the church. Ten minutes later the Japanese soldiers came out of the church and without a glance at their three previous victims, returned to their positions close to an inner lagoon.

The islanders fearing the worst crept into the silent church. Both Dutch priests lay sprawled in front of the altar that was surmounted by a large crucifix. The priests had been beheaded. Godwin sighed, distractedly he began reading the investigating officer's notes. In places the details were more explicit, yet impartial, clinical. Comments and observations helpful to the prosecution were added. This included the accused's attitude, remorse or arrogant, his penchant for lying or telling the truth and so on. Godwin's interest quickened as he noted Major Rafferty's signature as the investigating officer. He wryly smiled to himself while clearly understanding the Major's motive. He had learned more in a couple of hours reading a war criminal's case history and the procedures to be followed in investigations than he would have in a whole day's listening. Such was the analysis and depth of both interrogation and finally, proof. After all, a suspect's life could well hang in the balance.

Moving his empty cup aside Goodwin began reading the second file. It was thinner than the first but no less bizarre. There were no interrogation notes nor a case made out for prosecution. At the top of the first page and lightly underlined was the word deceased. His thoughts flashed back to what Rafferty had spoken earlier. 'One of these bastards was tipped off. He committed seppuku.' That guilt prompted the suspect to take his own life was not an issue. What murderous deed or deeds he had been involved in was. Intrigued, Godwin began to read the file. It only took half-an-hour because of the lack of supporting prosecution details. After reading the file he pondered deeply. What made a man personally kill fourteen people in cold blood? Was he a psychopath? Was he a genocidal fanatic?

Godwin rubbed his eyes before stretching back in his chair. His thoughts reverting to introspection and his own personal experiences as a prisoner of war. Isolated instances of murderous and unexplainable brutality along with wilful killings of defenceless people, could in context, be viewed as human aberrations and not representative of normal civilised standards. But this was an exoneration utterly at variance with the facts. The murders and massacres by troops in the field had all the hallmarks of ruthless consent sanctioned by the highest authorities of the Imperial Japanese Army and tacitly approved by Japan's wartime government.

He was well aware of wholesale massacres and instances of individual acts of slaughter by the Japanese. Had he not witnessed three beheadings himself and the clubbing to death of an elderly civilian? He took a deep breath, slowly expelling air from his lungs while attempting to come up with satisfactory answers. If there was no rhyme or reason to such killings inflicted upon conquered civilians or captured allied servicemen, then, there was no substantive motive. But such unsoldierly excesses – and they were in their tens-of-thousands, had to have an explanation. Murders of such mind-chilling proportions could not be generalised as isolated aberrations and motiveless. Common-sense and reason demanded answers. There could only be one conclusion Godwin thought, flicking a quick glance at his wrist-watch. Psychopathic genocidal fanaticism did not need motive or pretext. All it required was natural hate, a lust to kill and inherent sadism. This latter analogy being more than sufficient to justify in warped minds such murderous conduct.

Godwin's reverie was interrupted with the entrance into his small office by Major Rafferty. He was wearing his cap and held a briefcase in his hand. 'It's past 5.30, Godwin,' Rafferty smiled, 'Shall we stroll to our digs together? The walk will do us good.'

Godwin climbed to his feet. 'That's a good idea, Major, it'll help clear the mind after what I've been reading.' He reached for his cap. 'I note that you investigated both files. Your procedures and interrogation report were damned interesting. Perhaps if I just follow your style, I might do somewhere near as well.'

Rafferty stepped back into the passageway, followed by Godwin. 'On our way out I've got something for you. We call it homework,' he grinned. 'And yes, I thought it best to supply two completed files that were not too complicated.' He paused momentarily, 'We'd better return them to their cabinet. We don't want the cleaners gawking at them. It's all classified stuff.'

Nodding, Godwin stepped back and retrieved the files from his desk before following the Major into the secretarial office. Quickly Rafferty replaced the folios into their correct cabinet before unlocking a steel-door cabinet and removing a brand new briefcase. 'This is going to be your constant companion,' he grinned. 'Inside it there's an English-Japanese language guide and two-language dictionary. From what I know you understand the Nip dialogue and alphabet fairly well, but this lot will sharpen your skills.' He closed and locked the cabinet door before rising to his feet and passing the new leather briefcase to Godwin.

'Is this my homework?' Godwin's expression was quizzical.

'Sometimes it may be. Other times you'll be so caught up with what you're investigating, you'll find the urge to take the more difficult cases with you to study in the evening.' Rafferty's expression was sombre. 'You will encounter bare-faced lies and deviousness in many of the accuseds' "answers".'

The stroll back to the inn was enervating despite the jostling occasionally experienced where teeming crowds of civilians reduced walking to an enforced shuffle. After a leisurely but rather plain dinner (European menu), Godwin spent an hour relaxing and shooting the breeze (chatting) with other Allied officers in an ordinary but comfortably furnished public lounge. Major Rafferty had been invited to dinner at the British Officers Club by a Captain Richard O. Crewdson, a Grenadier Guards officer attached to the Intelligence Section of the British Liaison

Mission at Tokyo. He was also the chief arresting officer. Godwin
was later to meet this outstanding person and learn from him the
subtleties of the Japanese psyche and the political influences that
in a surreptitious way were helping war criminals escape justice.

It was Crewdson who told Godwin of his firm conviction that
his predecessor, Colonel C.H. Wild, the British Mission's Chief
Investigating Officer, had been murdered because he knew too
much. It was Colonel Wild who had insisted on investigating the
Emperor's cousins and brothers, all royal princes, who were no
less guilty than the officers and men they commanded. The Rape
of Nanking and the Germ Warfare Centre at Harbin in Manchuria
were both directed by royal princes in their capacities as lieutenant generals. Even the Emperor himself affixed his personal
Imperial Seal to the establishment of several Germ Warfare
Centres and where eventually, tens of thousands of prisoners of
war were transported and subsequently exterminated by inhuman
experiments. The Emperor was the arch-war criminal, but he was
protected from prosecution as were the Imperial Princes, by
General Douglas MacArthur.

Godwin was also to learn of the suspicious circumstances of
Colonel Wild's death, but which caused many people in high
places – both Allied and Japanese, to heave sighs of relief – not
regret. It is fitting at this point to recall the Colonel's sudden
death and how it occurred.

Colonel Wild was aboard a two-engined Dakota that lumbered
down the runway of Hong Kong's Kai Tak Airport enroute to
Singapore. His briefcase was full of incriminating documentation
that not only identified a new and powerful group of highly-
placed war criminals, but revealed – much to the embarrassment
of the Allies – particularly the British, that at least one Japanese
general had been wrongfully convicted of war crimes that he had
no involvement in. It was too late to turn back the clock as the
unfortunate general had been executed at Singapore some weeks
previously.

The man that Colonel Wild really wanted to lay his hands on was
a Colonel Masanobu Tsuji, a man who during the war had far more

power than his military rank bestowed. Wild had the evidence to prove that Tsuji had master-minded the Alexandra Hospital massacre, the killing of thousands of Singaporean Chinese – for which a Japanese general had been wrongly executed, and the slaughter of United States and Filipino Servicemen in the notorious Bataan Death March. But even more incriminating, was the evidence Wild had accumulated against Japan's Imperial Dynasty. Advice to Colonel Wild to back-pedal his investigations into the Emperor's role in war crimes and that of Imperial Princes, fell on deaf ears. 'Justice for one must mean justice for all' was this senior British officer's criteria. But it was not to be.

A few short minutes into its flight after passing over Kowloon, the Dakota – usually most reliable aircraft, shuddered in mid-air. Still at good speed but for no apparent reason, it nose-dived from 4,000 feet and crashed in a ball of flame into a hillside. There were no survivors. But, was there ever meant to be? Many a Japanese war criminal – those known and unknown, must have sighed with relief when told that not only had everyone been killed in the crash – including Colonel Wild – but that all of his vital and incriminating evidence had been destroyed. Thus did this single-minded and crusading British officer meet an untimely end. The date, 25 September 1946.

Captain James Godwin was to encounter considerable intrigue and prevarication during his three years at Tokyo, more particularly and blatantly noticeable during his final six months as an Investigating Officer. But during his first week no hint of collusion or collaboration with a former enemy was even thinkable. Outward manifestations of soft-pedalling by the Allies was not to become apparent until the beginning of 1949. Godwin assumed his appointment at Tokyo in early July, 1947. He would have a fair go for eighteen months before political and military corruption – better described as wheeling and dealing, slowly disillusioned him and like the late Colonel Wild, his crusade too, 'of justice for one justice for all', a dedication deftly foiled by an emerging Allied Japanese Conspiracy.

Solid proof and beyond rebuttal has, for the past half century,

eluded many historians searching for the truth that could explain
Japan's remarkable return to prosperity and the 'Big Lie' that all
War Crimes Investigations had been completely and successfully
prosecuted. Without evidence to the contrary, apologists and
collaborators alike have been able to rebut and condemn writers
and historians who have had the temerity and courage to challenge and question the true reasons for the inclusion of Article 14
in the San Francisco Peace Treaty signed in 1952, and the
disgraceful neglect of not insisting that Japan compensate the
many hundreds of thousands of Allied prisoners of war who
suffered cruelly at the hands of the Japanese.

The forces of avarice, a greed for power, money, influence and
total political immorality, these were the ingredients of an unholy
alliance that ultimately triumphed following Japan's murderous
war. But all of these things came to fruition and indeed were
plotted between MacArthur's headquarters and the Imperial
Palace – only a stone throw away, between mid-1950 and 1952.
The following were just some of the leading players involved in a
most cleverly contrived conspiracy of mutual interest and who
supported MacArthur as the supreme representative of the Allied
Powers in Japan. Without any doubt, Washington DC pulled the
strings as after all, MacArthur was its man. Then there was
President Harry S. Truman, John Foster Dulles and some big-
name political and business tycoons, all from the United States of
America. Others included Sydney G. Holland, Prime Minister of
New Zealand, Ben Chifley, Prime Minister of Australia and to a
lesser extent Clement Atlee, Prime Minister of Great Britain.
Generalissimo Chiang Kai-shek of China who was having
serious problems with the advance of Communism in his country,
but who despised Japan, was bought over by millions of dollars in
military aid and credits. How then could the conspiracy of political and other interests fail?

Captain James Godwin who was now twenty-three, knew
nothing of political wheeling and dealing. From late youth
through to his present age, his experience of the world centred
upon being a member of the Allied Armed Forces until his

capture and imprisonment by the Japanese. He did, however, have one major interest and that was to help bring to justice as many Japanese war criminals as fate might permit. His writings clearly define this dedication and are worthy of repeating.

'I declare,' Godwin wrote, 'my determination to bring as many of these cowardly bastards who beat up old men and women, to justice. I witnessed all the horrors of captivity, and endured them to a point and on many occasions, exhaustion. I was beaten and clubbed almost senseless many times over. I saw brave Allied servicemen beheaded and a very sick old man clubbed to death. At POW Camp 15D in Japan, I was almost starved to death and saw many fellow prisoners who simply died from forced labour, medical neglect and appalling malnutrition. To all those who suffered and perished I am resolved to do my best to atone their miseries and deaths, unlamented as seemingly they are. Fate has given me the opportunity to represent the victims of Japanese barbarity in a most privileged and sacred task. I will speak for all those who perished at the hands of the Japanese. I can do no less.' (Dated 30 June 1947)

Enlightened by Godwin's worthy dedication, but now made aware of the forces of expediency and collusion slowly nurturing in post-war Japan and which were ultimately responsible for the closing down of War Crimes investigations in early 1950, let us return to Captain Godwin's quiet evening in the public lounge of his billet and the end of his first day attached to the Second Australian War Crimes Section.

It was close to 10 pm and with the lounge almost deserted other than three officers playing cards, Godwin decided to listen to the American Armed Forces network on the wireless – in those days there was no television or transistors. As anticipated and exactly at ten o'clock, the 'Voice of America' shortwave broadcast came through. Keeping the volume low so as not to distract the card players, he listened to the news which was mainly depressing. Two more Nazi war criminals had been sentenced at the War Crimes Trials held in Nuremberg. Generalissimo Franco of Spain was claiming Gibraltar as part of Spain and the Iron Curtain across half of Europe was ensuring the freedoms of people living under Soviet domination – according to *Tass*, the official Soviet news-agency.

Suppressing a yawn, Godwin continued listening until a languid weariness overcame him by half-past the hour. The music from the wireless was good, but sleep beckoned. Rising from a comfortable armchair he switched off the music and repaired to his room on the first floor. An early night would stand him in good stead, he thought, as ten minutes later he slipped himself into bed.

6

Investigations Commence

REFRESHED and full of vigour after his quiet night, Captain James Godwin sat at his desk leafing through documentation that Major Rafferty had, five minutes earlier, deposited in front of him with the advice that it would keep him going for most of the day. Rafferty had also stated that he would be out of the building for the rest of the day because he didn't know how long it was going to take to interrogate a prisoner at Sugamo Prison, long sought but finally apprehended in the guise of a monk at a Buddhist monastery in Fukushima.

With Rafferty's departure, Godwin settled down to the task of familiarising himself with the names of war criminals listed in a separate folio and who were held in Sugamo Prison awaiting trial or, who were still being interrogated. The list he was studying is set out hereunder.

SUGAMO PRISON – 22 July 1947

FILE	NAME	REASON	DATE ARRESTED
158D	Baga Kihachi	Suspicion murder	Released
125B	Nagai Yasuo	Two murders	28.10.46
158A	Ryokai Tsugio	Nine murders	2.11.46
159H	Ito Suzuki	Ordered massacre	Escaped arrest
150	Kitamura Juchi	Involved massacre	12.11.46
150	Suzuki Tadashi	" "	"
150	Shirakana Mitsugu	" "	Suicided
150	Kitamura Yoshihiro	" "	28.11.46
150	Teshima Fusataro	" "	"
125H	Kaino Denroku	Three murders	3.12.46
125H	Fukaya Hiroshi	" "	4.12.46
125H	Miyakawa Kiyoshi	" "	15.12.46
125H	Sakamoto Sadatoshi	" "	Suicided
125D	Tamaki Wakichi	Missionary murder	29.1.47
125D	Hijama Kesao	" "	31.1.47

125D	Wakamatsu Shigeyoshi	"	"	14.1.47
125D	Fujie Giichi	"	"	15.1.47
125D	Meguro Tatsuo	"	"	Evaded arrest
125D	Yokoyama Ichizo	"	"	3.2.47
125D	Magata Isao	"	"	Evaded arrest
125D	Ito Toichi	"	"	23.2.47
125D	Kanda Masatane	"	"	3.3.47
125B	Shimotashiro Ko	Beheaded airman		Chinese custody
151V	Itsui Hiroshi	Executed 8 Aust. POWs		19.3.47
151V	Shiina Hirayasu	"	"	27.3.47
125F	Nakamura Haruo	Executed 1 Aust. Civilian		28.3.47
125F	Nakashima Katsuji	"	"	5.4.47
168A	Nishimura Takuma	Ordered execution of 151 Australian and Indian POWs. Others involved still sought.		9.4.47

Godwin stared as though mesmerised at File Number 168A. It was the sheer number of executed Allied servicemen that held his eye. He noted the date of the war criminal's arrest. Nearly four months had elapsed in the interim. Was the accused still being interrogated he wondered and by whom? He drew a military rank reference index towards him, curious as to Takuma Nishimura's Army authority and the unquestioning obedience it would command. He ran a finger down quite a long list before stopping at the name. Nishimura had been a lieutenant-general in the Imperial Japanese Army at the time. His rank gave him more than sufficient clout to order the execution of twice that number. Godwin pondered briefly. Were the Australian and Indian prisoners shot or beheaded? In the fullness of time and once completed interrogation reports were filed, the manner of execution would be known.

For the rest of the day and well into his second week, Godwin remained deskbound studying reports and files that seemed to emerge from a bottomless pit, though in truth they came from the bank of filing cabinets situated in the room designated as the Secretarial Pool Office. Major Rafferty was forever ensuring that Godwin was well-supplied with files for research and interrogation reports to study. It was a serious business investigating suspected war criminals and as Rafferty had quipped on Godwin's first day, his new briefcase would soon be the carrier of interrogation and investigative reports that might prove complex and difficult. Godwin did acquire the urge to study the more unusual files at the inn and secluded in the privacy of his room. Rafferty was not wrong about the homework.

Occasionally Godwin would take an evening off and socialize with other allied officers from various missions, but invariably, and as he became proficient at his work, he would hunger for the day when Major Rafferty might invite him to assist at an interrogation at Sugamo Prison. Within himself he felt ready and reasonably qualified to question suspected or known war criminals. The day that he might do so could not come quick enough.

Half-way through Godwin's third week, Rafferty stepped into his office holding a cup of tea. He wore a satisfied expression and spoke without preamble. 'Smoko's as good a time as any to convey good news, Jim,' he said softly. 'I've had a chat with our seniors at the Australian Mission and they've agreed with my recommendation to put you out in the field as from tomorrow.'

'Do you mean investigation and interrogation, sir?' Godwin's hopes lifted.

Rafferty nodded, 'Consider yourself a full-time investigator as from now. I must say you're a bloody natural when it comes to speaking Japanese and this is going to help you in getting into the minds of the suspects you'll be questioning,' he gave a twisted smile. 'More as the rule rather than the exception, they're a crafty and artful lot of bastards.'

Godwin finished his tea in one gulp. His reaction to Rafferty's decision was one of suppressed excitement. And then, the Major had addressed him by his first name! Was this an indication of equality insofar as being a field investigator was concerned? 'This is welcome news, sir,' he replied smothering his elated reaction. 'I feel confident that no nut will be too tough to crack, no matter how devious the suspects I encounter are.'

'I thought you'd say that,' Rafferty grinned. 'In cabinet H under "Inquiries" there's a file relating to atrocities committed in Bougainville. Pull it out and check it through. It's a fairly simple one to start with but will require your judgement and written opinion.' He set his empty cup besides Godwin's before glancing at his watch and continuing. 'I'm going down to Yokohama so will be away for the rest of the day. When you've finished your report, hand it in to the secretarial pool,' he grinned. 'They're fast, Jim. You'll have it back on your desk within thirty minutes and word perfect.' Turning he gave an encouraging nod, leaving Godwin to relish his elation alone.

Godwin sat at his desk savouring the moment. At last and after endless days of studying reports and examining countless files – many of which were signed by Major Rafferty as the Investigating Officer, he was now about to prepare his own, his first. An inner appreciation gripped him with the realisation that he'd had the benefit of a top investigator as his mentor. Before being commissioned in the Intelligence Section of the Australian Army, Major Rafferty had been a Detective Chief Inspector in the Federal Police at Canberra. He had volunteered in the Australian Army when Japan had entered the war and though still a major after six years military service, it was fairly certain that once the aftermath of the war was over, and if he cared to, his job would be open in the Commonwealth Police with the strong likelihood of his promotion to a superintendency. His active service would count.

Godwin rose from his chair and headed for the filing cabinets determined to follow the guidelines exampled in the major's many reports that he'd studied, and almost bumped into a lass who was about to enter his office to retrieve his discarded morning teacup. 'You'll find the major's cup here too,' he smiled. 'There'll be no need to go to his office.'

Returning his friendly smile, the lass stepped past as Godwin selected the right key from a bunch of fourteen secured by a ring in his left hand. Within a couple of minutes he had the correct file before eagerly returning to his office. Plumping himself back into his chair he sighed in anticipation as he carefully leafed back the folio cover.

It was close to five o'clock in the afternoon when the report Godwin had carefully documented in long-hand was returned by a typist from the adjacent secretarial pool. Godwin nodded his thanks before eagerly scanning the one-page report. It was neatly typed and presented and only required his signature. It was set out as follows:

REPORT OF INVESTIGATING OFFICER (Capt. J.G. Godwin)

Subject: *War Crimes at Bougainville*

1. I have checked files No. 125, 125Z, 120 and United States files on loan from American Section 'War Crimes Investigations' re brutalities and atrocities committed at Bougainville.

2. Check-sheets for the undermentioned Japanese involved in the deaths of United States Airmen and a Padre at Numa-Numa in July 1943 have been forwarded.

Major Goto (FNU)	– 1st Engineers, 45th Regiment
Captain Yuda (FNU)	– 3rd Engineers, 45th Regiment
Captain Keneko (FNU)	– HQ 45th Regiment
Additional: 1 Officer and 1 Senior NCO: 45th Regiment	

3. Check-sheets for the undermentioned Japanese involved in the alleged execution of a United States Airman in October 1943, the decapitation of a native police-boy in August-September 1943, and the beheading of a Padre in November 1943, have been forwarded. These executions happened in and around the KIETA area in Bougainville.

Major Yamawaki	– HQ 45th Regiment
Lieutenant Kobayashi	– HQ 45th Regiment
Captain Uda	– HQ 45th Regiment

4. Check-sheet for Second Lieutenant **Noboru Nishino** who was the interpreter to Lieutenant-General **Masatane Kanda** has also been forwarded for appropriate action.

5. It is my opinion that many new cases will be revealed when the above-mentioned personnel are interrogated.

> J.G. Godwin (Captain)
> Investigating Officer
> 2nd Australian War Crimes Section
> 8th August 1947

Godwin sighed with satisfaction as he read the typed report.
It was clearly in Rafferty's style with the accent on brevity.
Earlier in the afternoon, the check-sheets had also been typed
and promptly despatched to the United States War Crimes
Investigative Section on the floor above. He was not to
realise it then, but later he was to investigate or complete very
close to 300 reports on atrocities, individual murders and
massacres. He was also not to know that when the War Crime
Trials and Investigations were closed down – at General
MacArthur's orders, there would remain many hundreds of
atrocities and massacres still to be called to account. The
war criminals involved and eluding apprehension, would go
unpunished and justice would have a holiday – thanks to
MacArthur.

From 1 August 1947 onwards, Godwin's workload really
began. If he was not interviewing suspects or interrogating prisoners personally, he would be back at his office consulting with
Major Rafferty or filing reports. Occasionally and sometimes in
the company with opposite numbers from other Allied missions –
usually arresting officers – he would be on hand when a sought
after suspect was arrested. Quite often the arrested person would
deny his true identity and claim to be someone else. This would
incur further inquiries with the Records Section of the Japanese
Army, a good example of which is as follows and occurred
frequently.

The suspect's true identity and the alias supplied would be
referred to the Japanese Army Records Section. In due course,
back would come the reply. The alias was that of a soldier –
usually a private, who was certified as either missing or killed in
action. The true identity and name supplied of the suspect was,
often as not, confirmed as being correct but with the advice that
he too was listed as killed in action – the 'missing' syndrome
being astutely avoided. There was little wonder that Allied investigators became cynical of Army Records. Clearly, they had been
tampered with to protect the futures of war criminals in a post-
war and defeated Japan.

This deviousness and falsity, indeed protection, was not confined to the Japanese Army alone. The Imperial Japanese Navy had many atrocities to hide and did likewise. Even the Japanese police proved on occasions to be obstructive and unhelpful in tracking down most wanted war criminals. In many cases – until Allied investigators got wise, advance information concerning a suspect's whereabouts would be relayed to the police of a particular precinct. Quite often this information would be extracted from another suspect during interrogation. Certain of their man and his hide out, full details would be supplied including the wanted man's name, serial number and service rank; even alias names, if gleaned, would be supplied. Armed with arrest warrants and having notified the local police to keep a close watch on the house the suspect was hiding in, the investigating officers would arrive and swoop.

If the suspect was a former private or NCO, the chances were good – but not always, that he would be taken by surprise. If the suspect was a former senior officer – and most wanted for heinous acts, the chances were that quite strangely, he had either fled or, committed seppuku (suicide). Such frustrating occurrences were not isolated in their enactment and pointedly suggested police complicity in the suspect's sudden departure or, his long delayed suicide. No other conclusion could be drawn.

Godwin would encounter many such frustrations in dealing with people who were naturally devious, but it didn't weaken his resolve, it strengthened it. He further learned that with most of the accused he interrogated, they had no conscience. Remorse or apology seemed to be utterly alien to their nature. It was an enigma quite unexpected from a so-called civilized race. As the weeks turned into months and with accumulating experience standing him in good stead, Godwin's success rate climbed, much to Major Rafferty's satisfaction. Being able to converse in Japanese and without the need for an interpreter he would nonetheless take one along when dealing – for the first time – with a suspect who had held high military rank. This was a ploy that was a method of counter-intelligence enabling surprising results and even more surprising consequences. The following portrayals example this.

A Japanese cruiser captain who was proving difficult to pin down, appeared likely to get off scot-free for war crimes committed ashore – which were usually hard to prove, and for which he was responsible. In company with an interpreter seconded from the American Section and whom he had not worked with before, Godwin sat down in one of the interview rooms of Sugamo Prison before politely greeting the already seated ex-naval officer. 'Good morning, captain,' he said. 'I'm afraid I know little Japanese so must ask you to bear with me and communicate with the interpreter.'

The interpreter translated Godwin's apology. In response, the Navy captain jerked a short nod of understanding before addressing a quick comment to the interpreter. 'What does this oversize buffoon want? Tell him I'm not feeling too well today, so he'd better make his questions short.'

The interpreter smiled his appreciation of Godwin's description but merely translated, 'The captain is off-colour and asks for a short interview.'

'Of course, of course,' Godwin replied readily. He glanced at a note-book that he'd opened in front of him. 'Ask the captain if he authorized a landing party from his ship at Buto Island in the New Hebrides for the purpose of executing twelve islanders, three nursing nuns and the island's priests?' He added softly, 'It was September 1942, and his cruiser was known to be in the area.'

The interpreter translated the question into Japanese while Godwin sat in polite silence though vaguely glancing around the otherwise empty room as if he couldn't understand a word of what was being said. However his ears understood everything and he was not amused by either the captain's sarcastic retort or the Interpreter's unauthorized advice that followed.

'Tell the buffoon my ship was not in the area,' the captain almost hissed before smirking and added, 'Where's the witnesses? I never went ashore. They can't prove a thing,' he added hastily, 'Don't repeat what I just said. Tell that idiot I deny everything and am wrongly accused.'

'Have you thought of saying you were on leave or were sick at the time, captain?' the interpreter volunteered adding, 'They know it was your ship in the area because of Naval records they've dug up.'

'Are you sure?' the captain quickly asked.

'Yes!' the interpreter's reply was as quick. Turning slightly in his chair he smiled apologetically at Godwin. 'The captain expressed his regret but cannot accurately recall after five years where his ship was stationed. He denies any involvement in the executions alleged and begs to inform that he is wrongly accused. Also,' the interpreter added with an inscrutable expression, 'the captain does remember being very ill with malaria in September 1942.'

Godwin had difficulty containing himself. Never had he been a witness to such connivance and bald-faced lies. Masking his feelings he shrugged. 'Well the captain will get his wish. Please tell him that this interview is over.'

It was difficult for Godwin to contain his anger during the drive back to his office from the Sugamo Prison. The interpreter sat beside him blissfully unaware that before the day was over he would be dismissed by an American colonel in charge of the United States Investigative Section and to which he was attached. It was Godwin who recommended the dismissal on the strongest grounds of collusion and collaboration with a suspected war criminal. When Major Rafferty heard of the incident the following morning he chuckled with a type of perverse appreciation and expressing the opinion that maybe now Godwin was becoming too sharp for the Japanese and was playing them at their own game.

The ploy of pretending not to understand the Japanese language was put to good use a few weeks later when Godwin was especially invited by the United States Investigative Section to interrogate a Japanese former major-general. He was accused of ordering the beheading of eight Australian prisoners for the intentional purpose of cannibalism. But further, the accused was alleged to have ordered the execution of five American airmen. Of reason or motive there was none. How could troops be expected to behave when their own generals stooped to such barbarity? At the arranged time, Godwin entered Sugamo Prison and confronted the general in the interview room.

Intentionally so, an interpreter from the large War Crimes Investigative Section staffed by American investigators, was seconded to assist Godwin. Unlike the previous dismissed interpreter who was not under suspicion, this one was. It was Godwin's task to pretend that he was the most incompetent Allied investigating officer in Tokyo and with little or no ability in the Japanese language. Clearly the ruse worked. Supplying paraphrased questions from a well-thumbed notebook to the interpreter, Godwin would then sit back and stare vacuously at the ceiling, even to successfully contriving a couple of bored yawns. His performance was well rewarded.

The proof against the general was overwhelming. His guilt had already been established beyond doubt. This was not the intention of the interview. It had been decided earlier to ask spurious questions of a minor nature but which had no relevance to the evidence already obtained. As Godwin plied the questions the interpreter translated – but there the thrust of the questions were adroitly turned to suggestive helpful answers for the general's past authority and total command of thousands of men. His manner of translating the questions was respectful, almost servile. But his unsolicited and gratuitous advice was improper and proved beyond doubt where his true loyalties lay.

Godwin was not interested in the general's answers that were obligingly slanted by the interpreter. However and for appearances' sake he wrote down some replies while seething within himself. He could understand every word being said and knew duplicity for what it was. Closing his notebook he rose to his feet with a sigh before instructing the interpreter to inform the general that the interview was over. Needless to say and before the day was out, another interpreter had been dismissed.

This major-general was kept in Sugamo Prison for two years before a trial date was set. In late 1949, he was found dead in his cell. No autopsy was ordered. Instead and because he was not a convicted war criminal, his body was returned to his family for private burial. If he had been given the means to commit harikari by ingesting poison, then, the book was closed. There was no postmortem.

It is important to return to Captain Godwin's crusading endeavours and to his rather small office where authenticated and indisputable evidence was gathered, collated and presented subsequent to long hours of investigations and research. This material is intended as the main substance supporting the recording of a dreadful era in history that the chronicles ahead are intended to convey. With this resolution, attention centres upon Godwin's documentation.

REPORT OF INVESTIGATING OFFICER (Capt. J.G. Godwin)

Subject: *War Crimes at Bougainville and Buka.*

Files 125, 125A, 125B, 125C, 124D, 120 and 125Z.

1. I have been collating all useful information contained in statements by Major Uchiyama restrospective to crimes committed at Bougainville and Buka areas.

2. Check-sheets requesting the undermentioned information have been forwarded for appropriate attention.

   (A) The military and biographical histories of Lieutenant-General Hyakutuke, Lieutenant-General Kanda, Lieutenant-General Akinaga and Major-General Magata, all of whom were VIP's of the 17th Army stationed at Bougainville.

   (B) The Garrison and the area commanders of Buka and Tarlena areas as well as a list of Army and Navy units stationed in those areas. The names of these respective Commanding Officers have also been requested.

   (C) The location of Headquarters 38 Brigade attached to Bougainville as well as the names of the Commanding Officer and Staff Officers attached to Headquarters 38 Brigade.

3. A Check-sheet for Sgt-Major Shimamura, a senior NCO of 17th Army Kempetai unit at Ereventa-Buin area Bougainville, has been forwarded for appropriate action. This NCO is stated to have beheaded two Airmen in the above-mentioned area.
4. A signal to Army Headquarters, Melbourne, has been forwarded requesting large scale maps of the Bougainville and Buka areas.

J.G. Godwin (Captain)
Investigating Officer
2nd Australian War Crimes Section
15th August 1947

For a young man of just twenty-three, Godwin displayed an excellent grasp of his responsibilities as an investigating officer and showed his ability for meticulous detail. The world must concede that had it not been for Godwin's crusading dedication – right to the bitter end – all the cover-ups of Japanese atrocities and thousands upon thousands of murders would have forever been swept under the carpet, and where literally speaking, they have been concealed for fifty years.

In the absence of hard factual truth and with memories being dimmed by the march of time, justice has indeed been perverted. Historians have in the past been pilloried for chronicling murderous terror committed by the Japanese. Historical and indisputable documentation has, alas, been methodically destroyed – and not by accident but rather, by an agenda of conspiratorial interests whose God has been Mammon.

But now! Dare I say it? By the grace of God, a small but vital segment of honest and truthful history has survived the passage of time. It cannot be disputed backed as it is by documentation that was once guarded closely in the Supreme Command Allied Powers Headquarters at Tokyo. This privileged and extremely rare documentation will have the Japanese collaborators and apologists utterly dismayed. The arrogance of denial and blatant betrayal has now been exposed. Politicians who have sold their souls to Japan and preach its virtues while selling off a nation's heritage and identity must attract the contempt they deserve.

Justice, a much abused virtue, has had its voice stilled by a small coterie of heartless mercenaries joined in an international conspiracy with an agenda of mutual greed and power. The world is no different today excepting that economic conquest – not military, holds sway. A careful study of Captain Godwin's writings and official reports reflect these parallels so plainly. Where greed prevails there is want. Aggression promotes oppression. Power crushes the weak. Conquest, be it military or economic, only succeeds if ardently supported by egocentrics. The humanities like compassion, sharing and love, would find a barren refuge against such dominating parallels.

Thus did the Japanese war machine triumph for a time. Defeat in the military sense did not extinguish Japan's ambition to first own, then control the world. Instead of being punished it was allowed to launch a new conquest, an economic one. All the parallels of avarice were once again given full rein. Godwin foresaw this progression with foreboding. He well understood the Japanese single-mindedness and psyche, a combination of factors too close to fanaticism – given the circumstances, to ignore.

Not being a politician or captain of industry, Godwin evaluated only that which ordinary people cherished. He was a man of extraordinary perception and talent and embraced all that was decent in life. Anything evil or inhuman was anathema to him. Perhaps his brutal treatment at the hands of the Japanese as a prisoner of war instilled in him the desire to ensure that in his lifetime at least, those responsible for atrocious war crimes would be brought to justice. Alas, much more powerful men had other ideas. Power, greed and political expediency triumphed over justice. Unaware of what the future held, Godwin gave his everything to the task entrusted. With this concept of making the world a better place to live, a civilised planet that would emerge as a momument to those who had perished in war, he devoted his energies.

Throughout Godwin's appointment as a war crimes investigator he invariably completed a weekly report, the exception being if he was investigating war crimes that entailed travel to distant places such as Hong Kong or Singapore.

Because of their historical significance, selected official reports, summation and comment, should be included in this documentation and in their entirety. To omit any of this material purely for the limitations imposed by the chronicles opus would detract much substance and continuity of this rare documentation. Therefore and with the objective of reporting the full story – as the opportunity may never present itself again, and to honour the memory of James Gowing Godwin who originally wrote it all down, it is felt appropriate to collate the selected official reports as the final chronicles to this book.

The privilege of recording Japan's twentieth century history of unrelenting expansionism and the cost in human suffering and loss of possessions by its victims is a challenging task. However and thanks to Captain Godwin's archival dedication, what may forever have been lost to history emerges half-a-century later providing a first-hand insight that is utterly irrefutable. As a former prisoner of war of the Japanese and subsequently a war crimes investigator at Tokyo, Godwin's experiences and writings (diaries) provide the essential veracity and authenticity demanded by historians and the general public. As the author of this documented era in history I feel moved to declare – from personal experience gained through the course of considerable research – that only politicians resent any attempt to expose the collusion, corruption of justice, treachery and betrayal that over-shadowed General Douglas MacArthur's role as the Supreme Allied Commander in Japan.

In one of my earlier works titled *The Allied Japanese Conspiracy*, many years of research went into gathering information and eye-witness accounts of Japanese barbarity and murderous slaughters that made chilling reading. Alas, I did not have the benefit of sworn testimony. This allowed apologists – for their own special reasons, to attack the credence of what that book conveyed. Now however, everything reported in the previously published documentation is officially confirmed in this book with considerable sworn testimony in support and file numbers for each and every investigation carried out by war crimes investigators.

Apologists and the like will be confounded by the revelations exposed in this book and will find it utterly impossible to repudiate such officially sanctioned documentation that unintentionally but providentially authenticates much of the researched barbarism recounted in *The Allied Japanese Conspiracy*. Truth will have at last and after fifty years triumphed.

Returning to James Godwin's major contribution to this book, it is important to understand the following. In keeping with his meticulous approach to events and interviews he was also a born archivist and set down on paper his own first-hand accounts of impressions and honest opinion in comment and interesting summaries. Ever prone to call a spade a spade and liberally laced with colloquialisms indicative of his Antipodean upbringing, he held no reservations or compunction in expressing his true feelings. The niceties of grammar had no place in his forthright vocabulary – particularly his private writings. Consequently Godwin's personal summations are quoted intact to capture the moment and circumstances of this truly unique part of history.

As days turned into weeks then months and ultimately years, Godwin's duties as a war crimes investigator consumed most of his time and dedication. Being a very young man it was indeed surprising to learn that apart from several excursions – to get his mind off the depressing investigations at Sugamo prison, he lived a rather quiet life, socialising only occasionally. Fortunately for these chronicles, not only were his official weekly reports dated in faithful sequence, but also his on the spot private writings. Therefore and to correlate sequenced events with official reports providing ready reference, one to the other, each activity summation – in Godwin's private capacity – is dated to coincide and precede the official investigation reports at the conclusion of this book. Hereto is a summary of his private recollections in the following chapter.

7

The Tokyo Experience 1947-1950
(Captain J. G. Godwin)

AUGUST 29 1947, 'What an eye-opening revelation this month has been. Never would I have imagined the prevarication and deceit that I would encounter. It has been my recent task to interrogate several war crimes suspects who in my opinion are total strangers to the truth. I expect resentment and ill-disguised hostility, but not calculated falsehoods. One character in particular, former Sergeant Major Nobumitsu Shimamura is a case in point. The arrogance he acquired as an NCO in the Kempetai (military police) lingers in him. In the glory days of easy conquest – by sheer weight of numbers – the Kempetai were a law unto themselves and were specialists in torture and murder. I tried my very best to extract the truth from Shimamura regarding the beheading of a native police-boy. I had all the facts but this mongrel persisted in denying everything, even going so far as to state that at the time of the atrocity he was indisposed with malaria. Despite sworn testimony identifying Shimamura as the executioner, this drongo would have me believe the police-boy decapitated himself. The Japanese mind-set is indeed challenging.'

Fortunately for Godwin he was able to let off steam in his private writings and on infrequent occasions in social encounters with other war crimes investigators he would confide some of his most vexing and difficult assignments. By sharing interrogating experiences and citing the stubborn obstinacy of war crimes suspects, an understanding and appreciation of mutual benefit would emerge. The following is a typical example of Allied co-operation and social goodwill.

There were times when Godwin would accept invitations to

socials and well-chosen restaurants that were emerging from
Tokyo's war-ravaged metropolitan area – and it was whispered
darkly, were serving the finest foods obtained on the black-
market, the compliments of but unknowingly, Uncle Sam. It was
during one of these mind-restoring excursions and at the end of
an excellent dinner that Godwin shared an interesting conversation with a British major along with Major Rafferty.

Invariably and when a meeting of minds ran out of current
topics to discuss, common interests and frustrating challenges
relating to duties as war crimes investigators would enter into
their discussions. It was colloquially referred to as 'talking shop'.
Sipping his imported American beer, Godwin listened fascinated
as the British major described the undoubted ability of a former
British prisoner of war who had helped General Percival in the
difficult and demeaning task of surrendering all the Allied Armed
Forces based at Singapore to Japanese Lieutenant-General
Yamashita Tomoyuki.

The officer being discussed was Major Cyril Wild, Percival's
interpreter. In circumstances not dissimilar to Godwin's, Major
Wild suffered the vicissitudes of being a prisoner of war, though
for twice as long as Godwin. At war's end and after necessary
recuperation, Wild, with his ability to speak Japanese and with the
experience of being imprisoned by them, was promptly accepted
by the British War Crimes Liaison Mission at Singapore – established after the war, to hunt down the perpetrators of dreadful
atrocities and mass murder at Singapore. The Chinese, who were
the largest ethnic group on the island, had been the people targeted
by the Japanese for extermination – if at all possible.

Wild seemingly was hot on the trail of a war criminal who
would make Hideki Tojo look like an amateur. 'I have some
reference notes, just stencilled copies mind you,' the British
major remarked thoughtfully, 'that Wild made before his tragic
death in a plane crash near Hong Kong. It's damnably revealing
stuff that could be useful to you if this scoundrel's name ever
comes up.'

'Wasn't this mongrel a Japanese High Command colonel?'

Rafferty queried.

'Yes by jove! And a very evil and powerful one at that,' the British major agreed. 'Even Japanese generals were intimidated by him because of his influence within Tojo's government.'

'Mmmm, I know a little bit about Cyril Wild,' Godwin commented thoughtfully. 'I'd be keen to know more about this Japanese colonel though.' His eyes reflected his interest. 'Who knows, I may one day meet up with him. Er, what's his name, major?'

'It's on the tip of my tongue, captain, but for the life of me I can't remember it,' the major responded. 'Ah, if you like I'll send some of the copies I have to your office in the morning. You'll learn this colonel's name along with some interesting stuff.' He took a swig of gin and tonic before concluding. 'This criminal is not in Japan or Singapore I can tell you that.' He gave a wry smile. 'It would be a feather in your cap if you caught him.'

Rafferty who had been leaning forward listening offered an opinion. 'In my view there's hundreds like this bastard who have dived for cover. Brave and arrogant when they're on top, but scared as sewer rats when the tables are turned. They're nothing unless heavily armed and outnumber their adversaries ten to one,' he yawned. 'Well that was a corker meal, but I'm about ready to hit the sack,' he glanced quizzically at Godwin. 'It's nearly midnight, Jim, and there's always work tomorrow.'

Taking their leave of the British major who decided to sit at the bar for a couple of night-caps, Rafferty and Godwin returned to the inn by taxi and after bidding each other good night, repaired to their separate rooms replete with good food and slightly euphoric from the effect of the American beer. Within twenty minutes the lights in both their rooms were out.

As promised by the British major, a manilla envelope was delivered to Godwin's office the following morning. Because he knew it was not urgent Godwin placed it at the bottom of his desk tray before continuing to run through his latest typed check-sheets and report. He felt good within himself after signing the now official documentation and placing it in the filing tray.

Though the official report showed no startling confessions it nonetheless provided proof that progress was being made in interrogating war crimes suspects, a satisfying situation.

19 September 1947. It was a few minutes past the afternoon 'smoko' and with another weekly report concluded Godwin leaned back in his chair savouring the cooling breeze created by a softly humming wall-fan. The last three weeks had been uncomfortably warm and he longed for the anticipated drop in temperature that the imminent autumn season would provide. Though secluded and cosy, his rather small office could at times be oppressively warm and stuffy compelling him to remove his uniform jacket on a number of occasions. Seated in relaxed composure and with a loosened tie and unbuttoned collar, his eye caught sight of a brown manilla envelope still unopened in his 'in-tray'. Reaching forward while recollecting its origin, his thoughts reverted to an exhausting and most trying week that had just passed. He had visited Sugamo Prison six times in his capacity as a war crimes investigator and remained confounded by the wilful obstinacy and stubborn adherence to falsehoods resorted to by the war criminal suspects interrogated.

Never in his brief lifetime had he encountered such lies and denials to what was irrefutable by virtue of the sworn testimony of surviving witnesses. It required all his patience to relentlessly interrogate without losing his cool. Sighing inwardly, Godwin conceded to himself that the suspects questioned – and they were many – were masters at playing mind-games and in an inscrutable manner were adept at disclaiming reponsibility for war crimes they had authorised or participated in. Corroboration and confession was essential to parallel the evidential proof and facts from the suspects it was his duty to interrogate. He had no doubt that with most of the prisoners he was obliged to question, remorse or contrition was the furthest thought from their minds. Pseudo politeness and bows masked their inner villainy and lack of human decency. Prevarication, deception and artful guile attended most of their answers in reply to straightforward questions. They were, in Godwin's studied opinion, strangers to the truth and well-versed in jingoism and procrastination.

Sighing, he reached across and grasped the neglected envelope that had printed across its top 'British War Crimes Section'. It would he knew, contain subject matter supplied by the British major and which had been briefly touched upon at a restaurant dinner some nights previously. Casually he opened the missive and began reading its content. What initially caught his eye was a bold heading in the top right-hand corner, MOST WANTED. Curious, he flicked the stencilled copies to find that there were four pages. The material went as follows:

'Colonel Tsuji was attached to Japan's Department of Strategic Planning at the War Ministry. He was a man with a complete lack of conscience. Among the many war crimes attributable to him was the Alexandra Hospital massacre at Singapore, as well as the Singapore Chinese massacres. The following is a resume of Tsuji's war criminality as obtained by Colonel C.H.D. Wild.'

'Following his posting to Manila where American and Filipino forces were collapsing under the sheer weight of numbers of Japanese troops, he was responsible for the following. Beleaguered and surrounded in an exposed valley and woefully short of ammunition, three hundred American marines were on the verge of surrender when once more waves of Japanese troops hurled themselves onto precariously defended positions. But this was no ordinary attack. Colonel Tsuji, who was observing the unequal contest and well aware that the Americans must be getting desperately short of ammunition, gave an order that would seal their doom. 'When the Americans surrender,' he said, 'take them prisoner then execute them.

'To the horror of concealed eye-witnesses – indigenous rural peasants who watched from vantage points high in the surrounding hills – the surviving American marines who surrendered after their ammunition was exhausted were bound and formed in lines, all 280 of them, by their exultant Japanese captors. Imploring with prayers and tears, the peasant womenfolk called upon their faith to stop the carnage that followed. Bayoneted, shot or beheaded, every prisoner was dead within two hours.

'After the fall of Bataan and Corregidor, 80,000 American and

Filipino servicemen were herded into columns and forced to drag their weary, exhausted and some wounded selves towards captivity. This was known as the Bataan Death March. It was Colonel Tsuji who ordered this inhuman march while expressing the wish that for any pretext, as many prisoners as possible should be killed. In furtherance of this notorious death-wish he announced. "Japan is fighting a racial war and for the Emperor to triumph and to release our victorious soldiers to fight on other battle-fronts, prisoners must be executed."

'Tsuji partly got his evil wish. During the shuffling march that was to last for sixty-seven miles, the prisoners were subjected to appalling brutality. They were clubbed with rifle-butts, bayoneted and shot if they collapsed or fell behind the main column of prisoners. At the end of the forced march, 10,000 prisoners had been murdered. This left 70,000 to dispose of.'

'Fortunately, Tsuji was recalled to Tokyo before being sent south again, but this time to the Netherlands East Indies and Guadalcanal to impose a further reign of terror on more hapless prisoners. With his departure from the conquered Philippines, the survivors of the Bataan Death March were confined in harsh prisoner of war camps and though genocide was no longer the order of the day, they were nonetheless treated with vindictive and cruel treatment. In countless instances, intentionally starved to death, denied life-saving medical attention and forced to endure all the vicissitudes and miseries their Japanese captors imposed.'

'Colonel Wild had amassed a considerable dossier on Colonel Tsuji that if successfully prosecuted would most certainly have guaranteed his execution as a war criminal. All of this vital information and documentation was destroyed in the plane crash. Tsuji already had a head start as a fugitive from justice when Colonel Wild was tragically killed. By the time futher documentation and re-investigations were gathered and concluded, at least another valuable year would pass. Such a time-span had given Tsuji the opportunity to go underground somewhere in Asia, probably with the help of Siam's considerable gold bullion that he had ordered seized and which like him vanished.'

'On one singularly bloody occasion and following a desperate breakthrough on the Bataan Peninsula, close on 400 exhausted American soldiers without supplies of any kind, including ammunition, were compelled to surrender to overwhelming numbers of the enemy. Unknown to the Americans and only a day previously, a large number of American soldiers had surrendered to the Japanese, but only to be promptly butchered. Had this fact been known, it is doubtful whether this second surrender would have occurred. More probably the exhausted American troops would have preferred death in hand-to-hand combat.'

'After being taken prisoner and under heavy guard, a platoon of Takasago volunteers from Formosa was detailed to execute all the captured Americans. Such a large number of prisoners to suffer the death penalty must have pleased Colonel Tsuji who had arrived on the scene. "Kill them all" he ordered, adding, "chop their heads off." There followed a most gory and bloody massacre of close on 400 white troops that is probably best left to one's shocked imagination. These atrocities along with the subsequent Bataan Death March are now quite well-known but unlike ourselves, Washington is not pursuing the matter with the same vigour as our office.'

'We are aware that there were many evil Japanese but clearly, Colonel Tsuji was the most evil of all. We have learned that Tsuji, besotted by arrogance and fanaticism, brewed his own disgusting medicine from the livers of executed British, American and Australian airmen to drink for power and invincibility. During our interrogations of Japanese war crimes suspects, Tsuji's name keeps recurring. It has been recalled by other Japanese officers that at the South Pacific Hotel on the Island of Palau in 1942, Tsuji boasted about his special medicine and often with a request for further supplies of livers from beheaded airmen.'

'One more example of Tsuji's criminality should suffice. On 26 September 1944, Lieutenant Benjamin A. Parker of the 14th Airforce 25th Fighter Squadron, 51st Fighter Group flying mission F1027 and escorting Allied bombers, had his fighter aircraft hit by anti-aircraft fire. At the time Northern Burmese Japanese positions were being counter-attacked by Allied forces. Parker was noticed bailing out of his stricken aircraft by other pilots but was neither seen or heard from again.'

'Parker was quickly captured by a Japanese patrol and force-marched to the area HQ of a Japanese forward command post. It was his unenviable fate that the officer in command was none other than Colonel Masanobu Tsuji. There followed intensive interrogation with Tsuji playing a leading inquisitorial role. Despite dire threats and thuggery, Parker would only give his name, rank and serial number.'

'We have learned what followed from Japanese suspects being interrogated at Singapore. Enraged and with patience exhausted, Tsuji struck the defenceless airman with a slashing blow across the face with a steel bomb fragment. As blood welled from the deep wound he ordered Parker's immediate beheading with a blunt Burmese sword. At the first blow Parker slumped forward, his head only partially severed. With blood welling from a deep neck wound his arms were gripped by watching Japanese soldiers before being raised back to his knees. It required two further strokes from the dull blade before his head was finally severed. Thereupon and at Tsuji's orders, Parker's body was dismembered and the flesh taken for cooking and eating.'

Godwin read the short hand-written memo at the conclusion of the report. 'If you come across this monster, Jim, please let me know. Hanging will be too good for him.'

Arthur D. Pettigrew (Major)
British War Crimes Section
Meiji Building: Tokyo.

Godwin gave a long drawn-out sigh as he placed the stencilled information in the filing tray for indexing. The enormity of the crimes that Colonel Tsuji was responsible for was over-powering to the senses. Clearly, the British were keen to apprehend Tsuji, but why was the American interest so slack? The thought was intriguing. He wondered to himself where Tsuji might be hiding. The British major had previously stated that he was not underground in either Singapore or Japan, but then, with so much stolen gold he may have bought his freedom. There were intriguing connotations too disturbing to conjecture. Godwin's thoughts returned to more immediate matters of concern and which he was personally investigating. Quite often and during the past and succeeding weeks, he was involved in as many as a dozen investigations. Some were extremely difficult – made more so by the evasiveness of suspects, while others which appeared to have satisfactory explanations, did not ring true.

Among what appeared open and shut cases were the 'Good' – 'Roach' – and 'Weber' Files. The mystifying deaths of all three, and the manner of their disposal kept gnawing at Godwin despite the testimony of scores of witnesses called to make depositions. It would be preposterous to assume – without tangible proof – that all of the witnesses were lying, gathered as they had been from all parts of Japan. Collusion and a conspiracy to pervert the course of justice under these circumstances was unthinkable, yet, their answers to questions put were too pat, too similar, too suspicious when weighed against the information supplied by natives of the islands where the mysterious deaths occurred. It had to be accepted that the natives were mistaken in their testimony, not to the events alleged, but to the true identify of the victims killed. Then, there was the factor of dates when the atrocities were alleged to have happened. Few if any of the natives were educated. Months were described as 'bye and bye', years were exampled as following the hurricane or tidal wave. Not good enough when required to put a case together before a court of law.

And well did the Japanese know this. The natives' simplicity was their best defence. In spite of these difficulties, Godwin continued to believe the natives and remained determined to investigate the three baffling cases. As a consequence and despite the laborious paper-work involved and the calling of more witnesses ex the Imperial Armed Forces of Japan, he persisted in his inquiries, ever hopeful that he would at least satisfactorily resolve one of them.

7 November 1947. Godwin always looked forward to Sundays. He could unwind and relax in the company of Allied officers who, in the main, were engaged in the same intelligence work he was. Thankfully there was an unwritten rule that within the inn, 'talking shop' was avoided. Discussion usually centred upon the redevelopment of sport in Australia and New Zealand, including discussion on the friendly rivalry that existed between the two Anzac countries. It was a measure of pride to Godwin whenever the name of 'The New Zealand All Blacks' came into conversation. This rugby union team was considered one of the best in the world – if not the best, with Wales coming a close second along with the Springboks of South Africa.

It was just as freely conceded that Australia's rugby league teams were world-class. Australian Rules also had its supporters, particularly among the officers hailing from the Australian State of Victoria. A good supply of Australian beer had arrived at Tokyo which certainly helped the convivial atmosphere during the evenings and on Sundays at the inn. During this Sunday relaxation, Godwin would answer letters from his family in New Zealand, taking special pleasure in writing to his two adoring sisters. It was an unconscious substitute for his lack of female company at Tokyo. There were of course plenty of 'ladies of the night' available in newly established 'comfort houses', but this was not his scene or inclination. He held strong moral values learned from and imparted by his parents. Strengthening this attitude was the moral aspect. How could he consort with those who quite probably had given their favours to war criminals of whom a few, he was undoubtedly questioning? A schooner of ale and a good yarn, 'shooting the breeze' as Godwin called it, sufficed his puritan needs.

Sooner than Godwin wanted, Monday would dawn rekindling with it his dedication to war crimes investigations in the sordid world of murder and mayhem. A pattern gradually developed between limited leisure-time and the demands dictated as each new week began, stimulating his refreshed crusading endeavour.

14 November 1947. It was a cold wet afternoon and a few minutes before 5 pm when Major Rafferty popped his head around the partly opened door to Godwin's office. 'Jim,' he called cheerily, 'if you've got a few minutes would you like to come to my office? I've got some good news and dash it, I have to tell someone.'

'I'll just put these files into the cabinets, sir, and be right with you,' Godwin replied, beginning to rise from his chair. Assenting with a quick nod, Rafferty was gone. While Godwin was replacing the files in their separate cabinets he wondered what the major was all fired up about? Perhaps, just perhaps, his lieu-tenant-colonelcy had come through? Not before time he agreed to himself or to a more worthy recipient. Locking the last cabinet and with the chatter of typewriters stilled in the now vacated secretarial pool office, he pocketed the bunch of keys and briskly walked to the major's office. His soft knock elicited an imme-diate invitation to enter.

'Grab a chair, Jim,' Rafferty waved expansively, but then, he could afford to. His office was almost twice the size of Godwin's. He waited until Godwin seated himself before dropping the private bomb-shell that clearly pleased him. 'Well, I've got my marching orders,' he declared dramatically.

Godwin jerked upright. If it wasn't a promotion, why was the major still pleased? Marching orders didn't sound too good? 'Er, I don't understand, sir,' he murmured.

'I'm going home, Jim,' Rafferty announced, his eyes twin-kling. 'Captain Williams has received his majority and will be taking over from me at the beginning of next week.'

'Congratulations, sir,' Godwin was genuinely pleased but felt an inner regret at the major's pending departure. 'I know I'm going to miss you,' he said with feeling.

'You'll fit in well with Captain Williams, er Major Williams, Jim, and besides, you've worked well with him in the past. He'll be an excellent man to lead the investigation team, I have no doubt,' Rafferty smiled.

Godwin nodded. 'I fully agree, sir, but what about yourself? I mean . . .'

'Worry not, James,' Rafferty wore a satisfied expression. 'It's Canberra for me and probably my old desk job.' He shrugged. 'Who knows?' Possibly a superintendency, but the main thing will be that I'm posted back home to my old job. It will be good to go to the races and enjoy some home-life. I've really missed the family and even the bloody gardening,' he quipped jokingly before pointing to a small cupboard behind where Godwin was seated. 'Grab a couple of glasses, Jim, I reckon this calls for a splicing of the mainbrace.' Bending sideways he reached down and produced a half-full bottle of whiskey.

The next twenty minutes rapidly passed in light-hearted conversation during which James Godwin was to learn surprising snippets of political information that indirectly would have an influence on Allied war crimes investigations. Rafferty was of the opinion that the British would be the first to close down their war crimes investigations. With many of the more serious Singapore and Hong Kong war atrocities processed or under process, indications were that the British had no inclination to pursue the thousands of less notorious atrocities committed in other parts of Asia and the Pacific that were or had been, under their jurisdiction. He had gone one step further by opinioning when the British would pull out. Sometime around Easter the following year (1948) was his confident prediction.

Godwin with some astonishment raised the question of Colonel Masanobu Tsuji, Britain's most wanted Japanese war criminal. 'Surely they'll get that mongrel first?' he queried.

Rafferty shook his head sagely. 'They've already spent two years looking for him, Jim, and lost a damned good man in the process. This Tsuji is a cunning bastard and is well and truly underground,' he sighed. 'I believe they'll never find him. Colonel Wild may have, but he's gone. There are other major war criminals too, but what with changed identity supported with assumed names and their many sympathisers within the existing Japanese bureacracy, they can lie low for years. It's like looking for needles in a haystack.' He glanced at his watch. 'Crikey! It's about time to knock off.' Raffery recapped the now quarter-filled bottle and replaced it in his desk cupboard.

Godwin rose to his feet. 'Thanks for the drink and the natter, sir,' he smiled appreciatively. 'I guess you'll be looking foward to a return to civvy street.' He flicked a glance at the double-windows and constant rain pattering against the glass as well as noticing the fading daylight. 'Captain Ross is giving me a lift back to the inn. Would you like to accompany us, sir?'

'No, thanks all the same. I'm going to join Major Pettigrew in his office. We've got something planned,' Rafferty smiled impishly.

Nodding understanding Godwin took his leave and returned to his office to pick up an ever-full briefcase before heading for the main foyer where he knew Captain Ross would most likely be waiting for him. The newly installed American elevator transported him swiftly to the ground floor and to his waiting colleague.

The following days were no different to those preceding them. The sordid world of war crimes investigations exercised almost every waking hour except Sundays. Major Rafferty had returned to Australia and Major Williams occupied his former office. The same rapport continued within the Australian War Crimes Investigation Section as had prevailed under Rafferty. Only the duties differed, depending upon the subject files being investigated. The repetition was hum-drum though constantly challenging. It was this latter aspect that provided a continuous and stimulating interest, reinforced by Godwin's determination to call to account war criminals who deserved to answer for their crimes.

5 and 12 December 1947. 'Christmas is upon us again though I find it difficult to adjust to the fact that it is the third festive season since the end of the war. By the very nature of my duties I seem to be in a time-warp with my attention centred upon the past and a coterie of mindless morons whose cunning and guile has to be encountered to be believed. Deception and brazen lies yet supported by false politeness and bows is a bloody enigma I'm becoming used to. It's been a very trying two weeks as I was away with the arresting officer for a couple of days to escort back to Tokyo two wanted war criminals. We apprehended one of them okay, but the other must have been tipped off. Reaching his hideout we found that he had shot through (fled). It couldn't have been the local precinct police because they weren't informed of our intentions. It had to be the bloody Japanese 'underground'. These bastards operate from influential places and we know it. But with a hundred million Japs what can we do? Nothing! It would be difficult knowing where to start, though we have a bloody good idea.'

The above comments extracted from Godwin's private writings provides a clear indication of the intransigence and obvious unrepentance of those who it was the task of Allied investigators to apprehend. No official report or documentation articulates the frustration so ably expressed by Godwin. As the official reports extemporise – within the bounds of diplomatic propriety, the duplicity, intransigence, treachery, deviousness and falsehoods resorted to by suspects is commented upon – but only academically, clinical dissertation being the preferred analogy in official summations.

19 and 26 December 1947. Quite often and during the course of Godwin's investigations, echoes of Japan's horrific wartime past would surface and end up by way of memorandums on his now cluttered desk. It was not unusual for him to return from Sugamo Prison and find two or three reposing in the 'in-tray'. On one particular occasion and following the interrogation of a most devious suspect at the prison, he was thankful to plump down in his chair and try to mentally unwind. To help alleviate the mindset the prison invariably produced, he idly reached across for the latest Allied intelligence resumes awaiting his interest in the 'in-tray'. Cynicism, a seldom employed human mechanism when evaluating international politics, was to slowly influence his thoughts as he read the memorandum. It was a transcript from a newspaper report obtained from Singapore that proved most interesting:

'Singapore's Health Authorities are concerned at reports of decomposed and partly decomposed bodies along the foreshore of Blakang Mati's south-eastern coast posing a health problem. Shifting sands and recent high tides have revealed an extraordinary number of skeletal remains. A spokesman for the authority has suggested the human remains might be those of illegal immigrants from adjacent Indonesia killed by pirates. Another theory was more fanciful with the suggestion that it might be the result of an internecine massacre between local and warring Chinese secret societies. Not once was the possibility mentioned – and the most probable, that the large number of human remains could well be the consequence of Japanese wartime butchery. Forensic tests on the skeletal remains – but which were not ordered, would have cleared up this quite inexplicable lapse of memory.'

'A young Chinese doctor by the name of Ah Chee, who was studying pathology, undertook to conduct private forensic tests on the remains of three bodies. His findings rubbished the health authorities confusing speculation. "All three bodies," the doctor pronounced, "had been shot to death. One skeletal subject bore evidence of eight bullet entries per holes and shattered bones suggestive of death by machine-gunning." Dr Ah Chee determined the termination of life as being during the period 1941-42, a period coincidentally of the "Chinese Massacres" by the Japanese Imperial Army.'

Godwin put aside the memo, his mind questioning the unspoken, the obvious. Illegal immigrants and pirates was an outlandish claim and could not be sustained against the clinical and forensic conclusion evidenced by the Chinese doctor. He had heard rumours, whispers, of a surreptitious reconciliation between the Allied powers and Japan – for political reasons, a not unlikely plot and perhaps reinforced by the possible British decision to close down its Japanese war crimes investigations in the near future. Therefore, an admission by any authority that could be construed as being insensitive to Japanese feelings would not be helpful to such objectives. But why should the obvious truth be prostituted he wondered. Fact was fact and should not be the plaything of semantics. His brow furrowed as a feeling of cynicism intruded into his thoughts. Who, he speculated, was pulling the strings for such managed public deception? Chiang Kai-shek? Hardly. President Truman? Clement Atlee? Josef Stalin? Heaving a sigh he returned his attention to more immediate matters. There were always summaries and reports to write that in themselves and with regard to suspects answers, could at times be as ambigious and misleading as the recent event reported from Singapore.

9, 16 and 23 January 1948. One day and while awaiting his

latest summations to be typed up, Godwin received a memoradum from Major Pettigrew's office that though brief was quite interesting. It read as follows:

'This might interest you, Jim. I've learned from our office in Singapore that under the sands of Merah Tanah Besar Beach adjacent to Changi, are the remains of hundreds of massacred Chinese. What makes this information poignant is the news that under a proposed land development and reclamation scheme (envisaged for the future), this entire foreshore will be reclaimed for a civilian airport. This may well mean that runways will be constructed on top of hundreds, perhaps thousands of Chinese graves. It makes you wonder doesn't it?'

Regards: A. Pettigrew (Maj)

Nothing made Godwin wonder any more. He had matured beyond his years in the Army Intelligence Service and his constant duty-association with cunning and devious war criminals. There was now a cynical side to him adding to his investigative ability. He no longer took the word of war crimes suspects no matter how profoundly expressed. Bowing, scraping and hissing merely put him on his guard. The most innocuously polite suspects were, as often as not, the most dangerous and with the most blood on their hands. Shrugging off these morbid thoughts he slipped the memorandum into his briefcase to eventually join other unofficial and official communications that he ultimately intended would return with him to New Zealand when his tour of duty was over.

As expected, his latest investigative summation – all professionally typed – was delivered to his office within thirty minutes of conveying the long-hand report to the secretarial pool. As he glanced at the completed report he wished he could resolve his investigations as quickly.

6 and 13 February 1948. Another fortnight slipped by during which time Godwin flew to Hong Kong to assist an arresting officer to escort back to Japan a major war criminal who it was alleged, had ordered the execution of three United States airmen who had survived a Catalina crash off Tarawa Island. Also sought for a major atrocity on this same island was a Kempetai sergeant major. Without just cause or reason – other than an earlier but brief Allied air raid – he had personally beheaded twenty-three Allied coast-watchers, of whom some were British victims captured on Tarawa and who had been employed by the British Colonial Service. The remainder of the victims were – nineteen in all – young civilian employees of the New Zealand Post and Telegraph Department who had volunteered to act as coast-watchers in the Pacific Islands using their special skills as morse code operators. Japanese Army Records listed this latter war criminal as 'missing in action'.

Because a number of war criminals officially listed as 'missing in action' had fortuitously been apprehended – despite army records cover-ups – the propensity for the Japanese authorities to protect their own was well recognised, hence, a war criminal's alleged disappearance in action was largely disbelieved. It could never be proved but for many wanted war criminals, the 'missing in action' reports were a perfect cover. It allowed for a change in identity and safety back in Japan where many of these criminals became honoured pillars of their adopted communities. In Japan, duplicity and deception was admired and instrumented surreptitiously to the fullest advantage.

20 and 27 February 1948. On a rather quiet Sunday afternoon, Godwin decided to do a spot of reading in the ground-floor lounge of the inn. A group of off-duty Allied officers staying at the inn had arranged to visit Mount Fuji and though invited, he had elected to answer letters from home and to read some interesting material he had noticed in one of three book cabinets lining the lounge walls. With letters to his family in New Zealand out of the way, he was comfortably ensconced in a soft rather large armchair and studying with deep concentration several translations of Japanese manuals. The following are the publications that caught his interest.

The Imperial Rescript to Military Forces. This had been drawn up by Emperor Meiji in 1902. It was regarded by the Japanese as a sacred document containing fundamental guiding principles for members of the Imperial Armed Forces. A further publication was one issued by the pre-war Japanese Government as a supplement to enlarge upon the Imperial Rescript. Another, was a manual outlining the pre-war Japanese Army's Military Training Regulations. From the War Ministry's Manual, the following passages were highlighted.

'The essence of military discipline was obedience. Therefore, it is necessary that the officers and men of the whole Army should form a habit of sacrificing their lives for their Emperor's country, obeying their superiors with full sincerity and executing their superior's orders faithfully.'

Article two of the Military Training Regulations said in part, 'The duty of the military is to sacrifice their lives for their Emperor's country. It is a tradition inherited from the time of the old samurai. A samurai's loyalty to his country has been considered even more important than the worth of his own life. Remember the saying that life shall be considered as light and negligible as a feather, and loyalty as heavy and lofty as a mountain.' Article 50 of the same manual said: 'For the cultivation and maintenance of military discipline, it is necessary, first, to seek absolute obedience and, next, to make officers and men fully understand the significance, particularly the inviolable dignity, of the supreme command, so that they will sacrifice their lives willingly for their country at the order of their superiors.'

A further extract said in part: 'Subordinates should obey immediately the orders of their superior, irrespective of their nature. Such orders are irresistible.' When the Imperial Japanese Army was founded in 1902, the Minister of War made it compulsory for all soldiers entering service to take an oath of loyalty and obedience. It was to be understood that all orders came from the Emperor, a living god. A further passage confirms the moronic indoctrination instilled. 'Even under the circumstances of life and death difficulties, you shall respond immediately to orders from your superiors and yet you shall be glad to sacrifice your lives in the fulfilment of the orders. This is the expression of the spirit of

Bushido which is our tradition; it is the glory of the Army.'

Godwin was so taken by the fanaticism inherent in the manual
and the casually callous consideration of human life typified by
the remonstrance 'be glad to sacrifice your lives' that he copied
the above passages to be added to the material accumulating for
its eventual repository in New Zealand. His mind was ever
inquiring, ever searching for answers to help him understand the
psyche of a nation like no other on earth. Sunday passed all too
quickly as did the first half of March. The more Godwin pursued
his investigations, the more war criminals he was discovering. It
was, he conceded to himself, an up-hill battle particularly in
context with the inscrutable characteristics of many of those he
was obliged to interrogate. At times and when sharing his experiences with other Allied officers within the confines of the inn, it
was generally agreed that the sheer enormity and widespread acts
of inhuman conduct perpetrated by the Imperial Japanese Armed
Forces, would take at least ten years to investigate, and even then,
more than half of the war criminals would remain to be tracked
down. A most daunting prospect.

5 and 12 March 1948. The following are extracts from
Godwin's personal notes. 'I am now convinced that it was mainly
the worst elements within the Japanese Army who were assigned
military police (Kempetai) duties. The autocratic authority they
exercised was quite unbelievable in relation to their responsibilities. In sharing conclusions with other Allied officers, I am left in
no doubt as to the evil pervading their sadistic ranks. So far as
Allied prisoners were concerned, God help them if captured or
placed in the custody of the Kempetai. Instances of mindless
brutality and beheadings were widespread throughout the
Japanese Army and were pursued in complete disregard of the
Geneva Convention or justice to the point, or so it would seem,
that genocide was part of the Japanese conquering agenda.

'However and above all, the Kempetai were evil personified.
Instances of bestial torture and inhuman acts outweighing what
Japanese troops perpetrated in the field – if that was possible,
were carried out by the Kempetai. Time and time again I have

encountered conflicting testimony apportioning blame in the defence of 'no responsibility'. Either, the Kempetai were a law unto themselves, or had the tacit consent of superior officers. Whatever, I would have to acknowledge that these same members of the Kempetai, stripped of their authority and weapons, are a pathetic but devious lot. The junior ranks are included in this description but with the observation that many of them are of low intelligence and can lie against all odds, making even the devil smile in evil admiration.'

Japanese torture of civilians and POWs

25 March 1948. The weather outside was atrocious as Godwin
completed an endearing letter to his elder sister Moyra in far-
away New Zealand. The windswept rain lashed and rattled the
window-panes of his room at the inn as he carefully penned an
address on the envelope before affixing two postage stamps. It
was a Saturday evening but with the weather so foul he had no
inclination to visit the Officers' Club, feeling more comfortable
remaining at the inn. He had earlier put together as much information available to him concerning the disquieting disappearance of a Sergeant Andrew Hennessy, a New Zealander captured
while attempting to escape in a small boat from enemy-occupied
Nauru. Much of the information following Hennessy's capture
was vague and incomplete. However he had managed to write a
consoling letter to his widow, the mother of three children who
lived at Invercargill in New Zealand. From documentation
obtained Sergeant Hennessy did not survive imprisonment at
Harbin in Manchuria, indeed, no trace of him was ever found. It
was presumed that he had perished as a human guinea-pig at the
Biological and Germ Warfare Centre at nearby Ping-fan.

With these personal responsibilities attended to Godwin placed
his briefcase beside him and extracted several unread memorandums, pausing while he cleared his writing-desk. They were
enveloped and separate from his usual homework and were easy
to locate. Lifting them out, his eye fell on an envelope over-
printed with the words 'Australian War Crimes Tribunal'.
Instinctively he chose to read its contents first.

Without fail all the memorandums Godwin received proved
interesting. As he spread out the two pages they conformed to his
expectations. The memo read as follows. 'April 2nd, 1947,
Lieutenant-General Takuma Nishimura was sentenced by a
British Military Tribunal at Singapore to life imprisonment for
atrocities committed at Singapore by the Japanese Imperial
Guards and of which he was the commanding officer. This
sentence was confirmed on May 29, by Britain's Singapore-
based Commander-in-Chief, South-East Asia Land Forces, Sir
Neil M. Ritchie.

'But it was only too obvious from the reactions of Singapore's large Chinese population that they were outraged at the leniency of the sentence. Within hours a group of prominent members of the community began organising the Singapore Chinese Appeal Committee, and, through it, demanded not only the execution of Nishimujra but four other Japanese war criminals who had also been sentenced to life imprisonment and who collectively between them had been responsible for the massacre of 12 000 Chinese civilians. In addition, the committee insisted the authorities impose death sentences and carry out the hangings in public.'

'Countering the public outcry, British legal experts were obliged to announce that the constitution of the War Crimes Courts disallowed retrials with more severe sentences than the original ones.'

'On June 25, the punishments handed down at the conclusion of the Chinese Massacre Trial were officially promulgated. The executions of General Kawamura and Lt-General Oishi would be carried out the following day at 9 am. Mr Tay Koh Yat, Chairman of the Appeal Committee, told the *Straits Times* of his disappointment over the confirmation of the sentences which permitted five Japanese mass murderers to live. He further added that his committee would not be satisfied until all of the Japanese monsters paid for their inhuman crimes with their lives. As the authorities dismissed the demand for a public hanging, Tay Koh Yat demanded ten of his committee members be allowed to witness the executions the next morning.'

'In the event, eight representatives of the Chinese community – including two bereaved women – were allowed to attend. Unbeknown to the thirty-odd witnesses including the Press, who slowly walked through Changi Prison's main gateway at their appointed time, the military authorities had included a macabre addition to the morning's executions. Three Japanese war criminals were to be hanged; not just the expected two.'

'The third man on the gallows would be Captain Kosaki Goshi who had received a death sentence two months earlier at Kuala Lumpur. Goshi was the most evil unrepentant Kempetai

murderer ever let loose on defenceless civilians and was responsible for countless atrocities and massacres. He would be in most
fitting company on the scaffold.'

'As the three condemned war criminals, in ill-fitting prison
garb, were led from their cells at 8.45 am, other convicted war
criminals and war crimes suspects throughout the jail began
singing a Japanese version of "We'll meet again". High above
and across an azure blue sky, a Royal Airforce Meteor jet aircraft
screamed past as military guards manacled the wrists of the three
Japanese officers behind their backs and placed numbered, black
hoods over their heads. Three minutes before 9.00 am, the guards
ran the three bare-footed, hooded figures from the cell-block, up
a fairly steep wooden ramp to the scaffold's central stage.
Positioning the condemned men along an oblong trap-door, the
guards pinioned their ankles before swiftly slipping nooses over
their heads. Feeling the ropes in place, the defiant Japanese
muttered urgently to each other through their hoods, then began
muffled shouts in Japanese "Long live the Emperor" and
"Banzai". Abruptly the trap-door yawed open. The shouts of
fanaticism ceased. Ten minutes later, the three hanging bodies
were pronounced corpses.'

Godwin shifted to a more comfortable posture in his chair, so
compelling had the narration been he had disregarded the hardness of the wooden seat. There was half of the second page left
and his eyes swept through its content with continued avid
interest. 'The Singapore Chinese are not the only ones who feel
that all the convicted war criminals deserved death. The
Australian Authorities have already made representations to have
Lt-Gen. Nishimura sent to Manus Island in the Admiralty Group
to face trial before an Australian Military Court for atrocities
committed on Australian prisoners of war. The British
Authorities at Singapore have declined the request.'

[AUTHOR'S SUMMATION] After serving almost five years of his
life sentence in Singapore, Nishimura became part of a repatriation of Japanese war criminals back to Tokyo where, presumably,
they were to serve the rest of their jail terms. On 21 May 1950,

while the ship transporting him was temporarily in port at Hong Kong, Nishimura was transferred to the *SS Changte* on instructions of the Australian military authorities. From Hong Kong he was taken to Manus Island. In due course he faced trial in an Australian military court for ordering the massacre of Australian and Allied prisoners of war at Parit Sulong in Johore in January 1942. He was found guilty and hanged on 11 June 1951.

Many other Japanese war criminals serving life imprisonment in Singapore, and having completed five years of their too mild sentences, were repatriated back to Japan. Thereafter and intermittently, war criminals held in Japanese prisons received remissions of sentences and were progressively released. The last remaining war criminals were set free by a fully autonomous Japanese Government in 1957.

Godwin was not to know of the ironic twists of fate that ultimately and after his departure finally, from Japan, would see the realm of politics and collusion insidiously pervert the cause of justice whereby war criminals who should have been hanged, were given their freedom, and hundreds if not thousands of others were no longer in dread of investigation. Justice indeed, took a holiday when Japan once more and in 1952 returned to self-government. [END AUTHOR'S SUMMATION].

Before retiring for the night, Godwin read the remaining memorandums before placing them with his collection of personal papers. One of them was particularly intriguing as it dealt with an investigation of Imperial Japanese Army brothels – so widespread in its ramifications it was eye-boggling. It was a distasteful resume of debauchery and licentiousness that privately, he was pleased it was not his task to investigate. This matter was being handled by the American authorities. The last thoughts crossing his mind as he went to bed were the twists and turns his own investigations were taking. The vagaries of witnesses' evidence and the denials of suspects were the last enigmas pervading his tired mind as eventually, sleep erased his conjectures.

2 and 9 April 1948. [Comment] 'I cannot help but be aware of covert resistance to our War Crimes Investigations by both the

Japanese Bureaucracy and Organisations along with specific Societies. The fact that we are endeavouring to bring thousands of murderers to justice is lost to their obstinate mentality. The victims whom we represent – many posthumously – were victims of a killing machine that got out of control. No matter if those maimed or massacred were Chinese, Americans, Australians or Natives, war crimes remain crimes. It astounds me to learn that these bastards cannot comprehend the lack of such murderous activity by the Allied Powers and our revulsion at beheadings. It's as though such blood-lusting was expected from us.'

'The War Veterans Underground is a well-organised and well-funded outfit that exalts the mongrels we are searching for. I would have to comment that the refuge the Underground provides to wanted war criminals is linked to the fact that Japan lost its war of expansion. There is a deep-seated resentment and loss of face surrounding Japan's humiliating surrender. Politeness and many obsequious bows do not impress me. Such a rapid return to civilised norms and conduct is an artificial veneer well suited to their cunning and duplicity. I had personal experiences of these morons as a prisoner of war and am not fooled. I guess that thanks to a sympathic War Records Division of the former Imperial Japanese Army, a lot more of these murdering mongrels will be shielded. The Underground acts as a second protective buffer for criminals whom the War Records Division is unable to list as "killed or missing in action". Impairing our determinations and searching is the disadvantage of overwhelming numbers. So many Japanese, so few of us.'

16 April 1948. There was a feeling of spring in the air as Godwin returned to his office from a lengthy period of interrogating suspects confined at Sugamo Prison. He couldn't help noticing a new look of purpose on the countenances of many Japanese going about their business in Tokyo's congested streets. Perhaps, he mused, it was because of the British announcement that it was winding down its War Crimes Investigations in the Far East. Whatever, it would be certain that the war criminals harboured by the Japanese Underground would be greatly relieved at the British announcement. This and other thoughts filled his mind as flashing his ID to the provosts, he entered the Meiji Building. Reaching his office he instantly noted a tidy long-hand memo awaiting attention on his office desk. 'Come to my office as soon as you return, Jim.' There was nothing else excepting Major Williams' signature. Shrugging curiosity aside, he swung on his heel, placed his briefcase beside the wastepaper basket, before walking quickly to the major's office. Major Williams looked perplexed as after knocking and being invited to enter, Godwin was motioned to a chair. Something was bothering Williams and he didn't have to wait long to find out.

'Well, Jim, the "Brits" are closing down. Have you heard?' Williams didn't looked pleased as he added, 'The sake will be flowing tonight in the bloody Underground!'

Godwin nodded agreement to both comments. 'So I've heard, sir. That leaves just us, the Yanks and the Dutch to carry on.' He paused momentarily to find the right expression. 'I can't imagine that the British have investigated all the war crimes within their jurisdiction, or for that matter, prosecuted them. It does seem strange,' he shook his head.

'Bloody politics,' Williams declared. 'I've been talking to Major Pettigrew in the British Section. He's damned ropable! They have apprehended sixty-seven identified murderers and have even set trial dates, but all to no avail.'

'Er what do you mean by no avail, sir?' Godwin leaned forward in his chair.

'The bastards are all to be set free. No ifs, no buts!' Williams scowled.

'Perhaps we could take over the prosecutions, sir?' Godwin suggested hopefully despite a shake of Williams' head.

'Not a chance, Jim. More than half of them in custody are outside of Japan. Besides, their war crimes are outside of our jurisdiction. Something like the territorial understandings between ourselves and the Dutch,' Williams sighed glumly.

'Is this what you wanted to see me about, sir?' Godwin remembered to ask.

Williams nodded. 'Yeah, I had a bloody good reason. Once the Japanese we are interested in learn of the British pull-out, they're going to become arrogant and will resort to every prevarication and stalling tactic in the book.' His scowl changed to a twisted smile. 'They'll be waiting for us to follow suit, betcha!'

'Is there any likelihood of that, sir?' Godwin's expression was serious.

Williams gave a vigorous shake of his head. 'Australia and New Zealand are solidly behind bringing these bastards to justice, Jim. Just remember that it was only the battle of the Coral Sea that saved both of our countries from being partly occupied, or in New Zealand's case, invaded. Remember, Jim, there were 100,000 Japanese soldiers at Rabaul waiting to do just that.' He paused reflectively. 'I guess atrocities would have followed.'

'While the best part of our small army was in the Middle East,' Godwin concurred supportively.

'Well, that's the news confirmed, Jim.' Williams' expression steeled. 'It won't affect us too much, but fair dinkum, the fact that so many of these war criminals will be set free doesn't sit well with me. Then, there's the hundreds still being sought and who have evaded arrest? As I said, the bloody Underground will have every reason to celebrate.'

Major Williams was a Queenslander who bluntly spoke his mind. Godwin had no doubt of that as he more leisurely walked back to his own office after the brief discussion ended. It was he conceded to himself, damned unsettling. He would also miss the good fellowship of his British counterparts at both the inn and the officers club. Many were, like himself, dedicated to their duties as investigative officers. He resolved within himself to discuss the British closure of investigations and prosecutions with a couple of British captains he knew as well as Major Pettigrew over the coming weekend. Meanwhile he had more important matters to attend to, and that was preparing summaries for his never-ending reports.

23 and 30 April 1948. It was during a relaxed conversation over a meal at the officers' club and in the company of three investigative officers from the United States section that Godwin learned a lot more about the Biological and Germ Warfare Centre at Ping Fan in central Manchuria. It concerned two former Japanese soldiers who were part of a large garrison situated at nearby Harbin and who during the course of interrogation were discovered to be former members of a guard detachment that periodically was assigned to maintain discipline in various POW camps adjacent to Ping Fan. Under close questioning they admitted knowledge of horrendous goings-on with regard to many unfortunate prisoners of war who were murdered in their thousands at the Germ Warfare Centre and with the full approval of the Japanese High Command.

The number of prisoners murdered quite took Godwin's breath away. It was conservatively estimated that upwards of 60,000 prisoners were done away with in continuous mass experiments at the Germ Warfare Centre. The soldiers were not implicated in the actual carnage, but what they knew and had to say was a chilling litany of pitiless barbarism quite satanic in its implementation and which would pale by contrast the crimes of the Third Reich. Prisoners of all nationalities – but mainly Chinese – were experimented upon – always fatally, and which Godwin quietly thought to himself would explain the mystifying disappearance of Sergeant Hennessy to whose widow he had recently written a letter.

Usually 'talking shop' was avoided because of its predilection and genre, but the Germ Warfare Centre was so atrocious that he sat listening spellbound, pressing for more information that up until the moment he knew little about. The Japanese guards who did three-monthly stints at Ping Fan before returning to Harbin for less onerous duties, spoke of hundreds of prisoners each week being herded into the grim concrete complex, never to be seen again. In answer to questions at their interrogations, they both admitted that the bodies of the victims (all 60,000 of them) were cremated in crematoria and on much the same scale as the victims of Nazi tyranny. When the furnaces were cleared of masses of charred bone fragments and ashes, it was the duty of the guards to dump the remains into the nearby Sungari river. This procedure was followed over a period of several years.

The interrogated Japanese soldiers named the officer-in-command of the facility at Ping Fan as being former General Ishii, a leading medical scientist himself and under whom well over forty Japanese doctors worked. The Ping Fan Biological and Germ Warfare Centre was established in conjunction with General Ichii by an Imperial prince and cousin to Emperor Hirohito. A jarring and mystifying conclusion to the post-meal discussion was the uncertainty expressed by the American officers as to where their interrogations were headed. Both Major-General Charles A. Willoughby (SCAP's Intelligence Overlord) and the 'Supremo' General Douglas MacArthur, had personally intervened when requests – made through Colonel Alva C. Carpenter, a senior American officer attached to SCAP's Legal Section, for authority to apprehend the Imperial prince and General Ishii was formally requested. It was unaccountably denied.

It was further declared by the American officers that it had been reliably confirmed that the Emperor's personal 'Imperial Seal' had been affixed to the documentation authorising the establishment of this murderous facility to be constructed in the Mukden, Harbin, Ping Fan area of Manchuria and in the prior knowledge that victims for the proposed murderous Germ Warfare experimentation to follow would be helpless prisoners of war and of whatever nationality available. The fact that MacArthur and Willoughby were blocking the investigation was puzzling. It aroused concerns that because the Japanese Imperial Family including the Emperor was involved, political considerations prevented the just arrest of the Emperor for this and other war crimes. Clearly, the course of justice was being obstructed by the highest command structure of the Allied occupation. That America had stooped to such confounding practices of immunity from prosecution and blatant pardons per the all-powerful decrees of General MacArthur was difficult to comprehend.

Back in the privacy of his room at the inn and before retiring,

Godwin made notes of the startling information learned and added it to the private dossier of accumulating writings and official memos stored in his cabin-trunk. He wondered as he thought of bed and yawned tiredly, what would have happened if Adolf Hitler had been captured alive by the Allies? Would he have been treated to the same deferential and exonerating perversion of justice as was extended to Emperor Hirohito? He doubted it. But then, Eisenhower wasn't a MacArthur. An intriguing thought crossed his mind and which directly implicated Washington DC and indeed the Presidency. MacArthur could not protect Japanese war criminals of such prominent stature without the consent of President Truman. Was it fair to entirely blame MacArthur? Was the Supreme Commander at Tokyo merely obeying the orders of his Commander-in-Chief in the White House? More than probably, yes. Had political considerations corrupted and influenced General MacArthur's determination to seek justice and redress for Japan's wartime victims? On the balance of probability and with Truman's certain knowledge, yes. Who then was calling the shots and was the real Benedict Arnold? Tumbling into bed he promised himself that in his investigations and so far as his junior capacity allowed, justice, not collusion, would prevail.

7 and 14 May 1948. Though the weather was seasonably pleasant, Godwin caught a cold that confined him to his quarters at the inn for nearly three days following which he remained indoors until fully recovered and which required a further two days. His excellent physical condition helped him to recover swiftly from what was in effect a nasty bout of influenza. It was a relief for him to finally be given a clean bill of health by an Australian army doctor. With boredom behind him, his return to duty was eagerly welcomed.

For the following two weeks Godwin was out of Japan. He was required to fly to Hong Kong to appear as a witness in a prosecution involving eight Japanese war criminals and of whom six were convicted of involvement in a number of atrocities that included wilful murder. Two of the eight defendants were also wanted by the Australian authorities and after their conviction were to be extradited and escorted back to Japan for further questioning. Fortunately, the British authorities had no objection to the convicted pair serving their sentences in Japan.

From Hong Kong Godwin was sent to Singapore to escort, in company with three British officers, three suspected war criminals back to Japan for trial. All three Japanese had been discovered hiding in dense jungle-covered hills in the interior of Sabah, Borneo, in February 1947. It had taken the British authorities more than a year to investigate the wartime background of the three prisoners once it was known that they had been members of an infamous Kempetai Unit based in the Protectorate. All the legal documents, information and sworn statements were passed on to the 2nd Australian War Crimes Section at Tokyo for process. All three former Kempetai members were charged with the executions of many civilians and unidentified Allied servicemen who had been apprehended, tortured and then executed by them.

With the cessation of all investigations and prosecutions by the British in the Far East, it was most likely that the three murderers would have had to be released and repatriated to Japan as free men, but for Australia's willingness to apply the due process of law. It was during this brief Singapore-Japan assignment that Godwin was to learn of the political winds of change governing the British decision to devote its attention to re-establishing its colonial and economic influence in the Asian-Pacific region and a return to peace-time bureaucracy as quickly as possible.

So far as Nazi Germany – now vanquished, was concerned, it had been the bigger threat to Britain's survival than far-away Japan. Therefore, as it was more convenient, Britain pursued with vigour its participation in the War Crimes Trials at Nuremberg and was happy to maintain a sizeable occupation force in the country that once tried to rule the world. Howsoever, Japan was no less a threat to countries geographically closer and within reach of its marauding and brutal armies. New Zealand and Australia could never forget just how close the Japanese came to seizing parts of Australia and the almost certain and complete invasion of a poorly defended New Zealand. This perception of what was then referred to as 'The Yellow Peril' translated itself into an appropriate post-war desire to punish Japan and to hopefully ensure that all war criminals were brought to justice. Thus and with the British War Crimes Tribunals shut down, the Australian War Crimes Section could only deal with war crimes instigated within its territorial mandate and/or, where atrocities had been enacted upon Australian or New Zealand servicemen by the Japanese.

Where Godwin was perplexed, he believed that the British decision to pull out was ill-conceived, premature and a great relief to thousands of war criminals who would now, never be tried for their inhuman acts of brutality. It was futile to say that they didn't exist or, that all war crimes suspects had been dealt with. Clearly they had not. It was with this new perception that he returned to his duties at the Meiji Building. There was much to catch up on.

4 and 11 June 1948. 'In the temporary absence of Major Williams, I am fielding some of his files along with my own. As a consequence I will adhere to the continuation of his investigative reports but will have to condense mine to a slightly later date, probably mid or late July. Nonetheless my visits to Sugamo Prison – a bloody depressing place, continue as usual.'

'I've just learned that three mongrels have been released on express orders from the Supreme Command Headquarters in the Dai-Ichi Building (MacArthur's Central Administration Offices). I have personally interrogated one of them, (Eguichi Shinya: File 125E). At the time and with no admission of direct involvement in cannibalism, I was obliged to seek other witnesses and question several suspects. Though the practice of cannibalism was admitted as being known through hearsay, I couldn't nail anyone involved. However, I later learned that another suspect I had interrogated (Kamezawa Kiyoharu of the 2nd Battalion, 13th Regiment: File 125E) was identified as having boasted that he had eaten dead Australian soldiers and that further, he had implicated Eguichi Shinya in the practice. I find it frustrating to know that now I have tangible information and two sworn testimonies and could probably nail these two bastards, the file on cannibalism is officially closed. At least I've had the dubious experience of interrogating two cannibals before finally, they were freed.'

With the departure of the British Prosecuting and Investigative Sections, Godwin felt a sort of social vacuum. Perhaps it was because that as a New Zealander he assimilated more easily with the British than with the Americans and felt a bond with the British Empire. He liked the Americans and their generous openness, but not their brashness. The latter being exploitable to their cost. In matters connected to his work, Godwin was a workaholic and gave it total commitment. Long hours, energy and crusading dedication. It was with this sense of duty and the welcome return of Major Williams that enabled him to catch up on deferred reports and summaries that would keep his favourite typist in the secretarial pool busy.

16 and 23 July 1948. It was a Wednesday evening and with dusk closing in on a decidedly balmy night, Godwin felt it would be a pleasant change to shoot the breeze with fellow officers who might happen to be in the downstairs lounge. Even with the window open to the evening air, the confines of his bedroom felt oppressively warm. The thought of a couple of cold beers added stimulus to his decision. In less than two minutes he entered the lounge and almost immediately was pressed to partner a player in a game of cards for an hour or so before the card games finished. Thereafter he sat nearer the bar. Two newly installed wall-fans hummed and whirred behind where Godwin was seated in a very comfortable armchair. Soon he was in close conversation with Captain Ross, another investigating officer attached to the Australian War Crimes Section at the Meiji Building. Between them they were enjoying a back-handed joke that related to a comment made by Ross. He had declared that in most cases and with most people he could read their expressions or what was going through their minds, but the Japanese were a totally different kettle of fish. Their sphinx-like inscrutability and proclivity for lying made it hard to suss them out. Sometimes, he had suggested, they were so deliberately pathetic or naive he sometimes wondered if they would know their arse was on fire, yet, he had corrected as Godwin's chuckle faded, the same bastards were responsible for callous atrocities and cunningly contrived alibis. They were indeed a different kettle of fish.

Godwin nodded agreement. His mind flashed to his own investigations. There was Ebery, Roach and Weber; exhaustive investigations and scores of sworn statements were not the end of the matter. He had found, particularly with reinterrogations, that more than half the sworn statements would not stand up in court. Either they were conflicting, deliberately devious or, down-right lies. The cult of samurai was strong among the prison inmates – especially the war criminals. To deceive and mislead an interrogator was a practice resorted to by many, especially if it took the heat off a senior officer. It brought his thoughts to the vexing Weber investigation and moved him to comment.

'I understand where you're coming from on this, as a matter of fact I'm in the middle of several investigations that in context you've described quite well.' He sighed. 'I've questioned half the bloody prison on a suspected execution of a bloke named Ebery, but they either profess to know nothing or, feed me the same bloody line. A bloke named Roach is another case that has dragged on for as long as Ebery's, but,' he gave a determined smile, 'when I have some further confirmation, I'll crack both of 'em and nail the mongrels responsible.'

'That Father Weber one, Jim?' Ross took a pull at his pipe, 'have you solved it yet? That's taken or took a long time.'

Godwin shook his head. 'It's been a bloody headache that one. What's made the investigation so difficult has been what I believe, a jacked-up conspiracy and an orchestrated attempt to deceive me. Bombing a bloody plantation indeed! But then, every person I've questioned repeats the same story. It's as though it actually happened if only because I'm fed the same bull from all of them.'

'If your instinct is right and they're all telling lies,' Ross shrugged, 'it's a sure bet they're protecting someone fairly powerful. Someone they've been disciplined to respect,' he stroked his chin thoughtfully. 'A general maybe?'

'I'm questioning one at the moment,' Godwin answered, 'and yes, I think it's the answer. He looked bloody worried the other day when I questioned him.' His expression brightened visibly. 'Maybe he'll crack if I put some more pressure on him. But first, I've got to sort a cipher officer out. I think he's the bloody missing link, but strewth! He's a cagey bastard and of course suffers from AS. It's astonishing just how many of 'em suffer from this dubious disability when I put the screws on.'

'AS?' Ross raised an eyebrow puzzled. 'What's that mean?'

'Amnesia syndrome,' Godwin replied cynically. 'There's a lot of these Sons of Heaven who fake loss of memory when it suits them.' His expression grew serious. 'I've got to admit it's damned frustrating and the mongrels know it too. Then, there's their ploy of claiming to be ill with malaria when I produce absolute proof that they were known to be stationed at the scene of atrocities. God! They can lie like the devil.'

Ross nodded sombrely before pointing to his empty glass. 'Yeah I reckon, it's about as bad as waiting for a bloke's glass to be filled. Your shout I think mate?' His face puckered into a cheeky smile. 'Tell the drongo behind the bar that Aussies like chilled beer, not that warm brew he gave us before though it may suit you Kiwis'. Smiling at his own wit he took a long satisfying pull on his pipe as Godwin strolled across to the small house-bar.

The rest of the evening slipped by in small-talk before finally, Godwin returned to his room. Because it was a particularly warm night, it was some time before he could feel drowsiness overcoming his recumbent form as he lay on his bed covered only by a sheet. The evening had been quiet but pleasantly relaxing in the company of Captain Ross and earlier with other Anzac officers. Sleepily he recalled partnering Ross in a game of 500 against two other players, both of them from South Australia. Ross was adept at the game and was perhaps the fastest shuffler and slickest dealer he'd ever seen, but better still, between them they had won all three games. He was imagining how close the last hand had been when slumber finally stole his drowsy thoughts.

30 July 1948. [Comment] 'I am now utterly convinced that not only were individual Allied airmen captured after their aircraft were disabled but, an estimate of the number of Allied airmen captured collectively would exceed 600, probably more. The fate of most of these unfortunate pilots is too grim to conjecture. Only a few went down with their crashed aircraft. The majority parachuted safely, but where are they now? There is sufficient evidence to substantiate the belief that they were beheaded upon touching ground or soon after. Accordingly, I have no doubt that ninety percent of the still missing airmen will never have their fate resolved. The Japanese knew that executing prisoners of war, be they airmen or whatever, was insupportable and morally wrong, yet persisted in this widespread and barbaric practise. Undoubtedly many of these atrocities will remain concealed by the Japanese for all time.

'On a different matter. I have received a disappointing letter from the New Zealand Prime Minister, Peter Fraser. According to my notes and information learned, I felt there was a very good chance of nailing the mongrel or mongrels responsible for the decapitation of twenty-three civilians and servicemen on the Island of Tarawa, north of Fiji and on the equator. My interest was motivated by the fact that seventeen of the massacred victims were fellow New Zealanders most of whom were single and aged between nineteen and twenty-one. The latter were morse code operators stationed in the Pacific as coast-watchers and were employed by the New Zealand Post and Telegraph Department.'

'In reply to my letter offering to investigate and locate the criminal or criminals responsible for this murderous atrocity, the Prime Minister's reply was bloody negative. "The matter," he says, "has been resolved." By whom for God's sake? Is this another bunch of murderous bastards who'll evade punishment by ill-informed political default? I've checked the files upstairs and our own. Tarawa is only mentioned four times and then, in a matter totally unrelated. So far as I'm concerned and not begging Fraser's pardon, this slaughter has not been resolved or properly investigated. Unfortunately and without authority I am unable to proceed.'

'I have since learned that yes, some sort of useless inquiry into the Tarawa massacre was initiated by the New Zealand Labour Government in 1944 but, this was only a bloody Civil Service Commission, not a real War Crimes Investigation. Fair dinkum! I don't know what to think other than some people, particularly politicians, have bloody short memories.'

13, 20 and 27 August 1948. PERSONAL MEMORANDUM
Index 14B.   Interviews at Sugamo Prison.

Much of the testimony obtained from war crimes suspects was elicited from within the confines of Sugamo Prison. Witnesses of minor importance were interviewed within the Meiji Building. In this regard File 125F is a clear example of considerable time spent where there was no case to answer. Conversely, most of the investigations that absorbed months of endeavour and which were justifiable for prosecution encountered deception, lies and denials including discredited sworn statements that hindered the investigative process. Added to this difficult situation was the most frustrating problem of having key suspects elusively evading apprehension orders. There was undoubtedly a grapevine that kept the war criminals underground well informed. Consequently, if a suspect was successfully appre-hended, a confinement order would be immediately sought and enforced.

The following are examples of interrogations that took place within Sugamo Prison. The suspect being questioned was former Major Ito Toichi who was involved in the execution of three Allied airmen. The interrogating officer was myself hereafter referred to as Godwin. Opening the interrogation I asked Toichi whether, in his private opinion, the executions were justified?

TOICHI: After pondering deeply, I came to the conclusion that the three airmen deserved to die and that the decision was just. By taking up arms against our Divine Emperor, they had forfeited their right to live.

GODWIN: Would you say that the soldiers assigned to execute prisoners were in any way reluctant to carry out their task?

TOICHI: All soldiers of the Imperial Japanese Army obey orders. However, when it was found necessary to dispose of prisoners, orders weren't really necessary. At times I had difficulty in choosing the most deserving men from volunteers, particularly if the method of execution was by samurai beheadings.

GODWIN: You mention the disposal of prisoners. What do you mean?

TOICHI: Their execution.

GODWIN: Did it ever occur to you that these executions would be considered murder by the Allies?

TOICHI: It was war, hostilities meant just that. Prisoners required guarding and tied down our soldiers in non-combatant duties. We did not consider the disposal of prisoners as murder. What the Allies thought was of no concern. We expected at first to win the war, but then, as fortunes changed, we felt sure of an Armistice and with it, no inquiries as to how we waged war.

GODWIN: Why then, were the remains of the executed airmen so methodically destroyed and concealed immediately after Japan's surrender? Was it because that deep down your conscience told you that it was murder and that having lost the war, there would be retribution?

TOICHI: I was following superior orders. I do not feel accountable. What you ask requires a demeaning answer.

GODWIN: Was it any less demeaning for the Australian airmen to have been murdered?

TOICHI: From your perspective this may seem so. But they died honourable deaths and were released from the stigma of captivity.

GODWIN: Did it ever occur to you that they might have cherished life more?

TOICHI: They had no choice. I was following superior orders and as a soldier myself, would have chosen execution if the roles were reversed.

GODWIN: It appears you have a scant regard for life. Have you no feelings?

TOICHI: I am sworn to sacrifice my life for the Emperor and Japan. Soldiers no matter who, are expendable, ours and the Allies. It is an honour to die for one's country and to be exalted at shrines. The physical remains if buried in foreign lands are inaminate and best left undisturbed. Your desire to exhume the remains of those disposed of for reburial confounds me. To my mind it is decadent sentimentality.

GODWIN: Do you understand the word 'compassion'?

TOICHI: Yes, that is for women.

GODWIN: In the possible immediate future, have you thought of your own fate?

TOICHI: It does not concern me. I am a soldier of the Emperor. Whatever happens, I shall be honoured at shrines. Death is not an enemy but a friend.

GODWIN: You have evaded an earlier question. Why were the remains of the executed prisoners so carefully concealed? Was it because of guilt?

TOICHI: It was discussed and decided that the three airmen would be exhumed and then reburied together. There was no thought of guilt. How could there be? They had been disposed of with military approval.

GODWIN: Why the cremation and crushing of bones?

TOICHI: The flax mat was small and to contain all the remains it was necessary to reduce the larger bones and crush the skulls. The cremation itself was necessary because the bodies were only half decomposed.

GODWIN: Why a new isolated burial site of the ashes?

TOICHI: It was felt that their spirits would prefer the serenity of isolation.

GODWIN: You are implying that there was no thought of deliberate concealment?

TOICHI: This suggestion was never discussed. It just happened that way.

Godwin flicked a couple of pages of his personal interview notes and paused at Index 16R. This investigation had been dropped by a directive from the Supreme Allied Command Headquarters located at the Dai-Tchi Building. Nonetheless it was an interesting example of what was encountered when interrogating suspects who were evasive and less than honest. His eyes rested on one word 'CANNIBALISM'. Next to it for reference was File No. 125E. Because of the nature of the inquiry and the subject, the interrogation was held without witnesses. Despite this consideration, no important information, other than what was already known, was elicited.

Index 16R   Subject: CANNIBALISM.
Interview at Sugamo Prison. 5.12.47.

The suspect being questioned was a former member of the 13th Regiment and who was formerly stationed in the Solomon Islands and New Guinea. His name was Nagayama Ichiro and he had just been asked whether he had ever eaten human flesh or, could identify those who had.

ICHIRO: We did not always eat together. On occasions when a wild boar or other animal was shot, it would be prepared in a crude sort of way before being dismembered and roasted over an open fire. Never once did I knowingly eat dead enemy soldiers.

GODWIN: Would you agree that your army rations weren't adequate?

ICHIRO: We lived off what the jungle could provide to supplement the wild tapioca, breadfruit, yams and taro that were gathered when rice became scarce. We did hunger for fish but because we were inland for most of the time, it was unobtainable.

GODWIN: Could you say what was more important in the Japanese Army? Food or ammunition?

ICHIRO: Ammunition.

GODWIN: Can I put it to you that sometimes your platoon, or whatever, was starving?

ICHIRO: That is incorrect. If I said yes, you would seize upon this as a reason for cannibalism. Sometimes we would over-run an enemy outpost and capture their rations. Their tinned meat (corned beef) was very good. At other times we shot wild animals.

GODWIN: Did you not become suspicious that sometimes after a skirmish with Australian soldiers that perhaps, a special detail, briefed as an intelligence collecting platoon, would search around for freshly killed enemy soldiers?

ICHIRO: That was a rumour only.

GODWIN: Local natives have positively identified Japanese bivouacs and semi-permanent camps where cooked human bones have been found including toes and fingers. Surely you must have known what was going on?

ICHIRO: I have seen this alleged evidence myself, but it's nothing new. They were monkey bones.

GODWIN: Forensic and pathological reports say otherwise. These bones have been certified as human.

ICHIRO: The Japanese are civilized and honourable people. Have you forgotten? The natives of the South Pacific are not strangers to cannibalism. Some of our soldiers went missing too. Or, is it more convenient to blame us?

GODWIN: I'm here to ask questions, not to answer yours. You said earlier that you did not always eat together, why?

ICHIRO: Some of us would eat close to the cooking pieces of meat for convenience, others like myself, disliked the smoke and smell. We would eat apart.

GODWIN: These cooking pieces of meat? Could you identify their life-form even in dismembered portions?

ICHIRO: I am not a butcher, I suggest you ask someone better qualified.

At this point, Godwin discontinued the interrogation. Ichiro appeared to be callously indifferent and was perceived as being patently evasive.

3 September 1948. It was a welcome relief to have the next two days off. A party of Allied officers including Godwin had made arrangements during the week to go as a group to Sendai north of Fukushima for some sight-seeing and perhaps a spot of fishing. He had been reluctant at first but finally was persuaded with the realization that investigations, though never fully advanced, were at least on schedule and processed as far as humanly possible. Glancing out the single partly opened window of his office he noted that the weather was continuing brilliantly fine, a good augur for the weekend. It was close on half-past five and the thought of an unhurried stroll back to the inn in such glorious weather prompted him to call it a day. After closing the window he reached down and retrieving his brief case, clipped both locks before withdrawing the small bunch of filing cabinet keys from his jacket pocket. After securing the briefcase inside the rather ancient floor-safe that was situated next to the filing cabinets, he pocketed the keys and left the Meiji Building.

The next two days remained fine and settled and after departing Tokyo by train early Saturday morning, it was a relaxing pleasure to just sit back and take in the panorama that constantly changed. Apart from the fishing excursion on the clear waters of the Pacific that washed Honshu Island's eastern shores and which proved quite fruitless, the rest of the itinerary lived up to expectations. So interesting were the comparisons and customs that Godwin lost no time in jotting down his impressions and perceptions that are worth recording in this narrative. The following is what Godwin wrote upon his return to Tokyo.

'Japan is a land of festivals most of which are Shinto oriented and stemming from rice-growing rites, indigenous fertility cults and supplications for relief from plague and flood and on occasions, earthquakes. Buddhism has its celebrations, but most of these are performed in temples, whereas the larger Shinto festivals take place in public places. Sendai has frequent festivals where on occasions, one can dispose of much-used personal possessions such as needles and combs at a particular shrine.'

'We visited a shrine on Sunday morning. However despite the fine buildings and tranquil setting, there was a deserted atmosphere, like an empty rugby stadium. Had we visited at the time of a festival, it may have proved more interesting. We did notice a few other visitors, mainly sightseers like ourselves and other local people who had come for a special blessing or intentionally, to make votive offerings. I found out that ownership of these shrines is hereditary. The presiding monk and his family live in quarters adjacent to the shrine, some of which are opulent while others that were noticed on our tour, were quite shabby and poor. There are thousands of shrines scattered throughout Japan and it is astonishing how many of them manage to survive. Each shrine has an offertory receptable into which and during the four seasons, a few yen, multiplied hundreds of times over, are placed by the devout; especially during the New Year Festivals.'

'I found it particularly interesting to learn about the frequent moving of capitals. In 710 the Empress-Regnant Gemmyo made Nara Japan's first permanent capital, which it remained during seven reigns. By then the prosperous Buddhist temples of Nara were undermining the autonomy of the nearby Imperial Household and the capital was moved north to Kyoto. This was not the first or last transfer of the country's capital. Eventually it was established at Tokyo and remains so. There was much to see in and around Sendai. On Sunday afternoon we strolled through narrow streets cluttered with a variety of souvenir shops but of which, seemingly, every third one was selling painted wooden dolls, kokeshi, and which appeared much in demand. One sight that will remain in my mind was the number and variety of cast-iron cooking pots and kettles available to the local populace and tourists if so inclined to buy. Sendai is famous for its dolls and cast ironware.'

'Another lasting impression gained during our four-hour fishing excursion was the rocky coastline and high cliffs to the north, a sanctuary for numerous black gulls that screamed and swooped over jagged rock formations constantly beseiged by a tumultuous and boiling surf. The sheer cliffs to the north rose 900 feet in places, reminding one of the great depth of the Pacific, east of Japan and falling away to the Mariana Trench, the deepest place in the oceans of the world.'

Alas, this brief respite ended all too soon for Godwin. At 7 pm on Sunday evening the group was once more aboard a train and heading south to Tokyo. Brief as the weekend break had been, it had provided a stimulus of captivating interest sufficiently attractive to take his thoughts away from the task of questioning other Japanese who in the main, resorted to artful and mendacious answers. It was almost 11 pm when finally he returned to the inn at Tokyo. With a busy day ahead of him, Godwin wasted no time in seeking the solitude of his room and the intimacy of his diary to record the weekend excursion and all its interesting highlights. Always a person for detail, he faithfully included all of his impressions knowing that in the future mists of time much could be forgotten or only vaguely recalled. It was near midnight before finally, he closed the diary with an inner satisfaction.

10 and 17 September 1948. It is so utterly necessary to investigate every atrocity from all directions of endeavour. What appears plausible on the surface is quite often conflicting with various testimonies. Thorough and repetitive interrogations, sometimes involving as many as forty witnesses and suspects may be processed to get at the truth of just one atrocity. It is my unenviable experience and hardened opinion that known murderers are the most adamant in their protestations of innocence. If they were to be believed, the prisons would be empty though the murdered victims would remain very dead. I guess it's a conundrum of life whereby criminals having committed murder and knowing the enormity of the crime, think nothing of the lesser evil which is, to lie their way out of certain perdition and attrition.

Apart from the rare honest witness, not only do I get fed a pack of lies from prime suspects (usually proved guilty as sin), I now know that most of these mongrels have no compunction or conscience to tell the truth. Equally as bad and most unacceptable is the sworn testimony of witnesses who wilfully perjure themselves to aid a war criminal who once may have been their senior officer. The proclivity of suspects and some witnesses to lie is at times outrageous and tests my patience, especially when I know they are lying. I am not a psychologist but would have to conclude that their psyche generally lacks remorse, contrition or regret. If regret is visibly noticed, it is because they lost their bloody war and that the Allies put a stop to their senseless killings.

My contribution to war crimes investigations represents only one-thousandth of one percent. If the Government of China had the inclination and indeed the people of the two Koreas, Japan would have to answer for atrocities far in excess of those committed against the Western Allied Powers. The ensuing prosecutions could well collapse the country as a nation, so horrendous and prolific were the crimes perpetrated by the Japanese Armed Forces. One has to be here in Tokyo to understand the evil of Japanese ambitions. Often I wonder why Nazi war criminals are hunted down so relentlessly while their Axis pals here in Japan are let off the hook? I refer specifically to intelligence reports and directives that have confirmed the cessation of investigations into: (a) thousands of murders committed at biological and germ warfare centres by the Japanese; (b) the suppression of investigations into Imperial Army brothels where it is now known a quarter of a million women and girls were compelled to be sex slaves; (c) cannibalism in the South Pacific; (d) the Emperor's inexplicable immunity from arrest as well as a number of Imperial princes for war crimes ruthlessly carried out in Hirohito's name and to his certain knowledge. The general consensus of opinion among Allied officers charged with investigating ALL war crimes is one of disillusionment and dismay. I too feel and indeed know that these exonerations are an appalling travesty of justice and do no credit to Generals MacArthur and Willoughby who have directed that these serious concerns and investigations be discontinued. To my mind this is selective justice with which I disagree strongly, but then, neither MacArthur or Willoughby experienced the hell of being prisoners of the Japanese.

There are rumours of deals and collusion within high places that are disturbing. Hirohito nowadays is almost an honoured guest at MacArthur's headquarters. The Emperor is not an infrequent visitor at the Dai-Ichi Building. I hope there's no bloody sell-out and a return to facism in Japan. Come to think of it, I can't understand why there isn't a Four Big Power agreement administering Japan's post-war affairs the same as exists in Germany? Why the difference? I feel sure that if a Four Big Power agreement was in charge of Japan's affairs, instead of MacArthur (America) running everything, a more morally balanced consensus and justice would prevail including the lawful pursuit of war crimes investigations as categorised in the preceding paragraph and listed as (a), (b), (c) and (d).

Oh well, I have a heavy schedule ahead of me in my own investigations. I am determined to get to the bottom of the Father Weber mystery. There's more detail to come I feel sure. All I need is patience, lots of bloody patience.

25 September 1948. Godwin was relaxed and comfortably seated in the gaming room of the Allied Officers' Club. Around him visiting officers were playing darts, cards, ping-pong, billiards or indoor bowls. It was a pleasant change to chat with fellow New Zealanders who had arrived at Tokyo with a replacement contingent of occupation forces from New Zealand and known generally as the 'J Force'. It was a great opportunity to catch up with the news from 'down under' and to shoot the breeze on any number of subjects. Godwin's task of investigating war crimes under the auspices of the Australian Army and to be so commissioned drew surprised comment which was quickly blunted when it was learned that the Australians represented New Zealand's interests with as much dedication as their own.

Throughout the evening, Godwin conversed and listened with interest to accounts of news from back home. He learned the New Zealand watersiders were becoming troublesome, particularly at Auckland where demands for a higher return for their labour were being strongly resisted by the port authorities and shipowners. Many cargo ships loaded with vitally required imports, were swinging at anchor for days, sometimes weeks, awaiting berths. The ships in port, and they crammed every berth, were taking weeks instead of days to load or unload. Essential food exports to Great Britain, tens of thousands of tons, congested cool stores and wharf sheds. No longer was there urgency formerly attached to the much publicised 'Food For

Britain Campaign' despite the fact that food rationing was still in force in the British Isles. With the threat of Japanese conquest in the South Pacific removed, industrial labour long suppressed by the 'Manpower Act' that had now been repealed, was flexing its industrial muscle.

War and all its restrictions was a period of recent history that the country as a whole wanted to forget. Returned servicemen were also like-minded, preferring to remember the vicissitudes and hardships of war on just one special day of the year, known as 'Anzac Day'. Surviving prisoners of war, especially of the Japanese, were reluctant to tell their stories or relive their horrors. Too many of their mates had perished in forced labour camps from animalistic savagery and malnutrition while they, the survivors, were lucky to have escaped with their lives. With this reluctance to relive such horrors, a veil of ignorance attained ascendancy through such understandable default. This was very much to a defeated Japan's advantage, as the least said about their disgraceful wartime conduct, the better.

Between a few ales and good-natured banter, Godwin was treated to a recount of an alleged happening that was said to involve a British cargo-ship and the Auckland watersiders. It was narrated thus. 'Three gangs of stevedores were engaged in unloading three of the ship's holds. The first gang was required to unload pencil-lead and because of the nature of this cargo, demanded and received dirt-money as an extra payment. The second gang were unloading cases of scotch whisky and not to be outdone, demanded and received temptation money as an extra payment. The third gang felt quite mortified at missing out on these extra payments. Their hold was filled with sparkling white toilet bowls, clean and easy to handle. In view of this disadvantage, they held a stop-work meeting to explore ways of claiming a similar extra payment. Within ten minutes a solution was found. They demanded and received embarrassment money.

Godwin chuckled hugely at the comparisons with no thought of questioning the veracity of the alleged happening. It was too humorous and was better left in context. He was glad that his work was not discussed or questioned because of its depressing nature. It was good to relish the normal world and to remove his thoughts from the insanity of war crimes. Finding a moment to interrupt he asked, 'What was the name of the ship that brought your crowd to Japan?'

A second-lieutenant by the name of Earnshaw replied, 'The one that usually does the Lyttleton to Wellington steamer express overnight run, the *Wahine*, a damned fine ship too.'

'I know it's got heaps of accommodation,' Godwin remarked, 'But for such a long time at sea, didn't you find the cabins a bit on the small side? I mean they were only intended for one-night passengers.'

'We only used 'em to sleep in, Jim. The bunks were bloody comfortable and that's what mattered,' a major from Greymouth broke in, 'During the voyage, especially in the tropics, we spent most of our time on deck.' He mused thoughtfully, 'By golly for a veteran ship it was quite fast.' Thus did the evening pass, all too quickly Godwin thought as finally he took his leave to return to the inn. Interludes such as a quiet evening at the club, particularly with his own countrymen, was an occasion that helped to take his mind off a different kind of people whose past interest in life had been killing and destroying. To relax in a normal sane environment and to discuss sport and current events, even to exchange banter, was a necessary palliative and counter to such necessary duties as almost daily visits to Sugamo Prison. So tickled was Godwin by the joke about the Auckland watersiders, that before retiring for the night he wrote it in his second diary, smiling occasionally as he did so.

[Author's note]. The *SS Wahine* with a full complement of J Force soldiers aboard, struck a reef in the Arafua Sea between New Guinea and Northern Australia on 15 August 1951. No lives were lost but the ship became a total loss. Similarly a modern passenger replacement vessel, the *TEV Wahine*, struck Barretts Reef at the entrance to Wellington harbour on passage from Lyttleton in 1967. It occurred during the worst storm in local living memory. Fifty-seven lives were lost along with the almost new ship. The Union Steamship Company of New Zealand owned both of these ill-fated vessels.

For the next fortnight, Godwin was busily engaged in finalising details and testimony pertaining to the execution of Father Weber as well as expanding the inquiry into the 'GOOD' murder. He was not satisfied with the explanation that the Australian planter had committed suicide in the presence of a Japanese naval escort. Something didn't ring true. Just because the Japanese held a fondness for committing harikari didn't mean that this practice was generally widespread among Europeans. The Australian faced internment at Rabaul for the duration of the war, but this did not or would not have driven the Australian to such a desperate and irrevocable measure. Europeans, Godwin was inclined to think, were made of sterner stuff.

1 and 8 October 1948. It was a Sunday morning and just for a change Godwin decided to explore the area adjacent to the nearby Imperial Palace. Many times he had casually glanced in its direction between the gaps of obstructing buildings, but today on a cool autumn morning and with an English language guidesheet grasped firmly in his hand, he strolled in leisurely manner towards the picturesque moat that encircled century old walls. To inform himself better he had taken care to study the origins and history of the palace the previous evening in the quietness of his room at the inn. Accepting that the Imperial Palace lacked the history and grandeur of Buckingham Palace in London, he was nonetheless keen to take the opportunity of viewing the Emperor's residence at close quarters. There were others like himself who had come to view the imperial private domain, mostly Japanese subjects visiting Tokyo he presumed, as they dutifully bowed their heads in homage at the nearness of the Emperor's exalted person and to some who clung to traditional beliefs, his unquestioned mystical divinity.

Godwin trod a footway that followed the outer perimeter of the palace moat, his thoughts assimilating the simplicity and historical background that gave the palace an air of timeless mystery. Considering the city's big population and congestion, the Imperial grounds occupied a large area of central Tokyo and clearly reflected an era when the country was less densely populated. This would be the mediaeval period Godwin thought, when it was taken over from the Tokugawas by Emperor Meiji. The palace was originally a castle and to which this was obvious by the wide moat, striking gateways, white walls and stout timbered gates. It was easy to imagine that before the Meiji Dynasty it was the cloistered domain of Japan's last Shoguns. The palace was without doubt a fascinating drawcard for the city and by its very positioning, was a help rather than a hindrance to Tokyo's vehicular traffic. Inside the grounds a number of modest traditionally built dwellings and buildings could be seen dotted between gardens, lawns and ponds. To his perception, Godwin assumed that they were of very recent date judging by the modern materials employed in their construction.

It was close on 3 pm before Godwin finally returned to his starting off point. An unseasonably cold wind had begun to blow and the previously cloudy sky was now overcast, threatening rain. Quickening his pace he headed for the comfort of the inn. Somewhat footsore but energised by his rather long relaxing stroll he returned to the familiar surroundings and companionship of his fellow Anzac officers, a little wiser, better informed, but most importantly, mentally refreshed.

Just after a reasonably good evening meal, Godwin suddenly remembered an interview he had conducted with a Colonel Tashiro Shimazui at the Meiji Building on the preceding Tuesday. He had taken notes purely for his own information as the former colonel, after close questioning, was found to be unconnected with an atrocity that had occurred in British Borneo in 1942. He had in fact been closely associated with and stationed at Tokyo in the War Planning and Personnel Section of the War Ministry from 1941 to 1945. Quite often military ranks and surnames compared to others in the Imperial Armed Forces and required a lengthy process of elimination. However, useful information was often elicited from these eliminating interrogations. Shimazui was no exception.

Stimulated by his recollection of what the former colonel had revealed, Godwin headed to his room on the first floor of the inn, resolved to extract the notes from his briefcase and to transfer them to the cabin-trunk after reading and assimilating their contents. He knew that the information had been freely given and authenticated by Colonel Shimazui whose word and motive he had no reason to doubt. Once seated at his writing desk Godwin wasted no time in placing the neglected notes before him. Drawing a pad closer to him and with pen in hand he began to correlate the jumbled discussion notes into a semblance of uniformity. For ease of interpretation and continuity he decided to employ the interrogator-witness narrative to elucidate the surprising testimony. The following is the transcript he recorded in long-hand.

GODWIN: Let it be understood, colonel, that you are under no obligation to relate decisions taken by the War Ministry during your period of service in this department.

SHIMAZUI: This does not concern me, captain, as I already know that the Americans were quite aware of Japan's intentions from 1940 onwards.

GODWIN: Thank you for your candour, colonel. May I specifically refer to the 100,000 Japanese troops garrisoning Rabaul? Was this not a waste of valuable manpower with such a concentration of battle-ready troops?

SHIMAZUI: From a military point of view, no. Had the Battle of the Coral Sea been convincingly won by our Navy, this Army would then have been transported from New Britain to New Zealand via New Caledonia and Norfolk Island.

GODWIN: Why New Caledonia and Norfolk Island, colonel? Did they have some military significance for the Japanese High Command?

SHIMAZUI: Oh yes! An assigned number of troops would have been detailed to overcome resistance and garrison the new territory to deprive the Allies of port facilities and airfields. In fact it was intended to make New Caledonia our largest air-base in Southern Oceania.

GODWIN: You mentioned New Zealand. Of what strategic or

military value would this country have been?

SHIMAZUI: Militarily New Zealand was not a threat. However the War Ministry was aware of the country's potential to supply England with considerable amounts of food and other essential imports. By seizing the country Japan would assist Germany to overcome the English by denying them these valuable food supplies. Conversely the Japanese Army of occupation would be well supplied from New Zealand's abundance and could have ensured a vital source of food for Japan.

GODWIN: Was a tenacious resistance expected to a Japanese invasion of NZ?

SHIMAZUI: Perhaps around the larger cities but only for a time. We were aware that the country's national Army was small by our standards and that its most capable soldiers were overseas fighting in the Middle East. The Home-Guard and Territorials would have been quickly subdued by our overwhelming numbers and battle-experienced troops.

GODWIN: Did not the closeness of Australia geographically raise some concern?

SHIMAZUI: Not really. This possible threat had been considered but dismissed as improbable. It was our intention to base a heavy cruiser squadron and supporting naval units to operate from New Zealand and sufficient to deter units of Australia's small naval capability.

This example of currency was intended for use in conquered Territory such as Malaya, Hawaii and North America. Other currency, Guilders and Antipodean Pounds were available for use in the NEI, New Zealand and Australia following their occupation by invading Forces of the Imperial Japanese Army.

GODWIN: Were you privy as to how this invasion of New Zealand was planned?

SHIMAZUI: Generally yes. Our department assisted in collating all the information available which was considerable. We had thousands of photos of every public utility in the country including port installations, dams, cross-country power-lines, railways, bridges and the like including the location of military training camps.

GODWIN: How did you obtain such a wealth of photos, colonel?

SHIMAZUI: From Japanese nationals employed by the Oceania Division of Foreign Affairs. They were supplied with excellent Kodak cameras and sent abroad as tourists. Other photos were supplied by bonafide tourists after their return to Japan.

GODWIN: How was it proposed to administer the country after it was invaded? Would it have been a civil or military administration?

SHIMAZUI: Until the country was pacified or the war had been won, the country would have been under martial law. To this end an elite group of university graduates enrolled in the military and designated as the Tactical Section, had been trained to oversee the country's internal affairs and to prepare it for an orderly transition from military to Japanese civilian rule.

GODWIN: What about the local indigenous population? How would they have been treated, colonel?

SHIMAZUI: I really don't know, captain. New Zealand's future as part of the Japanese Empire was not of immediate concern. Japanese occupation currency would have replaced the current money supply within the country and it was envisaged that Japanese colonisation would have followed including the confiscation of farms and property deemed suitable for Japanese ownership.

GODWIN: Would there have been no compensation?

At this point Shimazui had shrugged and gave an answer that was clearly beyond his knowledge. 'A decision relating to the spoils of war would no doubt be made but at the highest level. Tokyo, not Wellington, would have governed New Zealand until

Japanese immigration surpassed the local population in numbers.'

GODWIN: Your answers have been frank and truthful, colonel, and support some information I already know. May I ask one last question? Clearly and with regard to Australia, Japan may have felt it was strategically contained until such time as it was targeted for invasion, but what about Canada and the United States? Was it honestly believed both of these large countries would have been intimidated by Japan?

SHIMAZUI: Initially yes, but only by an honourable armistice. In a protracted war and with North America's population and natural resources, it would have been impossible for Japan to win militarily. It was hoped that Japan's swift conquests and formidable army would help to persuade a new understanding of the status quo by the Allied powers. As the tide of war turned into severe reverses for Japan, the prospect of an armistice changed to one of unconditional surrender. The atom bombs just hastened the end.

Godwin lay down his pen before leaning back in his chair. What he had written from the notes was nothing new he admitted to himself. Informed people were well aware of Japan's wartime ambitions. Posterity he hoped would record them. Insofar as former Colonel Tashiro Shimazui was concerned he recognised the openness and honesty of the man. The earlier interview with him had clearly established his honourable credentials and lack of guile. It had been a most refreshing experience to meet up with a man of good character who, with nothing to hide, and harbouring no animosity or resentment, spoke the truth. Such occasions were unfortunately rare but at least assisted in providing a balanced perspective despite the proclivity of other witnesses and suspects to lie and deceive.

15 and 22 October 1948. I have discussed with Major Williams the obstructions encountered in my investigations. He is au-fait with my concerns as he is experiencing them himself. It no longer surprises me to have to listen to a constant flow of falsehoods delivered in polite self-effacing dialogues of contrived servility.

Strewth! These mongrels would have to be the world's best actors. Even their inscrutable expressions are impossible to fathom.

At times I find myself wondering just how these pathetic creatures once had Asia and the Pacific in fear of them. I guess it was their sheer inexhaustible numbers, something like the voracious ant armies of the South American jungle, overwhelming everything in their path.

File 125H is now another frustrating bloody enigma. War crimes suspect former Colonel Tsugio Ryokai denies everything even though he's been fingered in sworn statements. This is just part of the prevarication and obstruction encountered. Jacked-up testimony and wilful perjury is resorted to if it's thought there's a good chance of getting away with it. External scheming and plotting is all in a day's work for these mongrels. The supporters of former Lieutenant-General Fusataro Teshima and clique are a bloody good example of unprincipled morality. I wonder if they know the meaning of the world truthfulness or have a conscience?

Major Williams agrees that the underground is a highly organised coterie of sympathisers and supporters of the militarists. I'm chasing so many suspected war criminals, I've bloody lost count. What we need in Japan is an organisation like the Zionists in Germany. They would quickly find the mongrels we're looking for as from what I hear they're ferreting out Nazis in hiding far better than the Allied powers in Berlin. I have the feeling the Japanese police only go through the motions and are next to useless.

The Japanese police recently complained to the top-brass at the Dai-Ichi Building that all Allied Investigative Sections are impolite to them. This would explain the directive circulated from General Willoughby's office. 'We are to endeavour,' he says, 'to foster good relations with the police.' What crap! Doesn't he know or care about the police intransigence we are putting up with? We are investigating countless murders and atrocities, but seemingly, bloody politeness has a higher priority than bringing war criminals to justice. Or is this a devious ruse by well-placed underground supporters within the police to make us back off in the pursuit of war criminals harboured by the underground? After interrogating their ilk for well over a year, I wouldn't trust 'em as far as I could throw 'em. They're a bloody devious lot.

[Author's note]. Judging by Godwin's private comments he didn't mince words. He was the right man for the right job – after what he had endured at the hands of the Japanese as a prisoner of war. He was not easily taken in and preferred to call a spade a spade. Yet, and on occasions when he believed a witness was telling the truth, he had no reservations in pointedly drawing attention to this fact. The real problem was that for every honest witness, he would interview twenty that weren't. He was after all, only human. With such odds stacked on the side of duplicity and deception he had grown cynical. This reflected itself in his writings and second diary. We can be thankful that Godwin was such a determined and resolute man with a sense of history. Alas, much of what transpired in the late forties at Tokyo is now lost to that era of history which Godwin endeavoured to preserve. Thankfully his writings have survived.

29 October 1948. Due to the non-arrival of witnesses, I have been assisting Major Williams in the interrogation of witnesses called in connection with atrocities committed by the Fukumi Butai at Koepang, Timor. One of these witnesses (a war crime suspect) identified as Takeshi Sasaki, has confessed to having mutilated and beheaded a European prisoner of war. This prisoner, an Australian, was the only survivor from a ship sunk by bombs and was subsequently captured in a jungle ambush that killed three Dutch soldiers and eight Romushu natives. This action was successfully carried out by the Miyamoto Company near Besikama in April-May 1942.

Takeshi Sasaki perhaps, best exemplifies the needless, mindless urge to not only murder, but to inflict as much suffering and pain before death as possible and let it be remembered, there were thousands of other Takeshi Sasaki's in the Imperial Japanese Army afflicted with the same madness and desire to sadistically behead prisoners. In a peacetime environment such fixations would be quickly recognised by society as psychopathic insanity. Upon questioning Sasaki I was left in no doubt that I was talking to a psychopath. The following is an example of a typical interrogation of Takeshi Sasaki.

GODWIN: Is courage and bravery part of the doctrine of Bushido?

SASAKI: Yes, it is fearlessness and bravery that derives from Bushido.

GODWIN: Do you think it is right to execute an un-armed civilian or prisoner?

SASAKI: If it assists a military objective, yes.

GODWIN: Can you define a military objective?

SASAKI: Yes, the pacification of conquered territory and disposal of prisoners.

GODWIN: Disposal of prisoners? What do you mean?

SASAKI: Either forced labour or their execution.

GODWIN: Do you comprehend the sanctity of life and the permanence of death?

SASAKI: Life is just an hour-glass. It has but one purpose, procreation.

GODWIN: And death what does this mean to you?

SASAKI: I consider dishonour more important than death. Death is a void, no more. To execute the enemy is to release them from the ignomity of defeat and the dishonour of surrender.

GODWIN: I find this contradictory. Japan surrendered and lives with the dishonour of defeat. Do you have double-standards?

SASAKI: The Emperor has asked that we endure the unendurable.

GODWIN: As a human being, and imbued with the spirit of Bushido, which would you value more highly, your own life or a hundred prisoners of war?

SASAKI: To obey an order is more important than my life or that of prisoners. I merely obey orders.

GODWIN: Who ordered you to execute the Australian prisoner?

SASAKI: It was my decision. I was troubled by the enemy taking up arms against the Emperor and the circumstances dictated the prisoner be disposed of.

GODWIN: What circumstances?

SASAKI: The prisoner had to be constantly guarded and it was I who was detailed to this useless task. Our patrol left our makeshift bivouac to go on a reconnaissance and search for enemy coast-watchers. The natives too, had to be taken into consideration. Some of them were armed and unfriendly.

GODWIN: Are you saying that you were left to guard the prisoner on your own?

SASAKI: Yes.

GODWIN: You didn't carry a sword. Where did you find one?

SASAKI: Our sergeant major left his at the bivouac. I borrowed it.

GODWIN: What was his name?

SASAKI: I can't remember.

GODWIN: Do you know that two natives witnessed you executing the prisoner?

SASAKI: It didn't concern me. Most of the natives were frightened of us.

GODWIN: Why did you chop off the prisoner's feet?

SASAKI: So he could not escape.

GODWIN: The testimony we have alleges that you securely bound the prisoner before forcing him to kneel. You then tied his legs together as well. Why?

SASAKI: I was filled with a desire to punish the caucasian and the enemy for starting the war. Japan at the time was winning glorious victories and I wanted to be part of this success in my own way.

GODWIN: You said previously that you wanted to prevent the prisoner escaping. Did you not realize that by severing his feet he would probably die?

SASAKI: He was going to anyhow. It was my intention to decapitate him.

GODWIN: Was there not an element of pain and suffering that you wanted to inflict first?

SASAKI: I prefer to call it punishment for taking up arms against the Emperor.

GODWIN: According to the natives' testimony, you waited for half-an-hour before executing the prisoner. Was this a deliberate delay to ensure maximum agony of the prisoner?

SASAKI: No. I had to wait because he lay on his side unconscious for twenty minutes. I wanted him in the kneeling position and alert to his fate.

GODWIN: Was this achieved?

SASAKI: Yes. He was barely conscious but managed to resume the kneeling position. I could tell by his pallor and the amount of blood on the ground that he had not long to live. I struck his neck once with the sword and beheaded him with one stroke.

GODWIN: Did you not consider your execution barbaric?

SASAKI: Japanese soldiers do not think such maudlin thoughts.

GODWIN: Now that the war is over, have you no remorse?

SASAKI: I did my duty as a soldier of Nippon.

GODWIN: You must realize that you will go on trial for this war crime?

SASAKI: I did my duty to the Emperor and my country. War is war.

Takeshi Sasaki was confined in Sugamo Prison as a B Class war criminal. This meant that A Class criminals (usually responsible for massacres) and there were numbers of them, awaited prosecution first. However and later, Sasaki died from alleged food poisoning. I rather think he ingested something difficult to detect but far more lethal than food poisoning. To my mind he was surreptitiously helped to commit seppuku (suicide). His crime would have attracted a death penalty and I believe he knew it.

Godwin continued investigating war crimes as they came to light. Some, he knew, would be successfully concealed by the Japanese themselves, but in other areas of war criminality, selective immunities from investigation were directed from the Supreme Command Allied Powers HQ (SCAP) located in the Dai-Ichi Building. The Mitsubishi Slave Labour Inquiry (using Korean forced labour) had been inexplicably shelved. Mitsubishi

Heavy Industries had acquired great assets and wealth through its employment of forced labour at beggar rates of pay. If ever a board of directors deserved to be put on trial, it was Mitsubishi's. But, thanks to General MacArthur, prosecutions were not proceeded with despite its awesome manufacture of weapons of war.

There was also the Germ Warfare Centre at Ping Fan in central Manchuria. It was common knowledge among Allied investigators, but for some other inexplicable pretext, MacArthur placed a virtual censorship on what would have been exposed as the most criminal act of war in Japan's disgraceful pursuit of conquest. We knew enough about what had been discovered from our American colleagues to shake our heads in wonderment and dismay at MacArthur's decision to exonerate war criminals responsible for the thousands of murders of, specifically, defenceless prisoners of war in cruel biological experiments.

Then there were the dark whispers and yes, proof, that close on a quarter of a million females were forced into prostitution (unpaid) servicing the needs of a lustful Imperial Japanese Army with the official establishment of countless comfort stations (brothels). These serious concerns were discussed between ourselves, but strangely, for an alleged American democracy, a blanket censorship and prohibition inhibiting investigations has been imposed. I have to ask myself. What the hell is going on? Oh well, it's back to work and unlike the top-brass, without fear or favour.

19 and 26 November 1948. Godwin spent a number of days in Formosa pursuing inquiries into the alleged execution of Allied prisoners of war in 1945 by a number of identified Japanese guards. What made his quest difficult was the fact that the records and files of the fourteen guards involved had been uplifted by British investigating officers in 1947. These important dossiers and files were the missing link. Without evidence to back up apprehension orders, the names of the war criminals, even though known, were of no use. Allegations, nothing more, would not suffice in a Court of Law. After fifteen fruitless days of exchanging inquiries and messages to and from Hong Kong and

Singapore, and twice consulting Major Williams at Tokyo, it was a welcome relief to be ordered to return.

What had earlier been predicted had proved only too true. With no British War Crimes Section to consult, fourteen war criminals would escape investigation and prosecution. That there were others Godwin was certain, including the infamous Colonel Tsuji. These and other thoughts crossed his mind occasionally as the aircraft winged him back to Japan.

Christmas was once more approaching as Godwin resumed his duties in the Meiji Building. The faint chatter (when his door was closed) of the secretarial pool typewriters no longer disturbed him. During his absence in the first two weeks of November, tradesmen had refurbished his office and at last, provided a new desk and swivel chair that clearly had his personal measurements in mind. The month swiftly drew to a close during which he came to the conclusion that the Weber and 'GOOD' investigations had parallels of conflicting testimony not dissimilar. In many respects it appeared an uphill struggle, but he was determined to get at the truth and expose what he knew were conspiracies of deceit.

8

A Litany of War Crimes 1949

A POWDERING of fresh snow crunched underfoot as Godwin strode briskly in the direction of the inn. Behind him the Meiji Building receded within the enveloping shroud of an early winter's evening. It was almost dark with a cold wind gusting and carrying with it particles of snow and sleet, a reminder of the winter solstice that had passed but a brief fortnight previously. It was now early January 1949, almost three-and-a-half years since Japan had been restored to sanity and acceptable standards of civilization. Skeletal structures reared like spectres in vaguely seen symmetry on either side of the dimly lit street, their presence an assurance that the rebuilding of the war-shattered city was well under way. Godwin gripped his briefcase tightly with one hand while with the other, clutching firmly the collar of his overcoat that protected and kept dry a thick scarf repelling the elements and the cold.

While the western world rejoiced and celebrated the festive season and the fourth Christmas of world peace, Godwin like many other Allied officers stationed at Tokyo, continued the never-ending task of investigating war crimes that though cleverly concealed by their perpetrators, more often as not, were discovered through cross-interrogation of other atrocities, and usually, committed by the same suspects. These thoughts filled his mind as he neared the inn. Perhaps the most disturbing intelligence that was doing the rounds was the clear evidence that monstrous crimes against humanity had been carried out in Manchuria by a bunch of Japanese scientists. In this regard however, the concealment, originally a Japanese exercise in deceit, was to the astonishment of those in the know and Allied intelligence officers, kept a close secret by the Supreme Command Allied Powers. A 'Directive' from the Dai-Ichi Building (SCAP Headquarters) was issued to the effect that: 'The Ping Fan Biological and Germ Warfare experimental facility in Manchuria is to be neither discussed, investigated or entered into War Crimes Files.'

Of course the matter was discussed amid puzzlement at the censorship of such obvious atrocities that had surreptitiously become known. General Douglas MacArthur, who imposed this blanket prohibition, was not dealing with schoolboys. Collectively, the Allied intelligence officers were astute men of the world whose wits had been sharpened through the discovery of treachery, deviousness and duplicity encountered in their questioning of Japanese war crimes suspects. General Charles Willoughby, MacArthur's second in command and Chief of Allied Intelligence in Japan, had appended his signature to the directive that must have had MacArthur's concurrence and authority.

Whenever 'Unit 731' was mentioned in veiled discussion between the investigating officers, it referred to the Ping Fan murder facility created and operated by Japan's most evil men and personally approved by Emperor Hirohito himself. The cover-up may not have bothered MacArthur, but it did tug at Godwin's conscience and sense of indignation. The exclusion of any mention or record of 'Unit 731' in official files was a clear indication of the corruption of justice and politics. With these thoughts in mind Godwin reached the inviting lights of the inn, resolved within himself to record in his private writings the suppression of the truth and justice by no less a person than MacArthur himself.

7 January 1949. There was a memorandum awaiting Godwin when he returned to the Meiji Building after a miserably cold afternoon at Sugamo Prison. Curious, he opened it without delay as since the British Investigation Section had closed shop, the number of such memos had fallen away sharply. There was a brief hand-written message above some printed content and was signed by Ralph Hewson (United States Investigation Section). It read as follows:

'Jim, this may interest you. It's documentation captured intact from the Japs.'

'APPENDIX D: OFFICIAL ENTRIES FROM A TAIWAN PRIS-ONER OF WAR CAMP.'

The following is a copy of the official translations from part of the camp entries, dated 1 August 1944.

'The following answer about the extreme measures for POWs was sent to the Chief of Staff of the 11th Unit (Formosa POW Security No. 10).

Under the present situation, if there were a mere explosion or fire, a shelter for the time being could be held in nearby buildings such as the school, a warehouse, or the like. However, at such time as the situation became urgent and it became extremely important, the POWs will be concentrated and confined in their present location and, under heavy guard, the preparation for their final disposition* will be made. The time and method of this disposition is as follows:

(1) The time:

Although the basic aim is to act under superior orders, individual disposition may be made under the following circumstances:

(A) When an uprising of large numbers of POWs cannot be suppressed without the use of firearms:

(B) When escapes from the camp may turn into a hostile fighting force:

(2) The methods:

(A) Whether they are destroyed individually or in groups, or however it is done, with mass bombing, poisonous smoke, poison, drowning, decapitation or whatever, dispose† of the POWs as the situation dictates.

(B) In any case, it is the aim not to allow the escape of a single one, to annihilate them all, and not to leave any traces.

(3) To: The Commanding General.

The Commanding General Military Police‡.

Reported matters conferred on with the 11th Unit, the Kiirun

Fortified Area HQ and each Prefecture concerning the extreme security in Taiwan POW Camps.

Dated 1 August 1944.'

The above is certified as exhibit O in Document Number 2687.
Sworn before me this 19th day of September 1946.

(Signed) P.L. Vine, Major, RM.

*Disposition (Execution) †Dispose (Murder) ‡Military Police (Kempetai)

Godwin did not need clarification as to what the official
'Directive' from the Japanese War Ministry intended. Should
Taiwan be invaded by Allied armed forces and the probable liberation of POW camps likely, this would be a sufficient pretext for
the Japanese guards to massacre every prisoner of war and to
leave no trace of their butchery. That any country could consider
such a barbaric retaliation on weakened and defenceless prisoners was horrifying, but then, Japan was not just 'any country'.
It was a killing machine that had no compunction in imposing its
evil insanity on the world.

Slipping the memorandum into his briefcase, Godwin recalled
the fourteen Japanese camp guards who had executed a number
of Allied prisoners in a POW camp at Formosa. If there was any
doubt, the memorandum dispelled it. A pity, he thought, that the
British had not pursued that unfinished investigation in Formosa.
It was vexing he thought to himself, that fourteen known war
criminals, but without evidence to arrest, had escaped just
punishment. He wondered, was trade more important in the Far
East than investigating war crimes? Sighing cynically he picked
up his latest typed report that was awaiting filing.

4, 11, 18 and 25 February 1949. There is much to distract our
thoughts from matters in hand, both within Japan and without.
North Korea is making threatening noises and clearly wants
South Korea as part of one unified country. The Soviet Union –
dogmatic as ever is obviously encouraging this political and military instability and it has the Yanks particularly, bloody
concerned. Mao Tse-tung and Chou En-lai between them, are
hell-bent on communising the whole of China and are undoubt-

edly encouraging North Korea in its expansionist agenda. This could explain – but not justify – the reapproachment and political understanding taking place here in Japan between General Douglas MacArthur (Washington) and Emperor Hirohito (Japan). As a neutral intelligence division we are well placed to appreciate what is going on, but the Emperor's visits to the Dai-Ichi Building, now bloody courtesy calls by the looks of it, and John Foster Dulles' pilgrimages to the Imperial Palace, are sounding warning bells hard to ignore. When a Secretary of State from the most powerful country in the world hobnobs with a mongrel like Hirohito, then, anything can bloody happen and probably will.

It's becoming obvious to us that powerful interests, political and economic, are forcing the winds of change in United States foreign policy insofar as Asia is concerned and with it, concessions from Washington via MacArthur, that are tooled to accommodate the growing concensus between Japan and the USA. We no longer discuss between ourselves some of the directives from the Dai-Ichi Building per Willoughby the Hun. He may be MacArthur's second-in-command and a serving member of the United States Armed Forces but we've learned this is not his ancestral name. Born the son of a baron in Heidelberg, Germany, on 8 March 1892, Karl von Tscheppe-Weidenbach changed his name to Charles Andrew Willoughby soon after immigrating to the United States in 1910. He became a naturalised citizen of the United States before enlisting in the United States Army.

I can well remember British colleagues here in Tokyo, opinioning their belief that Willoughby, the Tokyo-based United States Intelligence Chief, as being positively anti-British, an attitude they conjectured to his Germanic background. The thought crosses my mind when I think of recent events occurring in Tokyo, that not only is Willoughby an arch anti-communist, but he appears to share the extremist views of influential Japanese militarists who are well known to us. After all, was not Japan, Germany's Axis partner? What strange and unlikely bed-fellows methinks? Only time will tell.

I still find it incomprehensible not to proceed with investigations and prosecutions concerning the Biological and Germ Warfare Centre at Harbin, Manchuria. It is our job as intelligence investigators to dig out the facts, but strewth! To come across one of the largest wartime murdering establishments in Asia and then to do nothing about it begs the question. What the bloody hell is going on? Willoughby has slapped a prohibition on even discussing the matter. Honestly, General MacArthur as the Supreme Commander and whose orders General Willoughby carries out, is quite literally suppressing history. Why?

Every week we hear of newly discovered Nazi atrocities and with all the grisly details. Crikey! This mass Japanese extermination centre at Ping Fan and other locations, and run by an outfit known as Unit 731, was bloody horrifying and equally as bad if not worse than half-a-dozen Belsens. What has happened to the American sense of justice? To my mind and to my colleagues, the awful atrocities committed by Japan's insane scientists at these germ warfare centres, should be exposed and not suppressed by MacArthur. It would provide every justification, if one was needed, for nuclear bombing Japan. The sad part of this reflection is the certainty that the world in general will never know just how dangerous the Japanese were, and for that matter, what they got away with. It is a truism to aver, that nations who ignore history do so at their peril.

Another impression that comes through loud and clear, is the selective choosing of what will be prosecuted and what will not. We should know. General field atrocities (GFA), such as we investigate, and providing they only involve lesser gods of war, are okay to pursue. However, and so far as major war crimes are concerned, the show-case trials are over. Major war crimes that have since been discovered, such as germ warfare, brothels and cannibalism, just to mention a few, have been canned. Clearly, these directives have been instrumented to protect Japan nationally from embarrassment and humiliation and yes, worldwide scorn and condemnation. Thus, the major gods of war are untouchable including Imperial princes who have got away with bloody murder. I refer to the mongrel who was in command of the Imperial Japanese Army responsible for the 'Rape of Nanking in 1937', Lieutenant General Prince Asaka, a senior member of the Imperial institution and former commander of several infantry divisions in China. We can't touch him by order of MacArthur. A further excuse for a human being was Prince Fuminaro Konoye, a former Prime Minister and another scheming war criminal he committed seppuku. Then there was the Army Chief of Staff, Prince Kanin, and the mongrel who headed the Germ Warfare Centre in Manchuria, Prince Kuni. Not least is the Emperor himself. All of them are Class A war criminals and responsible for considerable bloodshed. But we can't touch them. They, all of them, were the major gods of war, but remain immune from investigation and prosecution on MacArthur's orders.

To date, not one of these bastards has been taken into custody, nor is it ever likely to happen. I'll bet a hundred quid* that if Tokyo was a Four Power Command structure like Berlin, the Soviets, if not the Chinese, would have by now, nailed these royal war criminals, and why not? Sometimes as I write down my thoughts I wonder and fear for the world's future when politics and collusion and aye, avarice, conspire to defeat the course of justice. In the years ahead, my experiences and personal knowledge suggest to me that Japan's evil war history will be whitewashed – unlike Germany's – and that a synthetic analogy of Japan's conquests – minus the barbarity – will be documented into history textbooks. Conversely and if not in my lifetime, then hopefully, and for future generations, the chronicles I am recording will tell the unmitigated truth if the material survives for posterity.

4, 11, 18 and 25 March 1949. Feeling the need to enjoy some recreation away from the depressing environment of Sugamo Prison and well overdue for a relaxing excursion away from Tokyo, Godwin toyed with the idea of applying for a full weekend's leave. It would be good for the soul he thought, to

*Australian pounds ($200)

have a break and visit a part of Japan he had only seen pictures of. His application was promptly approved by Major Williams despite the section's heavy work-load. With spring in the air and cherry blossom slowly giving way to young leaves and budding fruit, it was an excellent time during Godwin's two-day break to visit Hiroshima and see for himself the destruction an atomic bomb could cause. Renting a car early on the Saturday morning, he drove almost due west to a city now of universal historic interest. It was mid-afternoon when he arrived at what appeared a desolated city. Gaunt reminders of what had once been office blocks and shops jumped into vision as he halted the car on top of one of many hills partly surrounding Hiroshima.

Aware of the radiation factor and unsure of its extent, Godwin decided to park his car in an area east of the city and to explore an outer suburb that seemed unaffected by the atomic bomb blast or which, had been restored and was teeming with people. One of the first sights to capture his attention was the number of young volunteers standing with extended tins collecting money for the provision of medical treatment for the remaining Hiroshima victims, denied to them by the local Japanese authorities. The rattle of these tins was a dire reminder of human excesses that brought about the atomic bombing and which prompted almost emotional thoughts.

From a vantage point Godwin could see at close hand the epicentre of the atomic blast, the famous skeletal-domed building which survived the fusion of nuclear forces immediately over-head. It was a most telling reminder of 6 August 1945 and the death of about 200,000 people within a two-mile area. The total deaths were not as astronomical as the Rape of Nanking (300,000 people) but certain and immediate obliteration followed the atomic blast, estimated at 100,000. The other half died within eighteen months of severe burns or/and radiation sickness.

Godwin was sensitive to the cruelties of war and whilst wandering through back-alleys and congested streets, absorbed the atmosphere and fatalism of Hiroshima's inhabitants, while pondering the bombing of the city. He knew that the dropping of the atomic bomb was not some unique act dreamed up by the Americans on a totally innocent people. He felt that the bombing had to be viewed within its historical context (either attrition or retribution) for Japan's past horrendous wrongs. It could be interpreted as the last 'atrocity' in a chain of atrocities: the atrocities of the Imperial Japanese Army in Korea, South-East Asia, Manchuria and China, before and during World War II. The Japanese war machine with its millions of soldiers had to be stopped somehow. In concise terms, had not Japan embarked on its horrendous conquests and stayed out of World War II, neither Nagasaki or Hiroshima would have been nuclear bombed. An over-riding thought entered his mind as he turned away from the sight of the demolished inner city. War was inexcusable whether one was melted or burned to death in Hiroshima, or beheaded in a Japanese prisoner of war camp. The loss of life if not the parallels were the same.

The setting sun reminded Godwin to retrace his way back to the parked car before driving to Miyajima, a few kilometres south of Hiroshima, where he had an overnight booking at a highly recommended inn. Dusk had fallen by the time he arrived at the inn, but he was expected and shown to a small but comfortable bedroom where he deposited his overnight bag before taking a hot bath. Later in the evening and after a tasty meal including several dishes of mainly fish and rice, but involving different preparation, he stood by a quaintly latticed window in his room and peered out into the night and at the nearby shore of the inland sea. Here and there coloured lanterns swung gently in the soft night breeze whilst beyond the shore a number of flickering lights, barely visible, revealed the presence of small fishing boats harvesting the calm waters.

Early the following morning after a refreshing night's rest and an enjoyable English breakfast of fried potatoes, ham and eggs, Godwin farewelled his Japanese hosts and drove towards the nearby and famous shrine of Miyajima, the second of Japan's unique tourist venues. Parking the car Godwin alighted and strolled closer to the shore's edge for a more advantageous view of a famous and classic Shinto shrine with quaint and traditional buildings snuggled around its rear and side edifices and all built on a small island. As Godwin had been advised by the inn's hosts, Miyajima's tourist reputation must largely have been promoted by the great vermilion torii or Shinto ceremonial gateway that rose from the sea in front of the shrine. At high tide it would tower, reflected in the clear mirror of the surrounding sea. At low tide it reared above and from the sandy and pebble-strewn shore, its lofty cross-beams mirrored here and there in captured pools of water. It was low tide and with a firm path clearly revealed he passed under the gateway and walked unhurriedly towards the shrine in its magnificent isolation on the island.

At 11 am and having explored every aspect of interest on the island, Godwin made his way back to the shore through throngs of sightseers and past a lot more sea-bed depressions that were slowly filling with water. The incoming tide clearly was on its way. Once more driving the car, Godwin turned east towards Tokyo, hoping that with the continuation of fine weather he would arrive back in Tokyo no later than 8 pm. The drive was tiring but incident free and provided a sufficient variety of rural and village scenes that distracted his tendency to recapitulate difficult aspects of his work as a war crimes investigator. He ruefully acknowledged within himself that he had yet to learn the art of switching off, but then such was the nature of his duties, it was not that easy to dismiss from his mind what he was gleaning from war criminals, many of whom were artful and knew every trick in the book.

As anticipated, Godwin not only returned to Tokyo safely, but he had returned the car to the rental company and was back in his room at the inn by 9 pm. A cold collation that he had previously ordered for his return awaited him in covered china bowls including a welcome thermos of hot sweet tea. The supper was provided on a tray placed on his writing desk. Sighing thankfully he seated himself before the repast, but prior to partaking of the tasty looking food he secured a memo-pad and pen and thereafter between mouthfuls of food, jotted down the most memorable points of his weekend trip to Hiroshima and Miyajima. Ultimately these fresh notes would end up in the metal trunk under his bed.

1, 8, 15, 22 and 29 April 1949. Following a discussion with Major Williams I was astonished to learn that in excess of 600 war criminals continue to evade arrest. With the help of yakuza gangs and the underground, they remain hidden. I am gaining the distinct impression that the worse the crime, the greater is the chance of the mongrel responsible to be aided and abetted as a fugitive from justice. Clearly, there is no contrition or repentance from the Japanese population at large. We are still the enemy. The simple expedient of changing names and identities and moving to other parts of Japan is the evasiveness and deception most often resorted to by these bastards with guilty consciences.

I have been reading some notes taken by Captain Somerville formerly attached to British Allied Intelligence here at Tokyo. I can imagine the frustration he must have experienced in trying to track down vicious camp guards. A clear example concerns a brutal Japanese army sergeant by the name of Matsuhiro Watanabe. For three long years he was stationed at a POW camp on an island in Tokyo Bay. The name of the camp was Omori and held up to 600 American, British and Australian POWs. This mongrel regularly clubbed and beat prisoners to within an inch of their lives. At least fourteen POWs died as a consequence of these sadistic beatings during the three years Watanabe was stationed at Camp Omori. Following Japan's surrender this mongrel scarpered and has not been seen or traced since. He is classified as a Class A War Criminal. I would really like to hear of his arrest with the certain knowledge that with the evidence against him, he would be hanged.

I guess it's bad enough chasing war criminals evading arrest, but it's just as bad having guilty mongrels in custody, and then having to release them, not for want of prosecution evidence but rather because directives from the Dai-Ichi Building decree their liberty as free men. A good instance of this – and there are many – concerns a Japanese war profiteer by the name of Ryoichi

Sasakawa. This mongrel was in the same class of war criminals as those who directed and expanded Mitsubishi Heavy Industries with forced and prisoner of war labour. A number of these slave-labourers died from brutality, medical neglect and serious malnutrition.

Like Mitsubishi, Sasakawa was regularly supplied with prisoner-labour rounded up in Korea by Japanese troops and transported to Japan to work at hard labour and to what amounted to penal servitude. The mortality rate for these captive slaves was extremely high and in the instance of Sasakawa, wherever his manufacturing complexes produced high yields and slave labour occupancy, so did the local cemeteries. He was undoubtedly responsible for the deaths of many of his imported slave labourers.

This mongrel Sasakawa was held in custody for three years pending his trial on numerous counts of human rights abuse, exploitation of prisoners and deemed responsible for the deaths of fifteen Allied prisoners of war and over 800 Korean slave labourers, all of whom perished working as slaves for Sasakawa. The evidence against Ryoichi Sasakawa was irrefutable and damning, yet, his unexpected and sudden release from custodial imprisonment was ordered by General Charles Willoughby, no doubt approved by General MacArthur. All charges against Sasakawa were dropped. A classic example of the power of money.

Major Williams filled me in on another sinister intention of the Japanese military. Okunoshima, an island twenty-miles off the coast of Hiroshima, was discovered to contain within its three-mile diameter, a huge cache of chemical warfare toxins including 3,000 tons of mustard gas. Follow-up investigations by the American authorities revealed that earlier shipments of poisonous and mustard gas had been transferred by the Japanese to Sone, in the northern part of Kyushu Island in the mid-1930s and where shells and bombs were filled with the lethal material for use in China, which Japan invaded in 1937.

It seems that every week something more horrific and frightening emerges from Japan's past evil history. I realise that despite what I learn and convey to my diaries, the sheer enormity of Japanese criminal excesses are so vast in scope and dimension that what I chronicle for posterity is merely scratching the surface of Japan's evil intentions. Such so-called human behaviour makes me question if the Japanese can ever be trusted again?

On a more civilised note, I must make mention of an inspection visit by our overall commanding officer, Lieutenant-Colonel D.L.B. Goslett. If ever I have come across a fair-dinkum and true-blue Aussie, it has to be him. He epitomizes all the excellent characteristics of a serving Australian field officer, a trait admirably reflected by other Australian officers attached to this investigative section. It's good for the soul and my mental equilibrium to have fellow Anzacs in supportive roles and sharing the depressing duties of mixing with and interrogating some of the world's most cunning and evil men. Tomorrow and once again I'll be back at the coal-face – Sugamo Prison.

6, 13, 20 and 27 May 1949. While going through my notes recently I came across the name Benji Kawamura, a former colonel and senior judicial officer who had been interrogated on matters pertaining to allegations of illegal punishments handed down by Japanese military courts to Allied prisoners of war. So interesting were Kawamura's evasive explanations, I have collated the interrogation text into a question and answer interview which reads as follows:

The Japanese Army Courts
INTERROGATION OF FORMER COLONEL
BENJI KAWAMURA: (Condensed Form).

GODWIN: Were prisoners ill-treated prior to their court appearances?

KAWAMURA: At all times prisoners were treated fairly and honourably. (Sik)*

GODWIN: With regard to judgements, were the military courts lenient or harsh?

---

*(Sik) Questionable

KAWAMURA: Mostly lenient. (Sik)

GODWIN: Was provision made for a prisoner's defence?

KAWAMURA: The prisoners were adequately defended. (Sik)

GODWIN: Were transcripts of charges brought, supplied to the accused prisoners by their defending officer?

KAWAMURA: This was not done because the accused could not read Japanese.

GODWIN: Presuming the prisoners could not speak Japanese either, I have to ask, did their defending Japanese officer speak English?

KAWAMURA: Not always.

GODWIN: Would you call this a fair or adequate defence?

KAWAMURA: It was wartime. Justice had to be dispensed.

GODWIN: Please answer the question. Was the defence of the prisoners fair and adequate?

KAWAMURA: It was not a matter of proving guilt. Courts martial only convened when the charges were irrefutable. It was more a matter of determining a just sentence.

GODWIN: I put it to you again. In your opinion, were these Army trials fair?

KAWAMURA: Yes, according to the judicial guidelines. (Sik)

GODWIN: Most of these prisoners, as our records show, faced and were usually sentenced to death. Therefore, in what language was the prosecution and defence spoken?

KAWAMURA: Japanese.

GODWIN: Would you concede that the prisoners must have been greatly disadvantaged during their trial and not understanding one word of it?

KAWAMURA: This was unfortunate but could not be helped.

GODWIN: Are you affirming that justice was consequently compromised?

KAWAMURA: Not at all. The accused were given careful trials.

GODWIN: On average, how long did it take to prosecute and sentence a prisoner?

KAWAMURA: It depended very much on circumstance. Sometimes half-a-day, at other times, half-an-hour.

GODWIN: How on earth could a man on trial for his life and not understanding a word of what was being said, hope for justice with such a short trial?

KAWAMURA: The courts were consistent and correct in their judgements.

GODWIN: You are evading the question.

KAWAMURA: This question is unfair. These courts were not applying peace-time judicial process. They were Army courts obliged to process justice swiftly.

GODWIN: Conceding that Japanese Army courts were consistent, I am therefore obliged to ask. Would you affirm that the majority of sentences pronounced and by decapitation, were correct?

KAWAMURA: Death sentences for escaping or attempting to escape were delivered to discourage other prisoners from trying the same thing. It was a correct solution and considered a punitive measure.

GODWIN: In your experience. Was any mercy ever shown?

KAWAMURA: The decision of a court martial was final. There was no appeal court.

GODWIN: Surely, both the courts and yourself must have known that these death sentences were against the principles of the Geneva Convention re the treatment of prisoners of war. Why was this civilised Convention ignored?

KAWAMURA: I cannot say. I only followed procedures ordered by superior officers.

GODWIN: I put it to you. How would you feel if the present War Crimes Trials were conducted within half-an-hour? Would you consider this correct and fair?

KAWAMURA: I am unable to answer your question. It is hypothetical.

GODWIN: Can you not give an honest answer without being evasive?

KAWAMURA: What may be considered fair in war, may not be considered likewise in peace. The prosecution of justice must bend with the wind.

GODWIN: As a trained legal person, you must concede that justice is or should be inviolate. Why this pardox?

KAWAMURA: I do not wish to answer this question. You are compelling me to give ambiguous parallels.

GODWIN: Is it any more ambiguous to question the miscarriage of justice that was too frequently resorted to by Japanese Army courts?

KAWAMURA: Discipline and punitive measures controlled the findings of Japanese Army courts.

GODWIN: You don't mention justice, why?

KAWAMURA: Punishment was the first criteria.

GODWIN: By beheading?

KAWAMURA: Such sentences at the time, served their purpose.

GODWIN: I find it difficult to follow your logic. We seem to be going around in circles. This interview is over for the present.

Godwin sighed heavily as he placed the transcript of Kawamura's interview into a green folder that was used when assisting other investigating officers in their research of suspected war crimes. He had no doubt that the former colonel possessed an alert mind and like most Japanese encountered, was extremely talented. It was the twisted thinking that bugged him just as it was the difficulty in reconciling the prostitution of justice that he maintained was acceptable. If that was the Japanese Army's mentality as conveyed by Kawamura, then the taking of life meant nothing. It was indeed a hard act to follow as Godwin clipped his briefcase shut and headed from the Meiji Building to some temporary relaxation at the inn. Tomorrow he pondered to himself, would be another day as he thoughtfully left his office.

9

Disillusionment

Observations about Japan: James Godwin, 3 July 1949.

SINCE returning to Japan two years ago to exercise my commission as a war crimes investigator, opportunities to travel around this most interesting land have been singularly scarce. Whatever I have seen I have recorded however. For a change and to provide balanced perceptions of the country as a whole, I have collected many of my notes in an attempt to formulate a comprehensible background of what is now a peacetime Japan. There are social enigmas and circumstances permeating the very fabric of Japanese society deserving of more than just passing mention. Here then are my perceptions.

There are several areas of discrimination in Japan that intrigue one's interest. Much of what seems blatantly unfair, is conversely, the least discussed. Most Japanese choose to ignore discrimination as being for the greater good. It is a mind-set dating back to medieval times. As I see it, there are three main influences of discrimination in Japan, each one different but all to a large extent rooted in the all-pervading sense of national identity. The discrimination against a unique sector of the population known as the burakumin is the least comprehensible, because these people are pure Japanese whose genealogy dates back to the Heian period (794-1185). They are the descendants of ancestors who were isolated from the ruling cultism because they toiled as butchers and producers of leather goods. This segregation carries on to this very day and is evidenced by the burakumin ghettoes called dowa chiku.

The pure Japanese remain severely discriminated against, particularly in employment and marriage. I have learned that there are about 2,000,000 burakumin residing in up to 5,000 dowa chiku throughout Japan and which represents a little under two per cent of the country's population. Because of the rigid system of identity papers in Japan and as a consequence of the ghettoes, it is almost impossible for the burakumin to conceal their identity. The routine investigations checked out before employment or marriage are basically to ensure that such individuals are not burakumin.

Another instance of racial discrimination applies to the residence of 450,000 Koreans living in Japan, most of whom were brought across from Korea as forced labour between 1939 and 1945. Quite simply, these people are now displaced persons and are considered aliens and in every way are discriminated against socially, politically, legally and economically. What I found to be quite draconian was the fact that all Koreans, half-caste or otherwise, are not only regarded as alien but must be finger-printed and carry their alien registration cards everywhere with them or risk being imprisoned for six months. Jobs of the lowest status is their lot and they are not enrolled as voters. If this is the new democratic Japan, then it leaves a lot to be desired.

Few Koreans are successful in large businesses, the barriers take care of that. Those who have the inclination for business can not hope to aspire beyond back-street restaurants, secondhand stalls, gaming parlours or the scrap-metal business. A very few get into the sleazy industry of massage parlours and saunas, while others flirt with the notorious yakuza gangs in an existence of crime and shady wheeling and dealing. Education is another aspect that deserves mention. It not only applies to the Koreans but also to the burakumin. Both groups do not receive the same educational opportunities as the mainstream Japanese population. It is my view that when education is severely restricted along with the existence of ghettoes and enforced poverty and yes, prejudice, all these contributory discriminations exacerbate the natural progression of crime that as an example, is not confined to Japan alone. It is however, useful to understand Japan's culture and prejudice, it provides an insight into their values and an understanding of their dogmatism in adversity and in war.

14, 21 and 28 June 1949. Words fail me. I've recently learned that some of the top Japanese scientists involved in experimenting upon and murdering thousands of prisoners of war are not only immune from prosecution (MacArthur's orders) but the mongrels have been given top jobs in Japanese universities. I refer to the Biological and Germ Warfare Centres in Manchuria and elsewhere that operated under the umbrella of Unit 731. My colleagues in the American section of war crimes investigations consider this the worst war crime uncovered of either the former Axis powers. It does shake my confidence to learn that the more heinous the crime, the less publicity it attracts. But worse, and to quell some details that have leaked out about Unit 731, the United States Chief Prosecutor, Joseph B. Keenan, is bloody declaring that the Japanese were in no way preparing for biological warfare. Tell this crap to the thousands of murdered victims Mr Keenan!

I have to ask myself, what the hell is going on? American investigators may be silenced and obstructed in their investigations by conspirators MacArthur, Willoughby and Keenan, but human nature being what it is they will share confidences, even with Allied colleagues. I'm bloody astonished at the suppression of this major war atrocity, but worse, I'm angry at the fact that all those victims of these evil Japanese scientists, are victims twice over from a coterie of heartless Allied tin-gods who have ordered these mass murders and their perpetrators to go unpunished.

In discussions I've had with American colleagues, one of the major reasons for sweeping this huge atrocity under the carpet is because, if investigations were proceeded with, they would lead directly to the Imperial Palace and Hirohito himself. This would not only destabilise the Japanese nation, but would embarrass the Yanks and their plans for a new Japan within the American capitalist sphere of influence.

Nonetheless and so far as I'm concerned and other investigators as well, the tenets of justice should not be compromised by political or economic expediency. If Hirohito is guilty, and the evidence suggests he is, he should be tried as a war criminal. I am privy to knowledge that he affixed his personal imperial seal to the establishment of Unit 731 and approved the expenditure of ¥6,000,000 for its first year of operations. Yet, Keenan denies everything. Why then, Willoughby's directive to cease investigating the murderous activities of Unit 731? But Willoughby was only the messenger. It was General Douglas MacArthur who called the shots. Therefore it is my conclusion that a conspiracy of deceit and collusion exists to protect the Emperor and the Imperial Institution and to hell with murderous atrocities committed in Hirohito's name.

The politicians will no doubt manage and manipulate history. Thus I wouldn't be surprised if this travesty of justice doesn't even make it into the history books for future generations. Suppression is censorship, but at least my personal writings may endure into the future to warn the world of Japan's past evil history, but then I guess no-one will be bloody interested. The politicians, collaborators and economists will probably take care of that.

As always and having been a prisoner of the Japanese myself, I feel strongly that these mongrels should be made to pay restitution and compensation to those upon whom they inflicted their brutal barbarism. We can only honour the memories of those who were murdered in their tens of thousands and who perished in such bloody horrifying conditions. Mr MacGregor of the *MV Behar* comes to mind. I'm bloody glad that he cast his gold watch into the Indian Ocean. But there's the next-of-kin I'm thinking about and the surviving prisoners of war. What will be done for them? It's my belief that the short answer will be nothing. I have reached this considered opinion on the premise of America's current foreign policy towards Japan. The Yanks in my view have gone soft on the Japanese.

8, 15, 22 and 29 July 1949. Deciding to unwind a little by taking a Sunday train excursion to Yokohama, Godwin boarded an early morning commuter to the port city. It was a warm balmy day made refreshingly pleasant by a gentle off-shore breeze that cleansed the air for Yokohama's teeming inhabitants as Godwin alighted from the train focusing his attention on a double row of vacant taxis, most of them pre-war Fords and Chevrolets. Clutching a Yokohama tour guide, printed in both Japanese and English, he quickly struck a deal with an obliging driver for a half-day hire and with no limit on mileage.

The first point of interest was Yokohama's great port, one of Japan's largest and one of several naval bases that had been established by the Americans since the Allied occupation. Glancing at his tour guide that extolled everything about the historic city in both Japanese and English, Godwin reflected upon the greatness that might have been, if Japan had not started waging war as far back as 1904. There were still visible scars of the massive fire-bombing that had destroyed a good portion of the city in 1945. As the cab made its way around the perimeter of a vast shipping complex he observed everything with intense interest while casting his thoughts back to an earlier period in the country's history as a whole.

Little remained in Yokohama to recall the foreign settlement established there in 1859, only five years after Commodore Perry and his small American fleet had 'persuaded' the Japanese Government to start opening up the country to the rest of the world. Japan had ultimately embraced everything western and with considerable fervour, copied western industry and technology within a remakably short span of time. Its ability to achieve this phenomena was largely due to the natural intelligence of the nation as a whole. Talent aplenty was available, it only required the harnessing of such a naturally clever people to step into the twentieth century albeit with an education agenda that would at first astonish, then alarm.

Mid-afternoon was drawing near as Godwin turned his attention to a back-page in the sightseeing guide that announced simply, 'Places Of Special Interest'. His eye fell on something that would be unique, different. Speaking his best Japanese he asked the driver to proceed to the Soto sect monastery at Sojiji, a sprawling seminary situated on the outskirts of Yokohama. It was, as he discovered after reading a brief paragraph of the tour guide, the second largest Zen sect in Japan, the Rinzai sect being the largest. At his request the cab-driver parked the vehicle at a vantage point near the crest of a small knoll. Welcoming the chance to stretch his legs, Godwin alighted and strolled towards a point from where he could obtain a sweeping view of the cloistered monastery that had been reached within an hour of his decision to view it first hand.

The driver stood quietly beside Godwin before mentioning that the monastery was accessible to visitors, but only at appointed times though alas, and because of the lateness of the afternoon, a close inspection would not be possible. To nullify any vestige of disappointment, the driver proceeded to provide a wealth of detail about the monastery and its ancient past. It was surprising to learn that 300 monks were in training at any given time and that it required six years to achieve the disciplines demanded in their vocation. While Godwin took in every detail of buildings that though quite clearly belonging to an earlier era, were in such picturesque and excellent condition, it quite took his breath away. Then there were the broad sweeping lawns and manicured flower gardens. Everything had a pristine beauty and symmetry that exuded order and tranquillity. A good twenty minutes passed before reluctantly, Godwin thanked the driver and made his way back to the cab.

Trains operated frequently between Yokohama and Tokyo, day and night, but Godwin was anxious to avoid the mid-evening commuter rush where he might end up like a sardine in any one of a score of overcrowded carriages. The direct express he had been told by the cab driver, though a dearer fare, was faster and usually much less crowded. Godwin not only made a point of shaking the cab driver's hand upon being returned to Yokohama's central railway station, he offered to recommend him to the National Tour Guide Association for his obvious ability and courtesy as a guide in and around Yokohama. Cementing this esteem, he thrust a handsome tip into the driver's coat pocket before mingling with an incessant stream of people coming and going from the city's busy railway station. Behind him a humble driver bowed his thanks.

It was still a pleasant summer's evening as the express commuter neared the outskirts of Tokyo. Godwin had managed to secure himself a seat and sat idly gazing out of a window at the passing terrain. The first tinges of a purple dusk partly obscured distant rural scenes but not the magnificent summit of a remote Mount Fuji resplendently bathed beneath the rays of the setting sun. It reminded him of New Zealand's own Mount Egmont which was similar in height and with the same conical shape. The day had been a relaxing one for him, away from the travails of war criminality and verbal ambiguity. It seemed incredible that such a beautiful country with so many ordinary normal people could spawn a military regime that had terrorised nations in an insane ambition to own everything within reach and in the process slaughter countless thousands. He sighed inwardly as his mind flashed back to a comment he had overheard at the Allied Officers' Club the evening before. It was to the effect that it was quite on the cards that war crimes investigations and prosecutions might cease within a year, certainly not much beyond February or March 1950. Only within Japan was this probability suggested, but as some weird exonerations and pardons had of recent date been issued from the Dai-Ichi Building, the likelihood of a shut-down, the same as the British in 1948, could not be taken lightly.

Godwin quietly pondered the consequences if all war crimes procedures were canned. He would not continue as a serving member of the Australian Army, of this certainty he was deter-mined. A career in a peace time Army had no appeal. The British Colonial Service were looking for keen young men who had matriculated and who were single. He would fit the criterias he knew, and a career in the Colonial Service held considerable prospects for advancement. In the meantime he would continue his duties as a war crimes investigator, a dedication and resolve that he would carry out until told otherwise by SCAP. A secondary thought intruded into his mind as the train perceptibly began slowing. What about all the war crimes on file and the

thousands more still to be uncovered? Thousands of war criminals would get away with murders and atrocities scot-free? This
probability didn't bear thinking about. It would make all his past
work so pointless. Then there was the general view that if Japan
regained self-government and the Allied powers packed up and
left, it was felt certain that the Japanese themselves would stop all
war crimes investigations and prosecutions. Some senior Allied
officers were even offering the opinion that as sure as night
followed day, the new Japanese Government could be counted
upon to grant selective amnesties to Japanese war criminals
within a short time of regaining power and a quite likely general
amnesty not long after.

These latter thoughts were disturbing to Godwin as he prepared
himself for the frenetic charge from the carriage and onto a platform packed with people waiting for trains departing or arriving.
As he rose to his full height he towered above those around him.
His sheer size, now close on sixteen-and-a-half stone, assured
him that despite the crushing mass of humanity on the platform,
his bulk and height would assist his passage out of the central
railway station without much delay after which he would hire a
cab back to the inn. As if on cue, the train came to a grinding halt
indicating his Sunday excursion was over.

Once more back at the inn and before retiring, Godwin sat at his
small writing desk and with his diary in front of him, faithfully
entered the highlights of his day trip to Yokohama, the recollections of which he recalled with satisfaction.

5, 12, 19 and 26 August 1949. After a particularly trying day at
Tokyo's Sugamo Prison, Godwin was thankful to return to the
quiet sanity of his office in the Meiji Building, well removed
from war crimes suspects confined at the prison. In most of the
interrogations he could count on politeness and meekness, traits
that belied the fact of whom he was dealing with. Inscrutability
and an almost humble servility was a disposition that in context
was an incongruous enigma when viewed against the revelation
of horrendous atrocities committed by many of these self-
effacing suspects. Then, there were the falsehoods, albeit perjury,

wilfully uttered into sworn statements and which confirmed the perception of deliberate deviousness, duplicity and intransigence.

By far the most frustrating obstruction and employed to the fullest by the suspects, was their recourse to prolix, repetitious and irrelevant testimony that by its misleading nature and intentional phraseology, had little or no probative substance. Then there was the Japanese practice of minimizing dreadful deeds to misdemeanour similes, an artful form of verbal deception that was extremely trying to the ears of a questioner. Because of these predilections, it was found necessary to implement considerable cross-interrogation in an attempt to extract the truth. The Japanese language was also a trying experience insofar as literal translation of Japanese into English was concerned, or for that matter vice versa. As a consequence testimony had to be paraphrased, but even then, so confusing were the discrepancies of interpretation that even ATIS (Allied Translation Intelligence Service) were at times hard put to determine phraseology in context. Just to make matters more difficult was the Japanese alphabet, a hurdle all by itself.

Godwin's thoughtful analysis ceased as his eye caught sight of a familiar signature appended to a note awaiting his attention in the in-tray. Reaching across the desk he lifted it from the tray before muttering its brief message.

'Jim! I'd like to have a word with you after five this afternoon if possible.' – Major Williams.

Godwin glanced at his watch. It was five minutes past the requested hour. Leaving the briefcase on the seat of his chair and removing his cap to temporarily join it, he stepped out into the corridor and strode briskly towards Major Williams' office. Following a peremptory knock and an invitation to enter, he was quickly invited to 'grab a chair' by his immediate senior whose usual mild expression wore a touch of concern. Without preamble, Major Williams spoke what was on his mind.

'We've upset some jokers in the Prosecution Division, Jim, ah, to be precise, the Yanks. It's no big deal but,' he waved an inter-office memorandum, 'it seems like free expression in official reports is frowned upon. Particularly your contribution, Jim.'

'Mine?' Godwin stared perplexed. 'In what way, sir?'

Major Williams glanced at the memorandum before replying. 'According to book, chapter and verse, one of your most recent investigation reports and concerning Files 151G, 168 and 151H, included a personal observation by yourself that was considered inappropriate. Do you want me to read it?'

Godwin shook his head. 'If it's about General Nishimura, I meant every word I said. What do the Yanks find so inappropriate, sir?'

Williams sighed. 'I know what you have to put up with when questioning these bastards and can forgive your cynicism, Jim, but it will be best if you confine your observations to factual circumstance, er, not private opinions.'

Godwin forced a weak smile. 'Then it does seem that truth hurts, sir?'

'I'm not disagreeing with you, but we have to be bloody careful when it comes to criticising the Court, particularly the sentences they're been dishing out lately. As a matter of fact I've checked out the file on this General Nishimura and your comments appear well-justified. The bastard should have been hanged.' Williams leaned back in his chair, a sardonic smile appearing briefly. 'Ours is not to reason why, Jim. If eventually they let these mongrels go free, it will not be our problem or concern.' He rubbed his chin thoughtfully while deliberating his own assessment of the Allied Powers' future intentions. 'We know that the Yanks are going soft on past war atrocities for two obvious reasons. First, it's now over four years since the atrocities ceased with the ending of the war and secondly, there's a hell of a lot of wheeling and dealing going on between the Allied Powers, particularly the Yanks and the Japanese.'

'Are you implying, sir, that the scenario is tending towards letting bygones be bygones?' Godwin looked askance.

Williams nodded. 'Without a doubt. Sooner or later the Japanese will once again be masters of their own destiny. As a matter of fact I have it on good authority that no later than 1952, it's hoped to restore Japan to full sovereign self-government.' He shrugged. 'Among other things that will mean the end of War Crimes Investigations and Prosecutions,' he gave a twisted smile. 'That will mean you and I will not be bloody welcome by the new Japanese Government.'

'But surely, the Allied Powers must know that so far as war crimes are concerned we've only scratched the surface. There's thousands still to be investigated?' Godwin tugged at an ear. 'Surely war crimes investigations will continue much the same as they're doing in Germany?'

'This is Japan, old son. The Yanks badly want military and naval bases here. This is where the wheeling and dealing is playing a large part, rest assured. The Japs despise communism as much as Washington does.' Williams' eyes narrowed. 'I'll bet my life that even now, political discussions between Japan and the United States are afoot, and what's going on at the Dai-Ichi Building should convince us of that. These bloody war crimes exonerations of all the big fish in Japan should tell us something. It's only blokes like ourselves who know what is bloody going on and who can guess the sell-out that will be struck with the Japanese.' He leaned forward in his seat. 'Why do you think there's a bloody taboo on investigating any of the Imperial princes, eh?'

'To keep the Imperial institution intact I guess,' Godwin replied through puckered cheeks.

'There's at least three Imperial princes who have track records worse than that mongrel Nishimura. But we can't touch them by order of MacArthur himself.' Williams' grin was bitter. 'The major gods of war including the Emperor go free while the lesser gods, but then not all of them either, are given to us to investigate so that the world will believe the propaganda that justice is being done. And yes you're right, Jim, about keeping the Imperial insti-tution intact. Without it, the local socialists would uproot the militarists once and for all and given the present conditions, Japan could quite easily embrace communism.'

'Hell! The Yanks wouldn't like that considering what's going on in North Korea, China, Eastern Europe and the Soviet Union.' Godwin murmured thoughtfully.

'Precisely!' Williams cut in. 'That's why I believe the Yanks are cutting a deal with the Japs for strategic bases and installations over here and in return, are prepared to hop into bed with the bloody devil and to hell with Japan's wartime past which is every bit as bad as that of the Third Reich, in some instances, more so if that's possible.'

'But surely, Australia, the British and the Dutch, even New Zealand, won't have a bar of the scenario you're painting, sir?' Godwin shifted in his chair. 'What the Japs have done is too bloody bizarre and awful for even the Yanks to kiss and make up!'

'It's the fear of international communism, Jim,' Williams nodded sagely. 'I reckon that will be a sufficient stimulus for the Allies to accommodate the wishes of their most powerful partner. Morality, legality and justice will take a back seat, just mark my words, and in the process Japanese war criminals will be let off the hook, the whole bloody lot of them. It's shaping up that way from what I've learned.'

Godwin could sense that Major Williams was speaking from the heart. He decided to follow suit, but from a background of bitter experience. 'I was a prisoner of these bastards for eighteen long months, sir. They would have played for keeps had they won. You have my service record so must know what I went through. It was sheer hell! Forced labour, beatings, being bashed with rifle butts and bloody near starved to death. I witnessed beheadings and sadistic thuggery that resulted in an elderly man's death while being bashed. Not only were countless thousands slaughtered by these moronic bastards but thousands of former prisoners of the Japanese were so bloody traumatised and broken in mind and spirit that now, that is those who were liberated by the Allies, don't want to discuss or relive their dreadful and prolonged experiences as prisoners of the Japanese. What infuriates me quite frankly is this. Because most of the former prisoners consider their captivity a bloody nightmare, they are reluctant to revive such bad memories by talking about a living hell. I can understand this but, this reluctance to dig up grim and frightful memories, suits the Japanese bloody perfectly. The least said about their depraved behaviour, the better. The least said the soonest mended, if you get my drift, sir.'

Major Williams had given an occasional nod of agreement as Godwin expressed his views. It would have been hard to disagree. What Godwin had mentioned was undoubtedly true, made more so with the ring of sincerity in his voice. He cleared his throat. 'I hope, Jim, that one day you'll put pen to paper and will write down your experience, perhaps even,' his eyes twinkled, 'a summary of your work as an Allied Investigating Officer and where your personal observations will not draw the wrath of the United States Prosecutor's Office.'

Godwin's wry smile was brief. 'I already have a wartime diary, sir. It's back home in New Zealand and it records every atrocity I witnessed or endured as a prisoner of the Japanese. I risked my life in keeping this diary in the prison-camp at Niigata. Had I been caught with it I would have been beheaded as a punishment. Perhaps in the distant future I might do as you suggest and put pen to paper. My immediate concern is the matter of compensation from the Japs for gross cruelty and forced labour. I worked my guts out ten hours a day, seven days a week. Sometimes it was twelve hours a day and all to help the bloody Japanese war effort. There are scores of thousands of former prisoners who were compelled into slave labour by the Japs, but the way things are going, particularly if your predictions are right, sir, it could end up with the Japanese avoiding paying compensation, that is if the Yanks have anything to do with it. This compensation exoneration is one I'm sure the Japanese will really push for, otherwise, the mongrels will be working for the next 100 years in paying reparations as enormous as the murderous mayhem they sowed like bloody locusts throughout Asia and the Pacific.'

'On that concern at least, let's hope that justice doesn't take a holiday, Jim.' Williams glanced at his watch. 'Crikey! It's twenty-to-six. I'm sorry to have held you back, old son.' He gave a deprecating smile, 'For the sake of peace and to avoid ruffling Uncle Sam's feathers, let's keep your official observations to bare comment, minus opinions. It'll make my job easier.' He climbed slowly to his feet, a wide smile indicating where his sympathies lay.

Godwin hurried back to his own office. There were notes to be catalogued and files to be returned to their respective cabinets before he too left the Meiji Building. He conceded to himself that clearly, it was the Prosecution Division, not Major Williams who had complained about his forthright opinions. It was supportive advice that the major had offered, not a case of being hauled over the coals as the Prosecution Division might have wished. The discussion, understanding and the advice received would be heeded, he resolved within himself. In future he would confine personal opinion about court judgements and other contentious matters to his private writings, but record them for posterity he would. Ultimately and in the years ahead when opportunity presented itself, he would go through his diaries and any other relevant material applicable to his time in Japan and properly chronicle the mass of information available to him, warts and all. It would give him something interesting to do in his retirement years and would be educational to future generations if by some mischance the world had forgotten about Japan's past bloody history. With all the documentation safely stowed during his musings, he retrieved his cap and briefcase from the office chair and headed for the elevator, another day of officially consorting with some of the world's most evil war criminals behind him.

7, 14, 21 and 28 October 1949. I've got a feeling I might be in hot water again. This time for criticising the Legal Division. I have no difficulty in accepting that the courts have reasonably full case-loads but most of the mongrels who are appearing for trial are the lesser vermin. Of course, disillusionment does erode zeal. The most powerful gods of war and who were responsible for bloody awful deeds such as Parit Sulong's General Nishimura, seem to bear unbelievable charmed lives. The higher up the ladder of influence and responsibility, most especially nowadays, the less likely is the chance they will be nailed. Recently I learned that the Japanese commander of occupation troops in the Andaman Islands (Bay of Bengal) was charged with ordering the massacre of 680 civilians just hours before Japan surrendered. The penalty he received was not death, it was a bloody joke. The War Crimes Tribunal that sat in judgement of this mongrel, sentenced him to two years' imprisonment. He's done his time and is now a free man. What was the point of prosecuting this murderous bastard in the first place? It is mentioned by senior blokes in intelligence that this mongrel drew a light penalty because he was related to Hirohito. Nothing surprises me any more, but then, how else could this monster have escaped the gallows?

It's a sad indictment and admission to have to reveal that the United States per MacArthur and Willoughby, and yes, Keenan, have perverted the course of justice here in Japan. As Allied intelligence officers and war crimes investigators we are bound to secrecy and forbidden to reveal opinion, and for that matter fact, relative to our investigations of war crimes, this to include any classified files and documentation pertaining to our work. I fully understand and accept this prohibition providing that truth and justice is allowed to succeed. It is a bitter pill indeed to be muzzled. Pardons, blanket absolutions, etc. had everything to do with collusion and conspiracy and nothing to do with justice. I must admit to being a poor scholar of American history but I do know who Benedict Arnold was – with all its connotations.

[AUTHOR'S NOTE]. It is clear from Godwin's writings of nearly fifty years ago that apart from his puritanical code of ethics he held strong views when it came to either man's inhumanity to man and justice. He was quick to condemn anything perceived as betrayal, collusion or corruption. This is best typified by his blunt comments – thinly disguised, at the conclusion of many of his weekly reports and which towards the end of his service at Tokyo, culminated in his getting off-side with both the legal and prosecution divisions to whom his reports eventually reached.

Let us return to Godwin's revealing commentary and selected war crimes files that will follow and which, are absolutely astonishing.

Godwin continues: It's bloody confusing when we perceive and receive the wrong signals. One has to work at the coal-face of intrigue and wheeling and dealing to appreciate what I mean. But undeniably, it all stems from the top and from both sides of the fence. The blokes I work with in Intelligence are dedicated guys, there's not a galah among 'em, but I can't say the same for the drongos at the Dai-Ichi Building. As I've mentioned, it all starts from the top. Take General Charles Andrew Willoughby as a bloody good example. I've now learned that he knows all about the Imperial Japanese Army's former sex-slave industry. The gist of this reprehensible practice bloody near involves every Asian country Japan occupied. Scores of thousands of captive women and girls were forced to become unpaid whores to Japanese soldiery in specially created dives called brothels (Comfort Stations). Of course our boss, Willoughby, should know about this despicable aspect of the Japanese Imperial Army. But then, why shouldn't he? He's the undisputed Chief of Allied Intelligence here in Japan. MacArthur too, must know. Yet the instruction is, 'do not investigate'.

Then there's the cannibalism atrocities that have been effectively quashed. What a bloody waste of time investigating the mongrels who resorted to this barbaric and primitive practice. I can think of recent cover-ups directed from the Dai-Ichi Building that do no credit to MacArthur or Willoughby. However I feel compelled to refer to Japan's wartime pursuit of biological and germ warfare. The general public in the western world, even here in Japan, know nothing about Japan's attempts to assist its conquests with germ warfare. It's being deliberately denied by no less a person than MacArthur himself, ably supported by his side-kick von Willoughby. Strewth! The real bad things about Japan are being white-washed. Cannibalism, army brothels and germ warfare. Why the double standards?

German soldiers in the field or for that matter in North Africa, didn't go around chopping off people's heads after capturing them, but the Japanese did. I'm not saying the Jerries didn't do bad things. They bloody did, but at least all the European intelligence services are doing a good job in tracking down the mongrels who wrought such havoc and misery, they don't need General Eisenhower's permission. Even the International Zionist Organisation is ferreting out Nazis with considerable success. The Soviets too, are equally energetic. One can rest assured there will be no cover-ups or wheeling and dealing like what is clearly going on in Japan. MacArthur and Willoughby have no moral right to defeat the course of justice, but they are.

As intelligence officers it's our job to investigate and expose criminal wrong-doing. How the hell can we do this effectively when the very worst war crimes are protected from prosecution? Over 60,000 victims perished in the Japanese Germ Warfare Centres before being shoved into furnaces with their smoke-ash remains spewing out of tall crematoria chimneys. We constantly hear of the 'chimneys of Belsen', but not a mention of the Japanese ones at Ping Fan. It's bloody frustrating to know of these major atrocities that are being deliberately covered up by the top brass. I've checked with the prosecutor's office and scrutinised 'Cases In Progress' and 'Cases Pending'. There are four prepared cases of 'Cannibalism' marked 'Deferred', though I'm told it's unlikely they'll ever go to trial. 'Too humiliatingly sensational for the Japanese nation to bear,' I was told. But so far as germ warfare experimentation crimes and mass sexual slavery are concerned, the charge-sheets remain blank. It's as though these atrocities didn't happen or directives from the Dai-Ichi Building have perverted the course of justice and in the process, have saved at least fifty war criminals from the gallows including an imperial prince.

I find it bloody annoying to have to work in such an environment of deceit and covert obstruction. How can I be expected to respect MacArthur and Willoughby when I know that they are hand in glove with major war criminals? The protection from prosecution says it all. I guess that as the years roll by, history books will make no mention of the concerns I have expressed. But then, why should they? There is nothing documented, no investigations, no prosecutions and no justification for humanity to know so far as MacArthur and Willoughby are concerned. How lucky can the Japanese get?

Perhaps I need a bloody good holiday away from those evil bastards at Sugamo Prison. This may not be long in coming from what I hear. Word has it that with the British now long gone, it's only a matter of time before war crimes investigations and prose-cutions will cease in Japan altogether. I understand that the Australian and Dutch authorities may continue dishing out justice in their own territories outside of Japan for a while longer but the writing's on the wall and with a peace treaty in the wind, supposedly 1952, the doors of justice will finally be closed.

If these predictions eventuate into reality, then I will have no hesitation in declaring from my practical background and experi-ence that less than ten percent of all Japanese war crimes would have been prosecuted. A bloody shocking indictment! The Emperor, the imperial princes and all their bloody relations, as well as countless other gods of war, along with the germ warfare criminals and the mongrels who enslaved a quarter of a million females in Imperial army brothels, all of them finally, will get off scot-free, thanks to MacArthur.

At least my writings and diary will record what historians may well miss. My experiences as a prisoner of the Japanese, and then, my education as a keen Allied Intelligence Officer here at Tokyo, should confound those who in years to come may attempt to minimise Japan's evil past. Analysts and historians can only theorise where suppression replaces fact with conjecture. Therefore, I hope that in the future mists of time, what I have taken the trouble to faithfully chronicle, may one day fill in the gaps currently censored and suppressed. With MacArthur and Willoughby no longer around, the truth will triumph supreme.

4, 11 and 18 November 1949. Last evening I dined out much to my later regret. My companions, two army officers attached to the New Zealand J Force, phoned to inquire about my health today, but only because they were feeling crook themselves. I'm feeling better now, but in future I'll give that cafe a miss. With another winter solstice looming and the weather becoming decidedly cold and inclement with short days and long nights, there is little to attract my interest to outdoor pursuits or for that matter sight-seeing. Instead, I am slowly wading through copious notes in the privacy of my room and retaining only the most significant for posterity. There's that much of the stuff I'll need another large suitcase if intending to take it all back to New Zealand.

Last evening I spent some time writing to the folks back home and wrote an extra page to my favourite sister, Moyra. The knitted scarf she sent me is just the cat's whiskers for the present climate, but then, she was always a thoughtful sis. Captain Ralph Hewson attached to the United States Intelligence and War Crimes Section is no longer in Japan. He was transferred back to the States in August, so I guess we won't have his organisational flair arranging a festive party this Christmas, but no matter, from what I hear it's quite on the cards that all War Crimes Investigations and Prosecutions in Japan might soon come to an end. Not that I'm particularly concerned as I've had about as much as I can take. The whole scenario is both alien and depressing. I'm trying to remember when I laughed last. But in my line of work I guess, there's nothing to laugh about.

(Four days later)

Strewth! I've just had the lowdown on what MacArthur's Second-in-Command and Chief of United States Intelligence is up to. General Willoughby (known to us more lowly mortals as Baron von Willoughby) and General Seizo Arisue, the head of Japanese military intelligence, are well and truly working hand-in-glove. The information passed on to me is impeccable in its source and so it should be. It's from Allied Military Intelligence. It now seems that Willoughby through General Arisue, has created a cover operation under the guise of an historical research project, nominally to record Pacific war progress from the Japanese perspective.

This disguised cover for something else is not fooling anyone, least of all the Allied Intelligence Services. Surprisingly, it's been operating for some considerable time, but then, most covert operations usually start up and function that way and on specious pretexts, Willoughby's brainchild being no exception. What is astonishing is the number of Japanese involved and most of whom are of high military rank. Colonel Takushiro Hattori (not a war criminal so far as can be determined) heads this American sponsored 'Agency' that quite plainly is a camouflage to conceal a ready-made core of anti-communist Japanese army officers (should communism ever rear its head in Japan). From what I can gather, Hattori has his own suite of Tokyo offices, a fully functional staff, and an organisation of some seventy officers, salaried and positioned around the country. Naturally the whole exercise is funded by Uncle Sam.

I'm damned sure that if Willoughby or MacArthur worked at the coalface of war crimes investigations and encountered the track records of some of the mongrels we come up against, they might have second thoughts about too rapidly reviving the militarist cult in Japan. Or, is the paranoia about communism so overwhelming that a rearmed militarist Japan is preferable. Frankly, the Yanks' agenda has got me beat. Confrontation and conflict, even in embryonic form, is not the way to go. I wonder if deep down and because of what I have personally experienced in my short twenty-six years, if I now have such a revulsion of war and its bloody excesses that I have developed pacifist leanings? I think that subconsciously I have come to detest the concept of bloody conquest for what it is. Avarice backed by political and military greed, nothing more. If I need reminding, Sugamo Prison's inmates are a damned prize example.

For what it's worth I've been discreetly dropping hints unofficially with regard to the Japanese paying compensation once restored to self-government. It's an undeniable fact that hundreds of thousands of civilians and service personnel suffered unbelievably as prisoners or victims of the Japanese. The forced labour camps were a regimen of brutality and a bloody disgrace that demands just restitution. My mind goes back to the period I was incarcerated at Niigata here in Japan. Ten to twelve bloody hours a day forced to work for the Japanese war effort and expected to survive on a starvation diet. I still suffer from deep-seated aches and pain in my knees particularly when it's bloody cold as it is now. This malaise sometimes makes me limp and dates back to my imprisonment on the Japanese cruiser where I along with other prisoners was forced to kneel on sharp-edged timber (as unwarranted punishment) for hours on end. There's also the niggling discomfort that centres around the spine at the base of my neck. The medico describes it as an affliction I'll have to put up with for the rest of my life and in his opinion, brought about by being clubbed too often with rifle butts or wooden clubs while a prisoner of the Japanese.

I have a strong feeling that despite massacres and wholesale beheadings committed by the Japanese, that when the Peace Treaty (referred to already as the San Francisco Document) is signed, the Japanese won't have to pay one yen in compensation. Only time will tell but, if my cynical prediction is proved correct, then, in my opinion, Washington will have betrayed every dead and living victim who suffered at the hands of the Japanese. My information tells me that it will be the Yanks who will call the shots in formulating this treaty, not its less influential Allied partners. It's this probability that concerns me. I hope for the sakes of all those who suffered or perished at the hands of the Japanese that I'm proved wrong, but I doubt it with drongos like Baron von Willoughby and MacArthur currently wheeling and dealing with Japan's 'new look' militarists and industrialists.

Well, it's happened. I rather guessed it would. I've received an official letter from the Prosecutor's Office. This will definitely be added to my private collection of papers. Here's the gist of the admonition received. Quote: 'Captain Godwin, you are no doubt aware as per the recent circular FF/442, that personal opinions of investigating officers must be confined to the bare facts of cases under investigation or review. It is noted that you criticise the parole system of war crimes suspects in advancing your submission of custodial confinement. It is accepted that your comments

are well-intended and offered with respect, but it is also recognised that your criticism covers a wider spectrum of concerns
more properly within the jurisdiction of the Legal Dept. Please be
advised that a reconciliation of common objectives betweeen the
Occupying Powers and Japan embraces higher considerations
precluding agendas or criteria applicable to the years 1945-46-
47-48. With 1950 almost upon us, it is important to view world
events in perspective and to realise the desire of the Allied
Powers to contain, not exacerbate the process of investigating
Japan's past wartime excesses. Your adherence to the advice
herewith contained is expected to be followed. Yours etc.'

Well, all I can say is that none of the drongos in the Legal Dept
experienced the trauma of being a prisoner of the Japanese.
Judging from the gist of the letter, I get the distinct impression
that both Captain Scott and Major Williams are right. The
writing's on the wall quite obviously. It's just a matter of time
when all War Crimes Investigations and Prosecutions cease in
Japan. Softly, softly could be the new name of the game. I'm
going to make a point of having a chat with Major A.D. MacKay.
He works in the Legal Department and will know this colonel
bloke who signed the letter, but more importantly, Major
MacKay should have his ear to the ground and will know what is
going on and when the prosecution of Japanese war criminals is
scheduled to cease.

I managed to have ten minutes with Major MacKay this
morning before going to Sugamo Prison. I've been told all I need
to know to make up my mind. There's a sellout in the wind and
it's all coming from the Dai-Ichi Building. It's bad enough having
prohibitions placed on investigating the mongrels who set up and
ran the Imperial Army brothels everywhere in Japanese occupied
Asia with captive sex-slaves, but to grant exonerations to the
bastards who operated the Germ Warfare Centres is too damn
much. There's much more war criminality that's going to be
swept under the carpet because of its sheer bloody volume. I'm
damned shocked to learn that mongrels like Colonel Masanobu
Tsuji (the butcher of Singapore and the Philippines) remains free.

He's known to be in Japan (and has been for some time) but the Prosecution Division have no interest in him. Why Germany is being hammered so relentlessly for the transgressions of the Third Reich while Japan is being surreptitiously exonerated, beats me.

I have decided that I will not be part of the deception instrumented from the Dai-Ichi Building that proclaims the approaching conclusion of War Crimes Investigations and Trials faithfully pursued by the Allied Powers. What rubbish! Britain abdicated its responsibilities so far as the prosecution of Japanese war criminals was concerned in mid-1948 (that's why ex-Colonel Tsuji is free). I have no doubt that America's misguided pacification programme and democratisation of Japan will endure only so long as the Japanese power brokers want it to. Provided everything falls into place for Japan (favourably), it will go from strength to strength, I understand their psyche too damned well. However, if in future years it suffers reverses (probably economic), it will be just as dangerous then as it was in the past. America's aspirations for Japan might then backfire as the latter is such an unpredictable country.

Not without a sense of relief I will therefore resign my Commission effective February, and return to my country where power politics, conspiracies and the perversion of justice is not sanctioned and where sanity and decency prevails. Further, I will have no hesitation in gathering official documentation to take back with me. It may be risky taking classified files and documentation out of the Meiji Building for secret transfer to the southern hemisphere, but then and in context, it's a certainty that much of this material will be destroyed when deals between Washington and Tokyo are signed prior to the envisaged peace treaty. From my point of view, records of historical significance should endure for posterity and be available as indisputable testimony to what in future years may be denied. Historians and archivists will I feel sure, agree with this valediction as hard documented evidence is more acceptable and irrefutable than most other forms of testimony – usually branded as conjecture.

To this end therefore and as a forewarning to future generations, I will gather whatever documentation, classified or otherwise, that I can safely lay my hands on as I am now utterly convinced that with coverups and wheeling and dealing, the worst of Japan's wartime excesses will forever be suppressed if only for the political convenience of the United States and Japan, and to a lesser extent, the Allied Powers.

6, 13, 20 and 27 January 1950. Last evening and in company with some fellow Allied investigating officers, I spent a few enjoyable hours shooting the breeze and downing some good Australian beer. Oddly, I didn't mind chewing the rag (talking shop), but then, why should I? After a few more days I would be on my way home. How the feeling exhilarated my thoughts; it was like winning the Art Union, a very special event.

On 11 February I'm free to do as I please and with my army service technically over. There's a good swag of leave due to me before I return to civvy street. I intend to apply for a career in the British Colonial Service in the hope that I have all the necessary credentials to qualify. I bloody hope so. Now to more immediate matters. Sergeant Weston will be taking over my office at the Meiji Building and my investigative files will be carried on for attention or until such time as the combined War Crimes Section closes down and which general concensus agrees, won't be long in coming.

There's one aspect of the Intelligence Service that gives us the inside running as opposed to the general public and it is this. The world may be fooled by pronouncements from the Dai-Ichi Building, but not us. We work at the coalface so to speak, and are fully aware and up to the minute on the wheelings and dealings instigated from the Dai-Ichi Building. However, though occasionally we shoot the breeze between ourselves on matters that privately we don't agree with, we are constrained from expressing our views officially or unofficially. Our oaths inhibit contradiction or opinion. Proverbially, ours is but to do and die and not to reason why. Which brings me to a concern that has been tugging at my conscience these last few days.

I have managed to secrete a hell of a lot of files, etc from the Meiji Building and which are now clandestinely stowed in my luggage at the inn. Files covering the last three months and which may need to be referred to by my successor, remain available in the cabinets, but I have had copies typed in some instances, or have uplifted the carbon copies. Whatever, a complete record of my personal endeavours will return with me to New Zealand, albeit secretly. I guess that like anything remotely clandestine, the prohibitive nature of such an exercise lends an element of intrigue and subterfuge in the attainment of the objective. Not surprisingly, it also induces feelings of suspense akin to some secret agent working undercover. This is a scenario somewhat alien to my nature, however, because I'm certain that much of the material held in the buildings under SCAP's jurisdiction will eventually be destroyed (at the behest of the Japanese), and only selected documentation and directives retained for Allied archives, I find a mitigation and consolation in this prognosis.

What I will not be able to overcome will be official objection and pressure if I attempt to publicise (in book form) my clandestine cache. It will give the lie to Allied announcements that all war crimes were successfully resolved. Not only would this contradiction be embarrassing, the revelations exposed would anger the general public, particularly with regard to the campaign of murderous atrocities conducted by Imperial Japan and revealed from an inside source, warts and all. But most importantly, I would place my future at risk and could well be the subject of prosecution for unlawfully possessing classified documents, no matter my best intentions.

Therefore, I have decided to place all this historical documentation in a secure repository somewhere in New Zealand. It will be carefully packaged and sealed for at least forty years before it again sees the light of day. By then and with the healing veil of time and as I will be in my sixties, then will be the opportunity, in my retirement years, to recall and document the past that I have the sure certainty will be whitewashed by Japan's new-age collaborators. I have expressed my feelings and opinion before and solemnly repeat same. Factual history, no matter how unpalatable to Japan, must break the bonds of censorship and suppression and be publicly recorded.

By perusing the Geographical Index listing specific atrocities: catalogue BB/189B: (Referral: Identified Massacres: Decapitations: Murder), etc, I have been able to minimise a hell of a lot of paperwork and to condense such atrocities briefly and in alphabetical form. This index will simply identify areas, number of victims and manner of execution. For convenience I have retained the code index (BB/189B). Furtherto and in all instances, where possible, the year and date has been listed. I guess that a book of encyclopedia size would be necessary were I to include China, Manchuria and the two Koreas. Daunted by this certainty, I have been compelled to omit them and for the further reason that Japan's Imperial Forces had rampaged across the northern mainland of Asia throughout the 1930s where no reliable estimates are available, so numerous were the number of executions.

I feel moved to declare hushed-up testimony regarding the deliberate slaughter of POWs immediately prior to or following Japan's defeat. A couple of examples will suffice to confirm that in two instances alone close to 1,000 POWs lost their lives in savage acts of revenge carried out by the Japanese. I am defying a specific directive in revealing the following. Upon the orders of Field Marshal Hisaichi Terauchi and despite knowing that his Emperor had just made a surrender broadcast, Terauchi ordered the execution of 560 POWs in horrifying summary executions at Sandakan, North Borneo. The war criminals who carried out this massacre are still being caught. Hisaichi Terauchi avoided the hangman by dying of alleged natural causes at Rengam, Johore Bahru, Malaya, June 1946. The other murderous atrocity occurred at Aikawa POW Camp on Sado Island where 387 Australian, American, British and Dutch slave labour POWs were deliberately entombed at a depth of 400 feet in a worked-out mine which was collapsed by high explosives. The date, 2 August 1945. There were no survivors. These premeditated murders were nothing more than revenge executions.

On a personal note, I'm looking forward to the next few days at the Meiji Building if only because they'll be my last as a War Crimes Investigator. Paradoxically part of me regrets this parting of the ways. Probably it's because I won't be able to nail any more of those mongrels who fought so blindly for their criminal Emperor and who, in their fanaticism, stooped to the lowest forms of sadistic depravity previously unknown to mankind. Perhaps the chronicles I have faithfully set down will at least provide a glimpse of the deceptive psyche of the Japanese 'The Coalface' as I'm prone to refer, but succinctly descriptive of mongrels who in my considered opinion can only be analysed as untrustworthy avaricious opportunists who think nothing of wholesale killings to achieve what Japan covets. My main regret will be that a hell of a lot of these evil killers will walk free when the San Francisco Document evolves into reality as a bloody Peace Treaty. This is a prediction I feel convinced will eventuate.

Capt. J. G. Godwin
10 February 1950

General Seishero Itagaki (centre) signing the surrender on behalf of Field Marshal Terauchi in Singapore, 12 September 1945. The scene as depicted in the Surrender Chamber at the Sentosa Island Resort, Singapore.

Authenticated War Crimes Documentation

G.RTM   REPORT OF INVESTIGATING OFFICER
(Capt. J.G. Godwin)
Subject: War Crimes in Bougainville

1 KIETA

Execution of a United States airman at Kieta in October 1943.
(A) No interrogation.

2 Decapitation of a police boy at Kieta in Aug-Sept 1943.
(A) No developments.

3 NUMA-NUMA

Executions of eight United States airmen and one padre at Numa-Numa in July 1943, have now been confirmed.

(A) Mitsuomi Yuda, formerly the Commanding Officer of 3rd Battalion, 45th Regiment, threw light on the above-mentioned atrocities. With his reluctant assistance, the where-abouts of the murdered men's graves has been located. All nine bodies were exhumed for possible identification before being reburied in a proper cemetery. The skulls of the victims showed sword damage and were found separated from the skeletons. Conclusively therefore, all the victims were decapitated.

(B) The interrogation of Shigemitsu Nishida – a strong suspect, and formerly a sergeant-major of HQ 3rd Battalion, 45th Regt at Tenekau is proceeding. As expected he denies any involvement.

(C) Tsutemo Sakamoto, formerly the Commanding Officer (1942) of the 3rd Battalion, 45th Regiment, revealed no infor-mation relevant to war crimes at Numa-Numa. He has been released from custody.

4 EREVENTA

(A) Execution of airmen by Sergeant-Major Shimamura and Sergeant-Major Sakamoto, both senior NCOs of the Kempetai, continues to be investigated. The interrogation of Junichi Hayami, formerly a Captain in the Intelligence Section of HQ 17th Army, threw no light on the above atrocities. Hayami did however admit that he had in 1943, interrogated two United States airmen and one New Zealand airman at the Kempetai HQ at Maika. He had heard that these airmen were to be taken to Rabaul. Whether this materialised or whether they were executed at Ereventa, he was unable to say.

COMMENT

It is an undeniable conclusion that the indiscriminate killing of civilians and prisoners of war by the Japanese was intentional and executed with malice. Not once have I heard of a valid excuse because there are none.

Former Captain Junichi Hayami is quite intelligent and outwardly co-operative and polite. In my opinion he is too clever for his own good and knows much more than he cares to admit. As a former intelligence officer he could provide us with a wealth of information. I shall be interrogating him again.

J.G. Godwin (Capt.)
Investigating Officer
2nd Aust.War Crimes Section
5 September 1947

REPORT OF INVESTIGATING OFFICER (Capt. J.G. Godwin)
Subject: War Crimes at Buka and Bougainville
File 125E CANNIBALISM BY 13th REGIMENT IN 1944 AND 1945

(A) Interrogated Yukio Yoshida who denied he was a partici-pant but admitted he was an eye-witness. He avers that the eating of human flesh developed into a common practice and included the cooking of freshly killed soldiers brought back from the jungle. He was unable to say if the Australian bodies had been killed in action or intentionally executed.

(B) Interrogated Masuo Haraiwa who also had knowledge of cannibalism and who further admitted that army doctors would perform on-the-spot dissections of corpses. This entailed removing certain internal organs such as kidneys and livers. Occasionally a body would be rejected because it had been dead too long. Bodies that smelled or were fly-blown were left where they had fallen in battle.

(C) This testimony repudiates the assumption made in File 125E of the previous week's report regarding the belief that Australian soldiers killed in action were not cannibalised.

(D) Masuo Haraiwa's testimony also identifies that these atrocities were committed by members of the 2nd Battalion, 13th Regiment, near Jaba River and other places he cannot recall.

File 125F DECAPITATION OF AUSTRALIAN CITIZEN: Francis Roach, AT ROROVANA, JANUARY 1943.

(A) Continuing investigation.

File 158A It is now believed the executions of Flying Officer Bellert, Flying Officer Summons, Wireless Operator Schlenker, Sgt Brownlee and Flight-Sergeant Brown R.P.S. occurred at different dates in 1944 and 1945.

(A) Under continuing examination.

File 158D DUTCH NEW GUINEA

It is now confirmed that decapitation of an Australian airman and flying nurse (Sister Craig) occurred at Babo in early September 1945. Though this was a remote area the world had been at peace for three weeks. Isolation and poor communications could not be used as an excuse for this atrocity. These deliberate murders had no justification either at war or peace. Vengeance, or so it would seem, at Japan's humiliating defeat, would appear to have been the precursor to this heinous crime.

File 160 EXECUTION OF F/LT MOODY AND F/SGT AITCHESON AT IDORE IN SEPTEMBER 1944

(A) Under action.

J.G. Godwin (Capt.)
Investigating Officer
2nd Aust.War Crimes Section
26 September 1947

JGG:PJM   REPORT OF INVESTIGATING OFFICER
               (Capt. J.G. Godwin)
               Subject: War Crimes in Bougainville and Buka
File 125A   NUMA-NUMA

Execution of United States airman and one padre approximately July 1943.

(1) No suspects to interrogate.

File 125F   Decapitation of Francis Roach in February or June 1945.

(1) All suspects interviewed so far have incredibly remarkable denials and ignorance, but all to a common pattern. Either they have been well schooled or are telling the truth and not lies. I remain suspicious.

File 150   Execution of Flight-Lieutenant Moody and Flight Sergeant Aitcheson at Idore in September 1944.

(1) Interrogated Masataka Matsuyama. Many new undeveloped leads were elicited.

(2) Interrogated Keisuke Yasumura. He revealed most important information.

(3) A not completed interrogation of Tamekichi Uchida has brought me to the conclusion that he is the most consummate liar and hostile suspect I have yet encountered. His evasiveness firms my resolve to continue interrogating him.

File 158A   Execution of five Australian airmen between 1944 and 1945.

(1) Interrogated Tomio Kobayashi and Takeshi Uehara; both corroborate each other's testimony. No developments.

(2) Investigations to date unproductive. Will in future concentrate efforts on the naval element in areas concerned.

> J.G. Godwin (Capt.)
> Investigating Officer
> 2nd Aust War Crimes Section
> 7 November 1947

JGG:RTM REPORT OF INVESTIGATING OFFICER
(Capt. J.G. Godwin)

File 125B   Execution of one European at Kieta in December 1943.

(1) Interrogated Takateru Ijichi, the former batman of Major-General Isao Magata. No leads concerning the execution of a European in 1943 were elicited. The subject individual was the most honest but simple-minded I have yet interrogated.

File 125E   CANNIBALISM BY MEMBERS OF 13th INFANTRY REGIMENT:

File closed. Direction from General MacArthur's HQ.

File 125F   Executions of Roach and Ebery:

(1) Interrogation of Ex-Ensign Shitoshi Sugudo of HQ No 1 Naval Base at Buin has not yet been completed.

File 125G   Executions of Allied airmen at Buin:

(1) Awaiting arrival of several Japanese called for interrogation.

File 150   Execution of F/Lt Moody and F/Sgt Aitcheson at Idore, 1944.

(A) Reinterrogated the former G.O.C. 2nd Army, Lieutenant-General Fusataro Teshima. He denies knowledge of the existence or execution of prisoners of war at Idore. He claims that only once in Dutch New Guinea was the presence of Allied prisoners reported to him and that was at Manokwari in May, 1944. This massacre refers to a case concerning a captured Dutch captain and seven Indonesians. A sworn statement will shortly be taken from Teshima.

(B) Reinterrogated Tsugio Ryokai, the former Chief of Intelligence 2nd Army. Ryokai was questioned with the object of determining the true story concerning the passing of an oral and written message from him to Gen Teshima in Sugamo Prison in December 1947. Ryokai denies passing written or oral messages to his former general at the prison.

File 158A   Executions of five Allied airmen in the Manokwari Area:

(A) Former Sergeant-Major Sadakichi Yamada of the 4th Company, 1st Battalion, 221st Infantry Regiment was interrogated re the disappearance of Kittyhawk pilot (A29-464)

Flight-Sergeant Brown R.P.S. Yamada denied all knowledge of this aircraft or its pilot, but disclosed surprising information concerning the deaths of three Allied pilots, one American, one New Zealand and one Australian who he maintained were killed while resisting capture in a mountain forest to the east of Saoekorem during June 1944.

Aware that the pilots at best would only have a pistol each – no match for a company of soldiers with rifles, I am sceptical about the pilots dying resisting capture. The probability of instant execution after capture sounds more likely. I shall investigate this matter further.

(B) Interrogated Hajimi Nattori, ex-Naval petty officer of the 18th Naval Guard Unit at Manokwari. He strongly denied any knowledge of Allied airmen held and executed by either the Navy or the Army. However he did state that he had heard of some natives being beheaded for helping Europeans in the Manokwari region. I have referred Nattori to the Dutch authorities.

> J.G. Godwin (Capt.)
> Investigating Officer
> 2nd Aust War Crimes Section
> 20 and 27 February 1948

JGG:JFV   REPORT OF INVESTIGATING OFFICER
(Capt. J.G. Godwin)

I am initiating investigations into the activities of former members of the Kempetai Detachment at Vito during March-April 1945. Wherever their presence is revealed, it's usually bad news.

File 125F   Executions of Roach and Ebery:

ROACH   Interrogated Toramatsu Nishiro, a former superior petty officer and member of No 1 Sea Transport Unit based at Buin. This interrogation was conducted in an endeavour to ascertain the names and ranks of the Transport Unit (Lt-Cmdr Haraguchi Sumiji) of HQ No 1 Naval Base Force. It has been discovered that this unit had no direct contact with the Sea

Transport Unit. Nishiro was unable (or unwilling?) to supply the names of any personnel of Lt-Cmdr Sumiji's section. He recalls hearing in December 1943 that an enemy aircraft had crashed into the sea approx 8 000 metres from Buin and that the pilot had been captured and later taken to HQ No 1 Naval Base Force. This airman was held in custody for a period of between ten to twenty days, after which he was transported to Rabaul by a small escort vessel. Nishiro's informant was 1st Class Seaman Toyoji Saito of No 1 Sea Transport Unit.

EBERY   Interrogated Masani Hirahata and Munetoshi Mitsui, former petty officers and members of the command platoon of 6th SNLP. Hirahata was able to recollect the name of Miyoshi – full name unknown (FNU), a former warrant officer and senior NCO of No 1 Platoon of the 2nd Company of the 6th SNLP. Mitsui's interrogation elicited little information of importance. The knowledge that Miyoshi (FNU) was a member of No 1 Platoon in February-March 1943, should prove valuable in establishing and/or corroborating the facts surrounding the death of Ebery. Hirahata also relates seeing an airman prisoner at HQ No 1 Naval Base Force, sometime in 1943 or 1944. He heard he was a pilot who had bailed out of his burning aircraft over Buin. Hirahata failed to supply a military or biographical history of the captured airman and was unable to furnish any information concerning the prisoner's subsequent disposition.

File 158A DUTCH NEW GUINEA:

I have submitted a request for the interrogation of Japanese personnel stationed in or around Manokwari, Saoekorem and Warena airstrips. Investigations will be pursued into the fate of Allied pilots of Kittyhawks A29-821 and A29-901 and in the case of Kittyhawk A29-464. All airmen are now known to have bailed out above the areas aforementioned. Their disappearance is baffling and in this regard I am encountering a wall of silence. Presuming the worst, I can only fear they were instantly beheaded upon capture by Japanese soldiers or the Kempetai, of whom their identities remain unknown.

File 125C   Executions in the Tarlena and Buka areas:

Interrogated former Captain Kazusuke Inoue, a member of the 12th Shipping Engineer Regiment at Rabaul. He states that the HQ and majority of personnel of his regiment were situated in the Rabaul area. He adds that sometime between June and December of 1943 and after plans to invade New Zealand were seriously compromised by the Battle of the Coral Sea, a force numbering approximately five officers and 200 ORs (Ordinary Ratings) was despatched to Bougainville to strengthen the garrison forces there. This detached force came under the jurisdiction of the 17th Army as far as operations, movements and personnel were concerned. Information concerning the Rabaul area was elicited and should be of some value in the investigation of war crimes committed in that area.

File 125D   Execution of Father Weber in Arigua area, Easter, 1945:

I have now interrogated many suspects in this case, but feel certain that the answers I am receiving are a well rehearsed and confusing litany of lies. The conflicting accounts of Father Weber's demise, and to a pattern, suggest collusion and a cover-up. I will persist in this investigation until I achieve a breakthrough.

(A) Interrogated former Kempetai Sergeant Hajime Hino of the 6th Field Military Police Unit in Bougainville. Hino states that he was captured by natives at Vito three weeks before hostilities ended, and handed over to the custody of an Australian Military Police Unit at Torakina in early August 1945. Hino is in addition to the Weber mystery, being interrogated about the execution of a missionary at Kieta at about December, 1943 (Refer File 125B). Both interrogations of this likely suspect are continuing.

File 125F   Executions of Roach and Ebery:

(A) I interrogated and obtained a sworn statement from Haraguchi Sumiji, the former shipping officer of HQ No 1 NBV (Naval Base Force) at Buin. Sumiji claims that he made two trips north of Kieta in February 1943. The first trip was a combined operation in which he acted as an interpreter. The expedition comprised personnel of the 6th SNLP from Buin and soldiers from the Marine Garrison Unit at Kieta. The object of the operation was to capture several Europeans and wireless transmitters supposedly located in the hills to the north-west of Numa-Numa. The information regarding these coast-watchers was taken seriously by HQ No 1 NBF. Upon arrival at Numa-Numa by barges, the force split up into two components (Buin and Kieta) and on arrival at the designated enemy site, discovered only six or seven camp beds and no Europeans. The two components returned to Numa-Numa and made only one short stop in the Arigua area – for the purpose of an airfield construction survey. The expedition then returned to Kieta and the following morning, the Buin component returned by barge to Buin. One week later, Sumiji was ordered by Lieutenant Migita, the adjutant of No 1 NBF, to procure some roofing material (iron galvanised) and furniture for the barracks of personnel attached to the aforementioned headquarters. This raiding party comprised Garrison Unit soldiers and fifteen (Korean civilians) construction unit personnel. This party made three landings, one at Numa-Numa, one at Asitavi Mission and the last one in the Arigua area. Sumiji claims that no expeditions inland were made. After seizing furniture that was deemed satisfactory from buildings near the coast, the party returned via Kieta to Buin.

(B) Future interrogations will be launched into this picnic style and harmless foray as described by Simiji, particularly the activities of the Kieta Marine Garrison Unit who were one of the three parties landed separately. Probably and as an inducement for local natives in their area to cooperate, four of them were summarily beheaded but not to help with gathering roofing iron, but rather, to help in locating the whereabouts of the elusive European coast-watchers and possibly, equally elusive Allied airmen. It is known that Roach was captured in this area on or about the date coinciding with the unwarranted execution of four natives which coincidentally, occurred at the time of the second expedition to ostensibly obtain roofing iron and furniture. I feel sure that Sumiji believes he has deceived me. At the next interrogation I shall disabuse him of this notion.

J.G. Godwin (Capt.)
Investigating Officer
2nd Aust.War Crimes Section
7 and 14 May 1948

[AUTHOR'S NOTE:] Regrettably the continuity of the War Crimes Reports in this section has been disadvantaged because of the sheer volume available. To include every report would require an encyclopedia. Hence it was found necessary to reduce this documentation from 930 reports – many of them extensive, to a sample number that would suffice to confirm authenticity and to inform the reader.

JGG:BMF REPORT OF INVESTIGATING OFFICER
(Capt. J.G. Godwin)
File 125F   Executions of Roach and Ebery:
A request for an interview with former Petty Officer Torao Eno of the 2nd Company, 6th SNLP has been initiated. The subject Japanese is alleged to have crossed the river at the same time as Ebery.
File 125H   Execution of Sgts Martin, Florence and Cpl Yates at Maika:
The interrogation of former Major Toichi Ito, the CO of the 17th Army Kempetai Unit on Bougainville, is now completed. The sworn statement obtained from him has three appendices. The attachments are plans of (A): The headquarters area at Maika. (B) Exhum- ation and cremation sites of the remains of the three victims. (C) Burial site of the ashes. Map #3394, Kahili Drome, 1/25:000 series, was produced and shown to the subject Japanese who marked with an asterisk the place where he believes the ashes were buried. The grid and geographical coordinates are respectively as follows.

35953652
E.   155 45' 13"
S.   06 43' 31"

Eno's description of the burial site of the ashes is as follows. Approximately 550 metres to the north of the Kempetai HQ and near a tree fern. The skulls were fragmented with rifle butts, then, the crushed bones and ashes were wrapped in a native flax mat and buried at a depth of three feet close to a tree fern. (NB) This tree was located at a place about seven metres away from the right bank of a small stream and was the only one of its kind in the vicinity. I feel moved to mention Toichi Ito's astonishment at our determination to locate the grave and to again exhume the remains and provide Christian burial at an Allied War Graves cemetery. Clearly and to his twisted perception, the living were of little consequence, but the dead, of no importance whatsoever. An Arrest Order for former Lieutenant-Colonel Kiyoshi Miyakawa of HQ 17th Army has been prepared and forwarded to the appropriate authorities.

File 125C   Execution in the Tarlena and Buka areas:

(A) Interrogated former Naval Lieutenant Akira Saka, the ex-CO of the 211th Naval Civil Engineering Corps. This unit was situated between Tarlena and Porton in Northern Bougainville. Saka stated that he heard that the 57th Naval Guards Force commanded by Captain Nikichi Kato (executed at Rabaul) had captured Allied airmen on at least three different occasions. The first occasion was about January 1944, but he claims not to have heard of the nationality or number of prisoners. The second occasion was in May or June 1944, when he heard that an enemy airman had parachuted down near Bonis Airfield and had been captured whilst hiding in an air-raid shelter. He thinks that the nationality of the airman was American. After the termination of hostilities and whilst awaiting repatriation to Japan from Fauro Island, he heard that Captain Nikichi Kato had been removed from their midst because of a suspicion that he, Kato, had disposed of (executed) some Allied airmen. The revelation that former Lieutenant Honda (FNU) was the 2nd in charge of area operations and intelligence officer of the 57th Naval Guards Force, was very interesting since by the brief description of him as given by Saka he would appear to be identical with

Lieutenant Seiiji Honda who was the CO of the Kieta Marine Garrison Unit about the time Francis Roach was murdered. Seiiji Honda will be called for interrogation at a later date.

File 125D   Execution of Father Gerard Weber at Arigua, Easter, 1945:

Reinterrogated and obtained a sworn statement from the former cipher officer of HQ 38th Brigade, Lieutenant Kunihiko Yoshitake. He now (remarkably) recalls receiving a signal from HQ 17th Army, ordering the execution of Father Weber and believes that after decoding it he hand-carried the instruction to Major-General Kisao Kijima, the General Officer Commanding the 38th Brigade. He remembers receiving this signal in February or March 1945. He added that in either March or April 1945, he received for transmission to HQ 17th Army, a message stating that the missionary had been executed. Yoshitake states he received this message from Staff Officer Wakamatsu. He can't recall attending the secret conference to establish a conspiracy of deceit about Weber's execution at the 38th Brigade HQ after the cessation of hostilities. (Observation). In this denial I am sceptical.

File 125F   Executions of Roach and Ebery:

A memo covering the investigation into the death of Thomas Ebery has been forwarded to the Prosecution Division.

Files 150 & 150/1   Execution of F/Lt Moody and F/Sgt Aitcheson at Idore, November 1944:

Interrogated and obtained a sworn statement from former Colonel Kasusato Hojo who was the 2nd in Command of the Medical Section of HQ 2nd Army at Manokwari and Idore. He states that on the evening of the 8th day of either October or November 1944 he left Idore for Babo in the company of the Chief-of-Staff of the 2nd Army, Lieutenant-General Shikao Fujitsuka. Captain Suzuki (FNU) of HQ 2nd Army, also accompanied them. He is positive that the day of their departure was the 8th, but is not sure whether it was October or November. Hojo substantiates Gen Fujitsuka's earlier testimony in regard to the latter's state of health. This interrogation was conducted with a view to ascertaining the actual date of the Chief-of-Staff's movement to Babo and the state of his health prior to his departure. Suzuki (FNU), when his surname is established, will be called for interrogation.

File 125F   Investigation: Roach and Ebery:

Interrogated Torao Eno, a former superior petty officer and member of No 1 Platoon of No 2 Company of 6th SNLP at Buin. Eno was a member of the road inspection party that used Mr Thomas Ebery as a guide. Eno stated that he was crossing the river at the same time as Ebery slipped and lost his footing. In an instant he was swept away by the fierce current. Eno alleges that upon reaching the opposite bank, SPO Hatsumi Ihara asked if anyone would go after Ebery. Eno claims that he volunteered to do so as he was a good swimmer. After stripping himself of weapons, pack, etc, he dived into the river after Ebery. He stated that he swam after Ebery for a distance of eighty yards, but due to the swiftness of the current he was unable to close the distance. He claims to have lost sight of Ebery's head at a bend in the river at which point he decided it was useless and too dangerous to continue the rescue attempt. Eno added that the reason why it was dangerous was the fact that the surface of the river was dotted with protruding boulders. While attempting to rescue Ebery he never managed to get closer than fifty yards.

(A) No evidence substantiating the following points was elicited.

(B) That Ebery was relieved of his walking stick.

(C) That the marines and natives were prevented from saving Ebery.

(D) That the marines had bayonets fixed to their rifles during the crossing of the river.

[Observation]. I am impressed with Torao Eno's frank and open demeanor. Usually I become sceptical at such detailed testimony supporting loss of life. Therefore, I am of the opinion that Torao Eno is an honest witness and may well deserve a commendation for risking his life to save another.

(E) This investigation concerning Ebery's confirmed death by drowning is now considered closed. There is no further suspicion or tangible evidence to support a charge against any member or members of the Japanese road inspection party.

File 125H   Execution of Sgts Martin and Florence and Cpl Yates at Maika, 1943. Former Kempetai Captain Hiroshi Fukaya has now been interned in Sugamo Prison, Tokyo. His trial date has yet to be set.

Former Lieutenant Colonel Kyoshi Miyakawa was mistakenly given his freedom and despite calls for him to return for questioning, is clearly evading apprehension. It is probable the underground are helping him to evade arrest.

File 125L   The 'Good' Murder:

Former Commander Takemi Shimazui, the 23rd Destroyer Division Commandant has been called for interrogation. Information concerning Japanese naval vessels operating around the northern end of Buka Island in March 1942, has finally been obtained from official Japanese sources.

> J.G. Godwin (Capt.)
> Investigating Officer
> 2nd Aust.War Crimes Section
> 13, 20 and 27 August 1948

JGG:BEJ   WEEKLY INVESTIGATION REPORT: 22 July 1949 (Capt. J.G. Godwin)

File 151V   SOUTH BURMA

File 151W   Executions of Australian POWs at Tavoy, Mergui, Victoria Point

File 151X   South Burma mid-1942

Commenced the reinterrogation of former Captain Hirayasu Shiina who was the OC 3rd Company at Tavoy at the time of the execution of eight Australian prisoners of war. Shiina who is presently confined in Sugamo Prison, was previously interrogated by the British authorities at Singapore about the above atrocity but was released from custody for lack of evidence and a plea of innocence. Shiina has been closely questioned concerning his knowledge and participation in the execution of the prisoners. This interrogation has also elicited the certain complicity of Shiina and the arrangements made by him for the carrying out of this execution. Before this interview was adjourned, questioning had reached the stage where the eight Australians were being lined up, etc. preparatory to their being shot to death by firing squad.

File 151W Resumption of investigation into Tavoy atrocity. South Burma:

Interrogated former Captain Hirayasu Shiina who was named as being the officer commanding the firing squad by Australian witnesses including Brigadier Varley; the latter being compelled to attend the execution. The eight Australians had been marched to an area with eight waiting poles. Shiina avers that while the prisoners' hands were bound behind the poles he took particular care to instruct the firing party to aim for the hearts of their nominated targets. At such close range – fifteen yards – the execution would be accurate, merciful and swift made all the more certain by the placing of small white cards in close position to their hearts.

Shiina confirms Brigadier Varley's testimony that all of the Australians refused blindfolds, preferring to stare straight ahead at the firing squad. Immediately prior to the order to 'fire' Brigadier Varley and his adjutant, who was also ordered to witness the execution, snapped to attention and saluted the condemned prisoners. Shiina avers that following the order to fire he unholstered his pistol with the intention of delivering a coup de grace to any prisoner remaining alive. However one volley had been sufficient. The eight Australians had slumped forward and remained in a stooped lifeless position tied to their poles. After walking along the line of executed prisoners and satisfied that they were all dead, Shiina stated that he then reholstered his pistol.

Shiina then went on to detail the removal of the bodies from the poles and their immediate burial in a waiting mass grave at the cemetery adjacent to Tavoy Airfield.

COMMENT

This investigation will continue as others are involved in this major atrocity.

J.G. Godwin (Capt.)
Investigating Officer
2nd Aust.War Crimes Section
22 July 1949

File 151G   Weekly Investigation Report: 21 September 1949
151H   OPERATION PARIT SULONG

168 (1) Completed the interrogation of former Captain Shoichi Nonaka who held the position of personal aide to the GOC Konoe Division, Lieutenant-General Takuma Nichimura at the time of the Malayan Campaign. Nonaka admitted to having been a member of the convoy (HQ Konoe Division) that stopped at Parit Sulong in the late afternoon of 22 January 1942. According to Nonaka he and Lt-Gen. Nishimura were travelling in the same vehicle and upon stopping at Parit Sulong he, Nishimura and the Chief of Staff, Colonel Imai, and other HQ officers alighted from their respective vehicles and walked over towards some buildings on the right-hand side of the main road. About half-way there the said party was met by a junior officer (a 2nd lieutenant, name unknown) who reported directly to Lt-Gen. Nishimura. Nonaka states he is unable to recall the full details of this officer's report; however, he does remember him saying that a great number of prisoners had been taken during the battle for Parit Sulong and that most of them were confined in a large wooden building which he pointed out. After finishing his report this said officer led the GOC and accompanying officers towards the building identified. On arrival at the building Nonaka noticed about six or seven wounded Australian soldiers in various postures near the steps leading up to a wide verandah. He also recalls seeing the bodies of many dead Australian soldiers scattered about at differnt places in front of this building. Among the dead were some Indian soldiers.

(2) Nonaka then recounted how he, Lt-Gen. Nishimura, Colonel Imai and the officer-in-charge of the prisoners

climbed onto the verandah and peered through one of the building's two open doors at the mass of wounded POWs confined therein. After this short inspection had been made, the said party retraced their steps and rejoined the other HQ officers in front of the building. Nonaka stated that Lt-Gen. Nishimura turned and gave him the following oral order.

(3) 'Instruct the officer-in-charge of the prisoners to execute (Shobun Seyo) all the prisoners by firing squad. Kill them all.'

No sooner had Nonaka acknowledged this order than the Chief of Staff, Colonel Imai gave him the following additional order.

(4) 'The bodies of the prisoners are to be cremated on completion of the execution and all traces of their disposal obliterated.'

Nonaka confesses to having relayed these two orders to the officer concerned, following which and whilst walking back towards the parked vehicles, Lt-Gen. Nishimura directly ordered SO Supply Major Eisaku Morioka to remain behind and supervise everything. Former Colonel Kamejiro Imai has previously been requested for interrogation; however, the Japanese authories have officially reported this former senior officer as having died from sickness in Siberia on 22 March 1947. Thus and despite our request for official Soviet verification, of which none has been forthcoming, further inquiries to the Soviet authorities reveal the following.

(5) Colonel Kamejiro Imai had never been listed as a prisoner of war of the Soviet Union. His alleged captivity and death by sickness is completely unknown. This investigation officer discounts quite frankly the truthfulness or veracity of the notification received from 'Japanese Army Records', and is more inclined to believe the Soviet authorities as an impartial source of honest information.

[Observation]: At most times and whenever a Class A war criminal is finally identified, particularly if formerly a powerful and influential senior officer, we invariably encounter subtle obstruction to their apprehension by means of deviousness and duplicity. For a variety of dubious circumstances too numerous to mention, the coincidences of major war criminals effectively disappearing is no accident, but when such vanishing acts are unaccountably but officially confirmed without investigation by Japanese authorities, one is tempted to suggest the word, collusion. It is hard to avoid being cynical. This charade happens too often with regard to officially sanctioned Japanese fabrications. The second part of this priority investigation should shortly be concluded and entered into Official Weekly Reports as quickly as possible. I have only to add my disappointment that the powers that be (Legal and Prosecution Division) do not propose to proceed with a fresh prosecution against Lt-Gen. Nishimura, a most evil man. Perhaps the sheer horror of what he ordered against defenceless and wounded Australian prisoners, particularly the large number, would shock the world.

> J.G. Godwin (Capt.)
> Investigating Officer
> 2nd Aust.War Crimes Section
> 21 September 1949

JGG:BEJ   REPORT OF INVESTIGATING OFFICER
(Capt. J.G. Godwin)
File 151G   Massacre of Prisoners of War, PARIT SULONG 1942
(1) Interrogated former Major Fukashi Hinokuma who had a grim story to tell and which was recounted to him in full detail over a meal by Staff Officer: Supply, Major Eisaku Morioka. It was Morioka who was detailed by the GOC to remain at Parit Sulong and supervise the mass execution. This is what was revealed.

(2) 'One hour before dark, the prisoners were ordered to make their way to an assembly point at the rear of a row of damaged shops. Those who were unable to walk were carried by the walking wounded, while others, also walking wounded, were made to carry the bodies of their dead comrades who were laying in the dust. The pretext used to entice the Indian and Australian prisoners to drag themselves to what was in effect, the designated execution site, was medical treatment, water

and food. Concealed within the rear rooms of damaged shops, three squads of executioners waited behind tripod mounted heavy machine-guns. When all of the prisoners had arrived at the assembly point and were either sitting or laying prone, depending on the seriousness of their wounds, the machine-guns began their wicked thumping chatter of death. Such concentrated machine-gun fire cut swathes of carnage from three different points, enfilading the closely grouped prisoners, chopping flesh and limbs to pieces. When cries of pain and shock were silenced, so were the machine-guns. Morioka mentioned to Hinokuma that seven prisoners had to be bayoneted despite the concentrated gun-fire. They had still showed signs of life. Funeral pyres were quickly expedited per the simple method of collapsing six abandoned shops with mortars and hand grenades, following which 161 bodies were carried in an endless stream to the timber-dry debris and placed in piles where the engulfing flames would consume most efficiently. A considerable amount of paraffin obtained from captured forty-four gallon drums and some sixty gallons of gasoline, were then splashed and spilled over and around the corpses. To ensure total incineration, tyres and demolition material from the walls and verandahs of the collapsed buildings, were also heaped onto the quite large pyres. At 8 pm, according to Major Hinokuma and as related by Major Morioka, he, Morioka, gave the signal for everyone to stand well clear. Then a flaming torch was thrown. The demolished buildings erupted with a whooshing cataclysmic roar. In the event four adjacent dwellings and nine shops burned to the ground before midnight. As told to Hinokuma by Morioka, the stench of roasting flesh permeated the warm night air until the small hours of the morning when the fierce flames had reduced to mere flickers above piles of grey-white ash. But even then, radiated heat from concealed red hot embers could be felt twenty yards away. Without any doubt, the mass cremation, like the execution, was an outstanding example of efficiency. Morioka told Hinokuma it was 4 am before he snatched a few hours sleep. He awoke at a little after 10 am and stepping outside into the hot morning sunlight he stared across at where the shops had stood. Nothing remained except scattered mounds of grey ash little more than two feet high. Clearly, incineration had been total. After enjoying a good breakfast and self-satisfied at the report he would be able to give the Chief of Staff of HQ Konoe Division, now temporarily quartered at Batu Pahat, he left Parit Sulong at about midday and was driven south to rejoin HQ Konoe Divison.' This interrogation will continue as a high priority.

> J.G. Godwin (Capt.)
> Investigating Officer
> 2nd Aust.War Crimes Section
> 7, 14, 21, 28 October 1949

JGG:BEJ   REPORT OF INVESTIGATING OFFICER
(Capt. J.G. Godwin)

File 152   Bangka Island Atrocities, 17 February 1942:

Former Ldg Private Tanemura Kiyoshi of the 2nd Platoon, 2nd Company, Orita Butai, was called for reinterrogation concerning the fate of Mr V.G. Bowden (Australian Trade Commissioner, Malaya) on Bangka Island on 17 February 1942. Kiyoshi admits that his platoon took part in the successful assault on the lightly defended island and that some Europeans (amended to all) were captured, including a number of Australian nurses. Kiyoshi displayed a most worried attitude that was not lost on this investigating officer. His answers to questions were evasive and devious, similar in context to an earlier interrogation conducted by Sergeant A.H. Weston. Kiyoshi reluctantly admitted that after the male Europeans were rounded up, there were some rifle-clubbing incidents inflicted on the prisoners as necessary punishment for disobeying the orders of their guards. He strongly denied being one of the guards, alleging in his own defence that he hadn't quite recovered from an earlier attack of malaria and had sought permission from his immediate superior NCO

Sergeant Furukawa (FNU) to rest in the shade of some trees. This was granted and because the island's defenders had ceased all resistance he had no qualms in repairing to a quiet area for recuperation. This investigating officer felt that Kiyoshi was concocting an alibi but for the purpose of elucidating the truth, accepted his testimony without demur. Kiyoshi went on to say that once closeted in a thicket he dozed off into a fitful sleep and only awoke as early evening shadows began to lengthen. Feeling somewhat refreshed he emerged from his privacy to rejoin members of the platoon after reporting his recovery to Sergeant Furukawa. Kiyoshi admitted to hearing screams coming from nearby houses situated between groves of paw-paw and mango trees, and was told by platoon members that some officers and NCOs were pleasuring themselves (raping) some Australian nurses. He was told that after the officers and NCOs were satisfied it would be the platoon's turn. Kiyoshi states that he then asked about the male prisoners and was told that they had been beheaded and were buried adjacent to a deserted Chinese store. When asked if he could recall seeing any particular European of importance like the Australian Trade Commissioner (Mr V.G. Bowden) among the group of male prisoners, Kiyoshi shook his head and declared that all the Europeans looked the same to him. When asked if he knew why the male prisoners had been executed he shrugged and answered that only the officers would know the reason, however, as a lowly soldier he could only presume that it was punishment for resisting the Imperial Forces of Japan. Pressed as to the fate of the nurses he volunteered the information that the following morning after the nurses had been raped inces- santly he heard that they had been herded down to the beach and there forced to bathe (ostensibly) whereupon a machine gun opened fire and disposed (executed) them. Kiyoshi strongly denied participating in the decapitation of the male prisoners (by reason of feeling unwell) and claimed that because of his slight indisposition he did not feel inclined to join in the raping incidents during the night with the rest of his platoon. Asked for the names of other NCOs and officers he hedged around and pleaded that as the incidents had occurred more than seven years previous, he could not remember. He did however volunteer the information that most of the platoon, NCOs and officers included, were subsequently shipped to Rangoon, Burma, but on passage their ship was sunk with great loss of life. This investigating officer has corroborative testimony to this effect supplied by the Japanese authorities. Kiyoshi's interrogation will continue, to determine his own complicity or guilt in the above atrocities which he blithely describes as incidents.

File 125F (Disappearance) Changed to Execution of Francis Roach 1943:

Interrogated former Sub.-Lieutenant Nakashima Katsuji and a sworn statement was taken. Katsuji was formerly the officer commanding 3rd Platoon, 2nd Company of the 6th Special Naval Landing Party (SNLP) at Buin and at the time of the subject in question. His sworn testimony contains the most pertinent information yet elicited and extracts from same are as follows.

(A) 'I recall that early one morning in January 1943, I was given oral orders by my company commander, Sub.-Lieutenant Nishida Toichi, to the effect that my platoon was to immediately make preparations for a reconnaissance in a mountain area west of Vito on Bougainville. According to Toichi the reason for this patrol was the fact that two Australian soldiers and an Australian civilian had been reported by natives as sheltering in the area designated by him.

(B) After disembarking at Vito, my entire platoon was guided inland by two local natives. We traversed rough country all night through hilly terrain before arriving at the outskirts of a native village at about dawn the following morning. Both of the guides were absent for about forty minutes and upon returning one of them pointed to a hill approximately 300 metres from the village. I then deployed my platoon in battle formation around the base of this hill, and upon nearing its summit we espied and surrounded a native-built hut.'

(C) Katsuji explains the capture of a European living in this thatched hut. From his description of the captive, it would definitely appear as though he was none other than Mr Francis Roche [Roach] was a prior and inadvertent misspelling. More extracts are as follows.

(D) 'After spending about two hours in this native village we departed with the European prisoner and the two native guides on our return journey to the coast. After we had been slogging for three hours, the patrol rested on my orders near the sandy steeply sloping bank of a small but swiftly flowing stream to prepare our midday meal. I recall that during this march through the jungle I thought about executing the European as my feelings towards him and the two escaped Australian soldiers were very hostile on account of the fact that the enemy (Europeans) wanted to take back what we had rightfully conquered.

(E) It was while eating my midday meal that I finally decided on my own volition to have this Australian killed. After the meal was finished I invited members of the platoon to punish the prisoner for opposing our Emperor and for putting us to so much trouble to capture him. Most of the platoon then fell upon the Australian who was securely tied to a nearby tree. At first he was punched and kicked before bayonet scabbards and rifle butts were used. I had to stop this punishment upon seeing too much blood on the face and body of the prisoner. I feared he might die before being beheaded.

(F) I then ordered 1st Class Petty Officer Nakumara Haruo to decapitate the Australian with my sword. Though severely beaten and after being untied from the tree, the prisoner struggled desperately when told he was going to be beheaded. He was bound more securely before being forced to his knees at the top of a sandy knoll immediately above the stream. The Australian was positioned facing the stream and during a spasm of trembling asked for his life. I felt so angry at having lost many comrades who had died gloriously for the Emperor, I refused. Petty Officer Haruo took up a position on the right-hand side of the prisoner and raised the sword high before bringing the blade down in one forceful stroke. The Australian was beheaded cleanly with his head rolling down the sandy bank into the stream. A member of the platoon nudged the decapitated body with the toe of his boot causing it to tumble down and follow the head into the stream.'

(G) Katsuji claims that when he arrived back at Kieta, he reported Roche's death to both Lieutenant Ashiwara Suotare and Sub-Lieutenant Nishida Toichi. However he adds that as he feared punishment for what he had done without authority, he falsely told them that the prisoner was killed while attempting to escape.

(H) Testimony from two other interrogated members of this platoon substantially corroborates Katsuji's sworn statement, but with the damning appendium that whilst tied to the tree, the Australian was stabbed in the abdomen by a hand-held bayonet and by Petty Officer Haruo. There is now sufficient evidence in hand to confine Katsuji in Sugamo Prison and initiate prosecution procedures against him. An arrest warrant will be issued for the apprehension of former Petty Officer Nakumara Haruo.

OBSERVATION

In the many interviews I have conducted, I have never met any suspect so unrepentant as Katsuji. The interview with him was more like a political statement-cum-confession. The interrogation required was minimal. I fear that in Katsuji's almost defiant testimony is reflected a fanaticism and hatred of defeat. Of remorse I could detect no sign. He appeared to savour reliving the macabre details of the beating Roche endured and the suffering of this helpless prisoner along with his former authority and power over life or death. Recounting the trembling of the Australian – who was no doubt in shock, Katsuji obviously enjoyed relating his refusal to grant Francis Roche mercy. I sincerely hope the court recognises the evil of

Nakashima Katsuji.

File 173   BALLALE ISLAND MASSACRE: 1942

I assisted Sergeant A.H. Weston in the reinterrogation of former Lieutenant-Commander Isamu Miyake who is presently confined in Sugamo Prison. This was a particularly horrific and sadistic massacre – almost satanic, and which is a further indictment on uncontrolled Japanese depravity. Because of its impact upon the sensitivities of normal decent people, it is not proposed to extemporize the genocidal and depraved excesses discovered. It is quite apparent that sexual lust dictated the behaviour of many hate-motivated Japanese soldiers who relished the opportunities to humiliate and ravish prisoners, particularly women and girls of European origin. In this regard and upon sworn testimony supplied, this reprehensible conduct included selected boys held as prisoners in special 'Boys' Camps' in the former Dutch East Indies. Perhaps, General MacArthur was aware of this widespread Japanese conduct and realising the enormity of what would be exposed if investigations proceeded – particularly concerning Imperial Japanese Army Brothels, of which there were hundreds in conquered countries, the order not to continue with investigations into these widespread atrocities was issued to spare Japan the odium and contempt of the world. However, a separate (CC) Report will be filed in the appropriate Prosecution Index. A report on this interrogation, minus the (CC) classification, will be filed by Sergeant Weston in his own weekly summary.

File 85H, 85I, 85K   EXECUTIONS OF AUSTRALIAN AND DUTCH POWs, LAHA AIRFIELD, AMBON ISLAND, February 1942

Considerable time has been consumed in tracking down witnesses who clearly were deliberately evading apprehension because of the nature of this atrocity and their probable involvement. Of four witnesses (suspects) arrested, two are unhelpful and hostile.

File 85H, 85I, 85K   EXECUTIONS OF AUSTRALIAN AND DUTCH POWs, LAHA AIRFIELD, AMBON ISLAND,

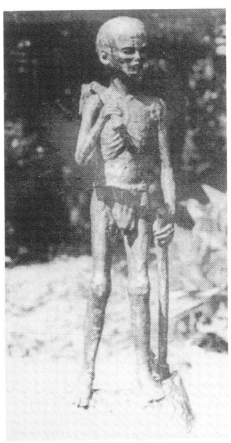

*Statue of 14-year-old European, Ambarawa
Concentration Camp, Middle Java, Indonesia*

4 February 1942

(1) Reinterrogated former civilian interpreter (Dutch and
Malay language) Saburo Yoshizaki of Kure No. 1 SNLP.
Yoshizaki was stationed at Laha Airfield from the morning of
3 February, until the morning of 10 February 1942. In regard to
the first executions at Laha Airfield (9 February 1942),
Yoshizaki admitted he, another civilian interpreter by the

name of Terada Okada, and 1st Class PO Tasuki Yamashita visited the scene of the execution on their own accord, the time of their arrival thereat being about 1800 hours.

According to Yoshizaki there were two prepared graves (holes 'A' and 'B') both circular in shape and of similar dimensions, namely six metres in diameter and about three metres deep. Grouped around the sides of each grave were one or two officers and about twenty-odd marines and soldiers including petty officers and NCOs. He states that just prior to the commencement of the executions, a marine (rank and name unknown) came over to where he and some companions were standing and requested the loan of his sword. Yoshizaki states he loaned his sword to the marine whereupon the latter disappeared among a group of marines standing about hole 'B'. Yoshizaki then described the execution of the first Australian prisoner at grave 'A'; this decapitation being carried out by Warrant Officer Kakutaro Sasaki. He recalls that after the fourth prisoner had been beheaded by individual marines keenly waiting their turn (ranks and names unknown) at grave 'A', several battery torches were procured to light the backs of the necks of each successive victim. After the seventh or eighth Australian had been decapitated at grave 'A', the marine who had borrowed his sword returned it to Yoshizaki commenting that it was blunt and the blade had unaccountably bent when he had beheaded a giant of a fellow. On receipt of his sword and scabbard, Yoshizaki stated he and his companions departed the scene of the killings and returned to their barracks. Yoshizaki denied having witnessed the executions of prisoners at grave 'B' as his attention was concentrated on the macabre drama at grave 'A'. Yoshizaki claims that he learned later that in addition to Dutch mortar unit personnel (about thirty prisoners), fifty-five Australian soldiers had also been beheaded on the night in question.

(2) Concerning the second executions, Yoshizaki states that on his return to Ambon township on 23 February 1942 (he had been absent on interpreting duties at Paso) he heard from, he believes,

1st Class Petty Officer Tasuki Yamashita that between 15-20 February 1942 (exact date not recalled), all the remaining prisoners (Australian) at Laha Airfield had been decapitated, some eighty-odd as related to him by Yamashita. Yoshizaki avers that he was told that this second execution at Laha had been carried out by crew-members of a Japanese minesweeper that had been sunk previously by an enemy mine in Ambon Bay. It was an act of reprisal and retaliation for the loss of their ship.

(3) Reinterrogated former 1st Class Seaman Miyataro Ichio who has been identified as having been present and to have participated in a further mass execution of Dutch and Australian prisoners at Soeakodo in early February 1942. He denied having been present at these executions, claiming to have been suffering from recurring 'malaria indispositions' at that particular time and all efforts to budge him from this dubious explanation proved futile. He was certain that his former Officer Commanding, Warrant Officer Kyusuke Yamashita had named him as being one of the dozen or so marines present at the said executions as he, Ichio, thought that the latter believed him dead and as such would not inconvenience other members of his platoon who did participate.

JGG:BMP REPORT OF INVESTIGATING OFFICER
(Capt. J.G. Godwin)

File 125M   A sworn statement in Japanese characters was obtained from former Lt Yoshiro Tsuda, formerly second in command of a forced labour camp on the island of Sado. This POW camp was the only one on the island and was based at Aikawa. To compound investigative difficulties in this inquiry it has been found that POW Camp 109 at Aikawa was an unlisted labour prison and of which records appear to have been wilfully destroyed.

The following information was extracted from Tsuda after three days of close interrogation at Sugamo Prison.

(A) Yoshiro Tsuda though evasive throughout his interrogation, answered most questions sufficiently helpful to enable this investigating officer to piece together the reason and cause surrounding the disappearance of 387 Allied prisoners of war and including the date of their mass execution.

(B) Tsuda maintains his innocence of complicity in the formulating of superior orders that was designed by higher authorities to appear like an accident. Because of the complexity of this investigation it is deemed best to recount Tsuda's own version of events leading up to the disposal of all the POWs.

(C) 'Tsuda's Testimony'. 'On the morning of 2 August 1945, I was ordered by Major Masami Sadakichi the Camp Commandant, to detail the usual working parties at the nearby mine but with the special instruction to ensure that every prisoner entered the mine. Usually fifty prisoners remained on the surface to empty the rakes of laden steel bins into nearby hoppers.

I pointed out this need to Major Sadakichi but he dismissed my concern with the comment that the mine was no longer viable and would be abandoned later that day. Superior orders decreed that all prisoners of war were to be herded into the deepest point of the mine, some 400 feet. Major Sadakichi further impressed upon me to ensure that the guard detail carried out their duties in normal manner and not to alarm the prisoners.

I was further advised by Major Sadakichi that a demolition detail had set concealed explosive charges inside the mine and at depths of 200 and 300 feet. This task had been carried out during the previous night. After the prisoners had been set to work hewing ore from the marked areas, I was ordered to instruct Sgt Major Mitsunobu Sakamoto, the NCO in charge of the guards, to order their discreet retreat out of the mine. The toiling prisoners were to be left oblivious to their fate.

Between 8.45 and 9 am on the morning of 2 August 1945, all of the guards emerged from the mine tunnel whereupon a number of wheeled ore bins were pushed to the mine's downward entrance and allowed to gather speed into its depths. At 9.10 am and with no further bins to dispose of, a signal was given to blow up the mine. I was watching from a distance of 100 yards and witnessed a rush of smoke and dust from the mine's entrance. While waiting for the smoke and dust to clear, every available guard was set to work dismantling the narrow-gauge steel track and then carrying portions of it into the mine's entrance. By 10.30 am or thereabouts, all traces of the steel track had been removed. From what I can recall, the demolition detail entered the mine to set more explosive charges just inside its entrance. It was while returning to the prison camp that I heard a loud explosion. Looking back I saw an avalanche of rock and earth completely cover where the mine entrance had been.

Knowing that the mine had collapsed in three separate places, I felt certain all the prisoners were doomed. Upon returning to the camp I immediately reported to Major Sadakichi that the mine had been destroyed and all 387 POWs entombed in its depths.'

COMMENT

Because of the lateness of the hour this questioning was discontinued until the following morning.

File 125M EXECUTION OF POWs, AIKAWA, SADO ISLAND, 2 August 1945

(A) Resumed interrogation of former Lieutenant Yoshiro Tsuda, the former second in command of Aikawa POW Camp, Sado. Tsuda was again closely questioned regarding his suspected complicity in the formulating of averred superior orders. He did not deny the Imperial Army Extermination Order of an earlier date that specifically provided for the swift disposal (massacre) of Allied POWs if the home islands were threatened with invasion or Japan with military defeat. Sado Island is the fifth largest island in Japan and only a few miles west of Niigata, Honshu.

(B) It was elicited from Tsuda that all of the Aikawa Camp POWs were European and comprised a mixture of American, Dutch, Australian and British Servicemen who had been transported to the island for slave labour from 1942 onwards. Tsuda claimed that because of the earlier Army Extermination Order he had no misgivings with regard to the disposal of such a large number of prisoners of war. Supporting this explanation

Tsuda pointed out that this Imperial Army Order had not been cancelled so far as Sado Island was concerned. Therefore he, like Major Sadakichi, was merely following superior orders.

(C) Yoshiro Tsuda reluctantly revealed under further close interrogation that following the murder of the POWs and for the next few days, considerable activity took place in dismantling the POW camp and removing all signs of its previous occupancy. Close upon the heels of this atrocity came the dropping of two atomic bombs on Japan and finally, its unconditional surrender.

Tsuda avers in his testimony that immediately following the dropping of the second bomb, all of Aikawa's camp guards and officers received official permission to return to their homes and await Army Transfer Orders. Because of the enormity of this secret atrocity and with the War Ministry's full knowledge, the Imperial Armed Forces Records Section subsequently issued notices purportedly stating prior transfers of all of Aikawa's military personnel to active service in the Kwantung Army. Deceivingly, officers were posted as missing or killed in action.

(D) While this investigating officer seeks authority to proceed with this investigation including an inspection of Sado Island, I have asked Yoshiro Tsuda to pencil a close sketch of the prison camp's former location and particularly the approximate area of the nearby gold mine. In the meantime Tsuda will be held in custody.

> J.G. Godwin (Capt.)
> Investigating Officer
> 2nd Aust. War Crimes Section
> 16 December 1949

OBSERVATION

This deception has endured for well over four years. To launch a full investigation and obtain evidence (the prisoners' remains) is a daunting but necessary task. It could take months with no guarantee of success. Major MacKay opinions, upon General Willoughby learning of this atrocity he could well prohibit any further investigation on the grounds that with Japanese-American reconciliation, it is no longer the time to revive or exacerbate public feeling on such evil.

File 85H, 85I   Execution of Australian and Dutch POWs, Laha Airfield, Ambon 1942

[Continuation of investigating a second massacre]

(1) I have completed the interrogation of former Warrant Officer Keigo Kanamoto, the Officer Commanding (L) Repair and Construction Unit of Kure No. 1, SNLP – Special Navy Landing Party. Kanamoto was the OC during February 1942.

(2) Kanamoto states that on or about 24 February 1942 and whilst stationed at the captured Victoria Barracks at Ambon, he learned from a fellow officer that a further 220 prisoners would be executed later that same day. Upon hearing that volunteers were invited to participate in this forthcoming mass execution, Kanamoto and three of his subordinates who had promptly volunteered, left Ambon by launch for Laha at about 1800 hours that evening. Only he, Kanamoto, was wearing a samurai sword. He recalls that 1st Class Seaman Shikao Nakamura and 1st Class Seaman Teruji Ikezawa were two of the volunteers who accompanied him.

(3) According to Kanamoto he and his said three companions did not arrive at the scene of the executions until about 1900 hours by which time it was almost dark. Several bonfires had been lit and cast dancing shadows on a spectacle reminiscent from the pits of hell.

(4) A large group of Dutch and Australian prisoners of war, all with their arms and hands securely bound behind them and heavily guarded, stood waiting in the shadows to be executed. The punishment site was situated in the same wooded area where the first mass execution of POWs at Laha had been earlier carried out. Kanamoto states that there were two large holes of similar dimension and situated about five metres apart, hereinafter referred to as grave A and grave B.

(5) Grave A was encircled by about thirty marines many of whom were carrying borrowed swords. Among them Kanamoto perceived one officer and a couple of senior NCOs whose names he could not recall. He was able to state posi-

tively that no soldiers or marines stood around grave B.

(6) Kanamoto then provided a harrowing description of what followed. He recalls witnessing the beheading of a young prisoner who shouted desperately and despairingly before being decapitated on the nearest side of grave A, followed seconds later by the beheading of another prisoner on the opposite side of the said grave. The flickering light from nearby bonfires was insufficient to properly illuminate the carrying out of the punishments (executions), consequently battery torches were produced and used to light the necks of each victim.

(7) After about twenty decapitations, curiosity impelled Kanamoto to step forward and peer into grave A. Some corpses were headless but several bodies with heads half-attached were jerking feebly and making faint gurgling moans. Kanamoto avers that a feeling of revulsion mixed with pity swept over him, but he could not interfere in the punishments that had been ordered by the Japanese High Command in the area.

(8) A little time later and with about forty executions carried out, subordinate 1st Class Seaman Nakamura borrowed Kanamoto's sword following which he beheaded four Dutch prisoners in quick succession on the nearest side of grave A. A short time later 1st Class Seaman Ikezawa took Kanamoto's sword and similarly beheaded three more prisoners, this time Australians. According to Kanamoto, Ikezawa then passed his sword to another subordinate (name not recalled) to behead more prisoners on the far side of grave A. Two further decapitations were successful, but on the third attempt that required two sword strokes, a strange sound and sparks concluded the sword's use. Kanamoto claims that he then recovered his sword which, upon inspection by torchlight, was found to be nicked at several places and slightly bent.

(9) After watching a dozen more beheadings and feeling somewhat uncomfortable witnessing such mass butchery, Kanamoto avers that the constant shouts of jubilation from watching marines mixed with ribald scorn as some prisoners begged for their lives, became too much for him. He and his

subordinates made their way to the garrison office (Laha Airfield) where he met Warrant Officer Rinnosuke Fukuda who was the relieving OC of the garrison unit of Kure No. 1, SNLP that was stationed at Laha at that particular time.

(10) Kanamoto avers that he admitted, when asked by W.O. Fukada if he had beheaded any of the POWs, that he had. Conversely and to this investigating officer, Kanamoto pleaded that this false admission to Fukada was to avoid 'losing face' in front of the latter. Kanamoto then stated that he and his subordinates returned to the Victoria Barracks at Ambon by launch at about 2230 hours.

(11) During luncheon the following day, Kanamoto heard that all the POWs (amended to 227) had been punished (executed) and that the incident was not completed until 0130 hours in the ensuing morning. He admitted, to avoid confusion, that though the two massacres paralleled each other at Laha Airfield, the dates were different and so far as the second massacre was concerned, the number of prisoners executed were far greater.

(12) Kanamoto was unable to provide the names of any of the executioners (there were so many of them), except those of his two subordinates; however, he did know that the crew of a destroyed Japanese minesweeper (No. 9) were responsible for slaughtering the majority of the Australian and Dutch POWs as an act of vengeance.

(13) Kanamoto strongly denied the adverse allegations made against him by other surviving members of Kure No. 1, SNLP and contributed such mendacity to their malevolent spite because it was known by them that he had broken the code of silence about the incidents. It is accepted by this investigating officer that Kanamoto is no doubt genuinely correct in his assertion, but the opinion is also held that Kanamoto may be deceitful in his denials of having taken no part in the beheading of prisoners which, by no stretch of the imagination, should be described as punishments or incidents.

(14) It is also noted that Kanamoto answered most questions in a paraphrastic and circumbagious manner. This investigating

officer appends his name to this report for the final time and for reasons known to Lieutenant-Colonel D.L.B. Goslett, Major Williams and Legal Officer, Major A.D. MacKay.

Quod Erat Demonstrandum

J.G. Godwin (Capt.)
Investigating Officer
2nd Aust. War Crimes Section
3, 10 February 1950
Meiji Building: SCAP
Supreme Command Allied Powers
Tokyo, Japan

[Referral: Identified Massacres: Beheadings: Murder, etc.]
Index: 189B, 189J: CC – Ref. 194A (Inter-Allied Investigations).
File BB/189B   31 January 1950.

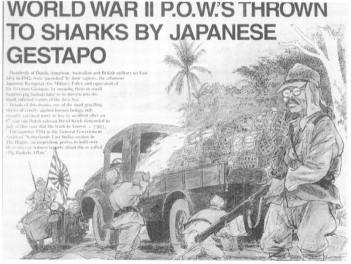

WORLD WAR II P.O.W.'S THROWN TO SHARKS BY JAPANESE GESTAPO

Hundreds of Dutch, American, Australian and British military on East Java in 1942 were 'punished' by their captors, the infamous Japanese Kempetai (the Military Police and equivalent of the German Gestapo), by encasing them in small bamboo pig baskets later to be thrown into the shark infested waters of the Java Sea. Details of this drama, one of the most gruelling stories of cruelty against human beings, only recently surfaced more or less by accident after an 87-year-old Dutch veteran David Kriek demanded in July 1993 that the truth be known. File number 5284 in the General Government Archives' Netherlands East Indies section in The Hague, on inspection, proves to hold over 60 sworn eyewitness reports about the so called 'Pig Baskets Affair'.

APPENDIX

The Japanese Killing Fields

Country	Area	Atrocity	Victims	Number	Year
Ambon Is.	Laha	Beheadings	POWs	312	1942
Andaman Isles	Widespread	Massacre*	Civilians	1 386	1945
Ballale Is.	Ballale	Massacre	Civilians	69	1942
Banga Is.	Serut	Beheadings/ Massacre	Civilians	103	1942
Batan Is.	Buyan	Beheadings	Airmen	4	1944
Borneo	Balikpapan	Beheadings	POWs	9	1942
Borneo	Banjarmasin	Massacre	Civilians	60	1942
Borneo	Loa Kulu	Massacre	Civilians	598	1945
Borneo	Pontianake	Shooting	Civilians	46	1942
Borneo	Sandakan	Massacre	POWs	560	1945
Burma	Widespread	Beheading/ Shooting	POWs	138	1942-44
Burma	Kwai Railway	Slave Labour	POWs	6 960	1942-44
Celebes	Widespread	Massacre	Civilians	213	1942
Formosa	POW Camps	Starving/ Shooting	POWs	170	1943-45
Japan	POW Camps	Sickness/ Brutality	POWs	2 315	1942-45
Java	Widespread	Massacres	Civilians	9 800	1942-45
Malaya	Parit Sulong	Machine Gunning	POWs	157	1942
Maritime	Widespread	Massacres	Ships' Crews	1 460	1942-44
Misool Is.	Binjap	Beheading	Airmen	5	1943
Moluccas Is.	Obi	Beheading	Airmen	3	1943
Neth East Indies	Maritime	Pig-basket Drownings	POWs	1 390	1942-45
New Britain	Widespread	Beheading/ Torture	POWs/ Airmen	388	1942-45
New Guinea	Widespread	Beheadings/ Massacre	Mixed	640	1942-44
New Ireland	Widespread	Beheading	Airmen	17	1943-44
Palau Is.	Palau	Massacre	Civilians	37	1942-44
Philippines	Widespread	Massacres	POWs/ Civilians	19 740	1942-44
Sado Is.	Aikawa	Entombment	POWs	387	1945
Sarawak	Widespread	Massacres	Civilians	290	1942-45
Singapore	Widespread	Massacres	Civilians	13 760	1942-45
Sumatra	Widespread	Massacres	POWs/ Civilians	14 000	1942-45
Sumba Is.	Widespread	Massacres	POWs/ Civilians	144	1942-44
Sumbawa Is.	Widespread	Massacres	POWs/ Civilians	290	1942-45

Tarawa Is.	Tarawa	Beheadings	NZ Coast		
			Watchers	23	1942
Truk Is.	Truk	Beheadings	POWs/		
			Merchant Navy	19	1942-44

* Massacre: Shooting, Bayoneting, Beheading.

COMMENT

As investigations are continuing to reveal more atrocities in the identified areas, the above totals should in no way be considered absolute. Furthero, many areas collectively or individually, such as Banga Island, Dutch New Guinea and the Solomon Islands, as examples, have not yet fully discovered all atrocities committed by the Japanese. There were many instances of isolated executions particularly of Allied airmen that the Allied War Crimes Sections accept will never be solved. This difficulty also applies to deliberate massacres of torpedoed ships' crews where they vanished without trace similar to the disposal of captured Allied personnel who were encased in bamboo pig-baskets by the Japanese, transported out to sea on coastal craft and heaved overboard to schools of sharks.

Atrocities perpetrated at sea and without evidence thereto though known of, are difficult to prove at law without live eye-witnesses and sworn testimony. Fortunately, a few survivors from torpedoed Allied ships were able to confirm, despite previous Japanese denials, that their lifeboats had been rammed and machine-gunned, but they could not identify the Japanese warships or submarines involved. In the instance of wholesale pig-basket drownings and being torn apart by sharks, there were no survivors to tell of these sadistic atrocities. So far as can be determined, 1390 POWs perished by this barbaric method of execution.

Finally, as intimated in the latter part of this chronicle, I have not attempted to correlate atrocities committed in the following areas. China, Hong Kong, Korea, Manchuria or Sakahlin. The task without proper documentation would be impossible, however, sufficient is known about the Rape of Nanking (1937) where 300,000 Chinese were massacred, and Harbin, Manchuria, where 60,000 prisoners lost their lives in biological and germ warfare experimentation, to realise that overall, the Imperial Armed Forces of Japan were responsible for the slaughter of hundreds of thousands of helpless victims wherever they rampaged.

In conclusion and to reinforce previous assessments, it would be no exaggeration to reiterate the appalling fact that so far as accountability is concerned, only one-tenth of Japanese wartime criminality, in an overall perspective has been uncovered. If, as present indicators suggest, investigations and prosecutions are wound down and cease altogether, then, for every ten atrocities committed by the Japanese, nine will escape punishment. The same parallel will apply (by deliberate default) to the lack of investigations into Imperial Japanese Army brothels. Approximately a quarter-of-a-million women and girls – some as young as thirteen – who were forced into sexual slavery, will be denied justice by a man who, for political reasons, chooses to keep the lid on a national scandal that would seriously embarrass his new Japanese collaborators. I refer to General Douglas MacArthur.

Epilogue

To my mind the preceding chronicles in this book reveal much of what has been suppressed and untold during the past fifty years. Courage, fortitude and dedication has countered brutality, mindless evil, sadism and hate. James Gowing Godwin was a rare New Zealander and patriot who fought and suffered for his country and then incredibly, was appointed to investigate Japanese War Crimes after that country surrendered.

From the first page to the last, this chronicle of history – like a flashback in time, compels attention and astonishment, and aye, conveys a warning against complacency. The major regret is that of the hundreds of documented and classified war crimes available, only a few examples are included. The rest perhaps, may be chronicled in a future publication.

I have done my best to present James Godwin's diary, writings and privileged documentation as faithfully parallel as possible to the phraseology and uniquely sincere style of this New Zealander who preferred to call a spade a spade. It is my hope and fervent wish that these chronicles of irrefutable horror should never be lost to history on the premise that a nation which ignores its history, is most likely to repeat it.

James MacKay

Biography

James Godwin was born in 1923 in the Province of Marlborough, South Island, New Zealand. His background was that of a typical country family of English descent who lived quietly and were regular church-goers. He had two sisters slightly younger than himself, but he was the only boy in the family. Godwin spent his formative years in the Marlborough Province and attended the Blenheim Borough Primary School before enrolling at the Marlborough Boys' College where he eventually matriculated with honours. It was his intention to study at the University of nearby Canterbury but with the Japanese surprise attack on Pearl Harbour and the Pacific suddenly plunged into war, he immediately enlisted in the Royal New Zealand Air Force.

In mid-1942 and having just turned nineteen, Godwin received his initial training as a pilot at Woodborne Airport adjacent to Blenheim before being transferred to Wigram Air-base in Canterbury. Being particularly adept at mathematics and quickly learning the skills of flying he was transferred to Canada for advanced training and a possible commission. As a pilot-officer and towards the end of 1943 he was posted to the Fleet Air-Arm, commissioned as a Lieutenant, and underwent intensive training gaining extra skills as an aircraft-carrier pilot. Within two months he received a posting to the British aircraft carrier HMS *Illustrious*. War service in the Indian Ocean followed entailing bombing missions over Japanese occupied Sumatra.

Following a well-earned but short spell of leave in New Zealand during the latter part of January and early February 1944, Godwin prepared to leave the country to rejoin HMS *Illustrious* which was stationed between Ceylon and India

patrolling vital Allied sea lanes in between attacking with its
aircraft nearby Japanese occupied territory. At this juncture the
chronicles in this book cover the following six years.

On 16 February 1950, James Godwin sailed from Japan for
New Zealand and from a country he had no wish to ever return to.
Following his arrival back to his home country and while
enjoying accrued home-leave he spent considerable time
commuting between his home town of Blenheim and the British
High Commission at Wellington. Just prior to being accepted into
the British Colonial Service he was summoned to Government
House at Wellington by His Excellency the Governor-General,
Sir Bernard Freyberg VC. Godwin must have impressed the
Governor, because and as a consequence, the following week his
appointment to the British Colonial Service was confirmed.

Godwin served in Malaysia, British Borneo and Sarawak for
the next twenty-five years before being posted to Christmas
Island as Colonial Administrator where he remained before
retiring from the Colonial Service in the mid-1980s. He returned
to New Zealand to finalize the disposal of some property before
proceeding with his wife whom he had met and married in Kuala
Lumpur years earlier, to Sydney, NSW, Australia. There he
bought a retirement bungalow in an outer suburb and with his
wife, settled down to a placid relaxed lifestyle.

The classified documentation that he had spirited out of Tokyo
in 1950 and without the knowledge of General Douglas
MacArthur, was removed from its long concealment in New
Zealand and also shipped to Sydney. One of the first tasks
Godwin set himself was to rewrite the content of his frayed and
yellowing diary as well as tackling the chore of condensing and
chronicling large amounts of Meiji Building inter-office memorandums, directives and exchanges before launching into redocu-
menting copious amounts of war crimes files. Sadly, barely a
quarter of this self-imposed task was completed when unexpectedly, he suffered a stroke.

Godwin never recovered full health nor the proper functional
use of his limbs. Despite devoted attention from his wife and

frequent visits by his sisters from New Zealand he gradually lost interest in his wartime and post-war chronicles as the first symptoms of Alzheimer's disease became noticeable. A further affliction that was becoming pronounced was an irregular spasm of neck jerking and head-shaking.

Following specialist medical examinations combined with head and neck X-rays. the medical specialists found that parts of the bone structure of Godwin's skull along with the neck spinal vertebra were crushed and mishapen. To their practised eyes the bone depressions of the skull were indicative of numerous blows to the head by heavy objects. This clinical diagnosis also applied to the neck vertebra. Godwin's war service record was shown to the specialists by his wife and upon learning that he had been a prisoner of the Japanese during World War II along with the information by his wife that her husband had often referred to being clubbed with rifle-butts by his captors, the specialists shook their heads knowingly; Godwin's bone damage was permanent and irreversible.

During the early 1990s, Godwin's Alzheimer's disease and head-jerking continued to deteriorate. By 1994 his memory recall was non-existent and in 1995 he no longer recognized his wife or sisters. He died peacefully at the end of Anzac week commemorations in 1995, at Sydney, aged seventy-two.

Index

A
A-Bombs 83, 171, 187, 252
Admiralty Islands Group 140
Ah Chee, Dr 132
Aikawa 220, 249, 251-2
Aitcheson 224-6, 233
Akinaga, Lieut-Gen 113
Alexandra Hospital Massacre 99, 122
All Blacks (NZ) 126
Allied Military Intelligence 213
Allied Powers 171-2, 202, 204, 216-8
Allied Prisoners of War 177
Allied Translation Intelligence Service
  (ATIS) 203
Allied War Crimes Investigations 129-
  31, 222
Allied War Graves Cemetery 232
Ambon Bay 249
Ambon Island 246-8
Ambon township 248
America 73, 146, 163, 168
American democracy 177
Amnesia Syndrome 152
Andaman Islands 209
Anzac 126, 191
Anzac Day 164
Aoba (Japanese Heavy Cruiser) 42
Arafura Sea 165
Arigua 229-30
Arisue, Seizo, Major-Gen 213
Armistice 171
Army Intelligence Service 133
Arnold, Benedict 147, 209
Art Union 218
Article 14 100
Asaka, Prince, Lieut-Gen: Mastermind
  of The Rape of Nanking 185
Asia 83, 92, 129, 172, 183-4, 207
Asitavi Mission 230
Atlee, Clement, PM 100, 132
Auckland (NZ) 163

Australian Army 86, 106, 163, 201
Australian Military Court 140
Australian Mission 105
Australian Occupation Forces 89
Australian War Crimes Commission
  101, 138, 149-50
Authenticated War Crimes
  Documentation 222-56

B
Babo 224
Baga, Kihachi 103
Ballale Island Massacre 246
Banga Island 241
Barr, Allen, F/Sgt 2, 41
Barretts Reef (NZ) 87, 165
Baron von Willoughby 213
Bataan 122
Bataan Death March 99, 123-4
Bataan Peninsula 123
Batavia 41, 45-6, 57, 61
Batu Pahat 241
BBC 1, 4
Behar, MV 1-9, 11-13, 15-16, 19-22,
  45-6, 49, 55, 60, 68-72, 80-1, 198
Bellert, Flying Officer 224
Belsen 184
Benge, R., Sub-Lieut 2, 41, 46
Berlin 172, 185
Besikama 173
Biological and Germ Warfare Centre
  138, 145, 162, 180, 184, 197
Blakang Mati 131
Blenheim 86, 261
Blenheim Borough Primary School 261
Bombay 1, 4-5
Bonis Airfield 232
Borneo 148, 167
Bougainville 105-7, 113, 222, 223-5,
  229, 231

Bowden, V.G., Australian Trade Commissioner 241-2
'Boys' Camps' 246
British Admiralty 86
British Allied Intelligence 189
British Borneo 167
British Colonial Service 134, 201, 218, 262
British Empire 150
British High Commission 262
British Liaison Mission 97, 119, 177
British Military Tribunal 138, 149
British War Crimes Section 122, 125, 180
Brothels 184
Brown, R.P.S. F/Sgt 224, 227
Brownlee, Sgt 224
Buckingham Palace 166
Buddhism 159
Buin 226-30
Buka 113, 223, 225, 229
Burakumin 195
Burma 235-6
Bushido 135
Buto Island 110

C

Calcutta 4
Camp Omori 189
Canada 171, 261
Canberra 106, 128
Cannibalism 149-50, 157-8, 162, 184, 211, 223-4, 226
Canterbury 261
Carpenter, Alva C., Col 146
Ceylon 1, 49, 261
Chang Dok Priok Harbour 41, 46, 55
Changi 133
Changi Prison 139
Changte, SS 141
Chief of Allied Intelligence 210, 213
Chifley, Ben, Australian PM 100
China 182, 185, 187, 190, 206, 220, 258
Chinese 185
Chinese Massacres 132, 145
Christmas Island 262
Class 'A' War Criminal 189
Coast-watchers 134, 153, 230
Cocos Island 1
Collingwood 86
Colombo 1
Colonial Administrator 262
Comfort Stations: Brothels 210

Communism 205
Cook Strait 87
Coral Sea 144, 168, 229
Corregidor 122
Crewdson, O., Major 97-8

D

Dai-Ichi Building: Gen MacArthur's HQ 149, 157, 162, 172, 176 180, 183, 189, 201, 205, 210-11, 216-8
Darwin 62, 69
Djakarta 41
Donaldson, Col 91
Dulles, John Foster 100, 183
Dutch 68, 206, 220
Dutch East Indies 246
Dutch New Guinea 224, 226, 228

E

Eastern Europe 206
Ebery 151, 226-31, 233-5
Eisenhower, General 147, 211
Emperor 68, 88, 98-9, 123, 146, 162, 166, 183, 185, 198, 212, 221, 244
Emperor Hirohito 83, 146-7, 162, 180, 182-3
Emperor's Imperial Seal 146
Emperor Meiji 134, 167
Empress-Regnant Gemmyo 160
England 2, 169
Eno, Torao, SPO 231-2, 234
Ereventa 223

F

Far East 148
Fauro Island 232
Fiji 153
Fleet Air Arm 261
Florence, Sgt 231
Formosa 74, 124, 177, 182
Four Big Power Agreement 162
Four Power Command Structure 185
Fraser, Peter, New Zealand PM 153
Fremantle 1, 3
Freyberg, Sir Bernard, Gov-Gen, VC 262
Fujie Giichi 104
Fujitsuka, Shikao, Lieut-Gen 233
Fukaya, Hiroshi, Capt 103, 235
Fukuda, Rinnosuke, W/O 255
Fukumi Butai 173
Fukushima 103, 158
Furukawa (FNU) NCO 242

G
General Field Atrocities (GFA) 184
Geneva Convention 22, 136
Geographical Index 220
Germ Warfare Centre 98, 146, 177,
  184-5, 211, 216
Germany 169, 183, 185, 205, 217
Goa 69
Gods of War 205, 208, 212
Godwin, James Gowing, Captain. As the
  principal character and mentioned on
  almost every page, the need to index
  Godwin is unnecessary.
Good (civilian) 126, 178, 235
Goodwood Park Hotel, Tokyo 90
Goshi, Kosaki, Captain 139
Goslett, D.L.B., Lieut-Col 191, 256
Goto, Major 107
Government of China 162
Government House, Wellington 262
Great Britain 163
Green, Percy, Capt, MN 4, 7, 41, 46, 70
Greymouth, NZ 165
Griffiths, Apprentice, MN 41
Guadalcanal 123

H
Haraiwa, Masuo 224
Harbin 98, 138, 145, 184
Haruo, Magata, Dr 53, 55
Haruo, Nakamura, P/O 244-5
Hattori, Takushiro, Col 214
Hayami, Junichi, Capt 223
Hennessy, Andrew, Sgt 138, 145
Hewson, Ralph, Capt 181, 213
Hijima, Kesao 103
Hino, Hajime, Sgt 229
Hinokuma, Fukashi, Major 239-40
Hirahata, Masani, P/O 228
Hirohito 162, 183, 197-8, 209
Hiroshima 185, 189-90
Hitler, Adolf 147
Hojo, Kasusato, Col 233
Holland, S.G., Sir, PM (NZ) 100
Home-Guard (NZ) 169
Honda (FNU), Lieut 233
Honda, Seiiji, Lieut 233
Hong Kong 98, 115, 129, 141, 147-8,
  177
Honshu 81, 159, 251

Huddart Parker Building 86-7
Hyakutuke, Lieut-Gen 113

I
Ichio, Miyataro 249
Ichiro, Nagayama 157-8
Idore 224-6, 233
Ihara, Hatsumi 234
Ijichi, Takateru 226
Ikezawa, Teruji 253-4
Illustrious, HMS 44, 49, 85, 261
Imai, Kamejiro, Col 137-8
Imperial Institution 185, 198, 205
Imperial Japan 219
Imperial Japanese Army 96, 104, 135,
  142, 177, 185, 187, 210
Imperial Japanese Army Brothels 141,
  162, 212, 216, 246
Imperial Japanese Navy 109
Imperial Palace 108, 166, 183, 197
Imperial Princes 98-9, 162, 184, 205,
  211-2
Imperial Rescript 134-5
Imperial Seal 98, 198
Index (189B) (189J) CC: Ref (194A),
  File BB (189B) 256-8
India 69, 261
Indonesia 131
Inoue, Kazusuke, Capt 229
Intelligence Section, HQ 17th Army
  223
International War Graves Commission
  82
International Zionists 211
Invercargill (NZ) 138
Ishii, Lieut-Gen 146
Ito, Lieut 60
Ito, Suzuki 103
Ito, Toichi 104, 231-2
Itsui, Hiroshi 104

J
J Force (NZ) 163, 165, 212
Jaba River 224
Japan 71-4, 81-4, 87, 100-1, 106, 120,
  125, 134, 142, 147, 168, 182-3, 217,
  251
Japanese Armed Forces 162
Japanese Empire 170
Japanese High Command 145, 254
Japanese Imperial Army 132, 210
Japanese Imperial Family 146

Japanese Imperial Guards 138
Japanese Police 109
Japanese Underground 130
Java 40, 45, 53, 72-3, 79
Johore Bahru 220

K
Kahili Aerodrome 231
Kai Tak Airport 98
Kaino, Denroku 103
Kanamoto, Keigo W/O 253-5
Kanda, Masatane, Lieut-Gen 104, 107, 113
Kanin, Prince, Lieut-Gen, Army Chief of Staff (ACS) 185
Kato, Nikichi, Capt 232
Katsuji, Nakashima, Sub-Lieut 243-5
Kawamura, Benji, Col 191-4
Kawamura, General 139
Keenan, Joseph B. (US Chief Prosecutor) 197-8, 209
Kempetai 64, 77, 118, 134, 137, 139, 148, 223, 227-9, 231-2
Keneko, Capt 107
Kershaw, L/Seaman 41
Kieta 107, 222, 226, 229, 230, 233, 245
Kiirun Fortified Area HQ 181
Kijima, Kisao, Major-Gen 233
Kitamura, Yoshihiro 103
Kitamura, Juchi 103
Kiyoharu, Kamezawa 149
Kiyoshi, Tanemura 232, 241-3
Kobayashi, Lieut 107
Kobe 74, 77
Koepang 173
Konoye, Fuminaro, Prince 185
Korea 187, 190, 196, 220
Korean Conscripts 58, 60, 65
Kowloon 99
Kuala Lumpur 139, 262
Kuni, Prince, Lieut-Gen (Head of Germ Warfare Programme) 185
Kwantung Army 83, 252
Kyoto 160

L
Laha Airfield 246-7, 249, 253-5
Lai, Chou En, Chinese PM 182
Li, Lai Yung, Dr 2, 28, 40-1, 60-1, 71
London 86, 166
Lyttleton (NZ) 165

M
MacArthur, Douglas, General 86, 98, 100, 108, 116, 146-7, 149, 162-3, 177, 180, 183-5, 190, 197-8, 205, 209-15, 226, 246, 262
MacGregor (civilian) 4, 7, 10, 12, 20-3, 29, 34-36, 39, 75-6, 80, 198
MacKay, A.D., Major 216, 252, 256
MacLeod, Bosun, MN 41, 46
MacWeir, Chief Engineer, MN 41
Magata, Isao, Major-Gen 104, 113, 226
Maika 223, 231, 235
Malaya 220
Manchuria 98, 138, 145-6, 177, 179, 180, 184-5, 187, 197, 220
Manila 122
Manokwari 226-228, 233
Manpower Act (NZ) 164
Manus Island 140-1
Mariana Trench 160
Marlborough Boys College 261
Marlborough Province (NZ) 86, 261
Martin, Sgt 231, 235
Mass Sexual Slavery 211
Matsuyama, Masataka 225
Meguro, Tatsuo 104
Meiji Building 90, 143, 149, 150, 154, 159, 167, 178, 180, 194, 202, 208, 217-9, 221, 262
Meiji Dynasty 134, 167
Melbourne 2, 4
Merah Tanah Besar Beach 133
Middle East 144, 169
Migita, Lieut 230
Mill-Hill Fathers 94
Mitsubishi 37
Mitsubishi Heavy Industries 176, 190
Mitsubishi Slave Labour Inquiry 176
Mitsui, Munetoshi, P/O 228
Miyajima 187-9
Miyakawa, Kyoshi, Lieut-Col 103, 232, 235
Miyake, Isamu, Lieut Commander 246
Miyamoto Company 173
Miyoshi (FNU) 228
Moody, DFC, F/Lieut 224-6, 233
Morioka, Eisaku, Major 238-40
Motueka (NZ) 86
Mount Egmont (Taranaki) 201
Mount Fuji 134, 201
Moyra (Godwin's sister) 87, 138
Mukden 146

N
Nagai, Yasuo 103
Nagasaki 187
Nairobi 4
Nakamura, Haruo 104
Nakamura, Shikao 253-4
Nakashima, Katsuji 104
Nara 160
Nattori, Hajime 227
Nauru 138
Nazi Germany 148
Nelson (NZ) 86
Netherlands East Indies 123
New Britain 168
New Caledonia 168
New Guinea 157, 165
New Hebrides 110
New Zealand 2, 5, 40, 47-8, 52, 81, 84, 126-7, 133-4, 136, 138, 144, 148-9, 163, 168-71, 201, 206-7, 212-3, 219, 223, 227, 229
New Zealand Naval HQ 85-6
New Zealand Post and Telegraph Dept 134, 153
Niigata 81, 83, 207, 214, 251
Nishida, Shigemitsu, Sgt-Major 222
Nishimura, Takuma, Lieut-Gen 138, 140-1, 204-5, 208
Nishino, Noboru, 2nd Lieut 107
Nishiro, Toramatsu P/O 227-8
Nonaka, Shoichi, Capt 237-8
Norfolk Island 168
North Africa 210
North Borneo 220
North Korea 182-3, 206
Northern Australia 165
Numa-Numa 107, 222, 225, 230

O
Officers Club (Tokyo) 144
Ofuna 77-8
Oishi, Lieut-Col 139
Okada, Terada 247
Okunoshima Island 190
Orita Butai 241

P
Pacific 13, 83, 92, 153, 158-60, 172
Pacific Islands 134
Palau Island 124
Parit Sulong 141, 208, 237, 239, 241
Parker, Benjamin, Lieut (USAF) 124

Parker, S.C., Lieut 2, 41, 43-44, 46, 68-71
Pascovey, Mrs 4, 27-8, 31, 41
Peace Treaty 212, 215, 217, 221
Pearl Harbour 54, 261
Percival, General 119
Perry, Commodore 199
Pettigrew, Arthur D., Major 125, 129, 133, 143-4
Philippines 123
Phillips, Chief Officer, MN 4-7, 41, 59
Picton (NZ) 87
Ping Fan 145-6, 177, 180, 184, 211
Porton 232
POW Camp 15D 101
POW Camp 109 249
Prosecution Division 203, 208-9, 217, 233
Provosts (MP) 90-1
Pyrmont Wharf (Sydney, NSW) 2

R
RAAF (Royal Australian Air Force) 4
Rabaul 83, 144, 166, 168, 223, 228-9, 232
Radio Australia 1
Rafferty, Major 89, 91-7, 103-9, 111, 119-20, 127-30
Rangoon 243
Rape of Nanking 98, 185-6
Records Section, Japanese Army 108
Rengam (Malaya) 220
Rhio Islands 74
Rinzai Sect 200
Ritchie, Sir Neil M. 138
RNZAF (Royal NZ Air Force) 261
Royal NZ Naval HQ 86
Roach, (Roche) Francis 126, 151, 224-7, 229-31, 233-4, 243-5
Romushu Natives 173
Rorovana 224
Ross, Capt 129-30, 150-2
Rowlinson, Radio Officer, MN 4
Ryokai, Tsugio, Col 103, 172, 226

S
Sabah 148
Sado Island 220, 249, 251-2
Sadakichi, Masami, Major 226, 250-2
Saito, Toyoji 228
Saka, Akira, Lieut 232
Sakamoto, Mitsunobu, Sgt-Major 251

Sakamoto, Sadatoshi, Sgt-Major 103, 223
Sakamoto, Tsutemo, Capt 222
Samurai 151, 155
Sandakan (Borneo) 220
San Francisco Peace Treaty 100, 215
Sasakawa, Ryoichi 190
Sasaki, Kakutaro, WO 248
Sasaki, Takesh 173-6
Soeakodo 249
Schlenker, R/O 224
Scott, Capt 216
Scotts Hotel (Melbourne) 2
Second Australian War Crimes Section 86
Secretarial Pool Office 104, 106, 128, 133, 150, 178
Secretary of State (US) 183
Sendai 158-60
Seppuku 92, 95, 176
Shaw, Mrs 4, 31, 39, 41
Shek, Chiang Kai, Generalissimo 100, 132
Shiina, Hirayasu 104
Shimamura, Nobumitsu, Sgt-Major 118, 223
Shimazui, Takemi, Commander 235
Shimazui, Tashiro, Col 167-71
Shimotashiro, Ko 104
Shinto 159
Shinya, Eguichi, (File 125E) 149
Shirakana, Mitsugu 103
Shoguns 167
Siam 123
Singapore 74, 92, 98, 115, 119-20, 122, 125, 129, 131-3, 138-41, 148, 178
Singapore Health Authorities 131
Sister Craig (Flying Nurse) 224
Snake, The 53, 67-9, 71-6, 80
Somes Island 87
Sojiji 199
Solomon Islands 258
Somerville, Captain 189
Sone, Kyushu Island 190
Sons of Heaven 22, 152
Sons of Satan 30, 35
Soto Sect 199
Sourabaya 62-4, 66, 72
South Africa 127
South American Jungle 172
South Australia 152
South-East Asia 187

South Korea 182
South Pacific 158, 162, 164
South Pacific Hotel 124
Southern Hemisphere 217
Southern Oceania 168
Soviets 211
Soviet Union 83, 182, 206
Springboks 127
Stalin, Josef 132
State of Victoria (Aust) 127
Straits Times (Singapore) 139
Sugamo Prision 92, 103, 105, 110-3, 117, 121, 131, 142, 149, 154, 157, 165, 176, 185, 191, 202, 212, 214, 216
Sugudo, Shitoshi, Ensign 226
Sumatra 40, 257
Sumiji, Haraguchi, Lieut-Cmdr 227-31
Summons, Flying Officer 224
Sundra Straits 40
Sungari River 146
Suotare, Ashiwara, Lieut 245
Supreme Command Allied Powers, (SCAP) 93, 114, 176, 180, 201, 219
Supreme Command HQ, Dai-Ichi Building 149, 176
Supreme Commander 147
Suzuki (FNU), Capt 233-4
Suzuki,Tadashi 103
Sydney (NSW) 2, 86-7, 100
Symmons, Capt, MN 4, 7, 29, 35, 41, 46, 60, 70, 80

T
Taiwan 74, 182
Taiwan POW Camp 181-2
Takasago Volunteers 124
Tamahine, SS 87
Tamaki, Wakichi 103
Tarawa Island 133-4, 153
Tarlena 113, 229, 232
Tate, 3rd Officer, MN 4
Taylor, 2nd Officer, MN 4
Tenekau 222
Terauchi, Hisaichi, Field Marshal 220-1
Territorials (NZ) 169
Teshima, Fusataro, Lieut-Gen 103, 172, 226
The Allied Japanese Conspiracy 116-7
The Emperor: A Living God 135
The NZ All Blacks 126
Third Reich 206, 217
Timor 173

Toichi, Ito, Major 154-6
Toichi, Nishida, Sub-Lieut 243, 245
Tojo, Hideki, Japan's PM 119-20
Tokugawas 167
Tokyo 77, 86, 89, 97, 99, 112, 114,
116, 119, 123, 127, 130, 140, 142,
147-8, 159-63, 166-7, 170, 173, 178-9,
183, 185, 188-9
Tome (Japanese Heavy Cruiser) 41
Tomoyuki, Yamashita, Lieut-Gen 119
Torakina 229
Toothy 47, 49-50, 52, 54-5, 57
Truman, Harry S., USA President 100,
132, 147
Tscheppe-Weidenbach, Karl von 183
Tsuda, Yoshiro, Lieut 249-52
Tsuji, Masanobu, Col 98-9, 122-5, 129,
178, 217
Tung, Mao Tse 182

U
Uchida, Tamekichi 225
Uchiyama 113
Uda, Capt 107
Uehara, Takeshi 225
Underground (War Criminals Haven)
130, 142-4, 172-3, 189, 235
Union Steamship Coy Ltd (NZ) 165
Unit 731 (Germ Warfare) 180, 184,
197-8
United States Army 183
United States of America 100, 203,
207, 218
United States Foreign Policy 183
US Prosecutor's Office 207
US War Crimes Section 108, 111, 112

V
Varley, Brigadier (Aust) 236
Vermilion Torii (Shinto Gateway) 188
Victoria Barracks 253, 255
Vine, P.L., Major, RM 182
Vito 227, 229, 243
Voice of America 101

W
Wahine, SS 165
Wahine, TEV 165
Wakamatsu, Shigeyoshi 104, 233
Wales 127
Wanganella, MV 86-8
War Crimes Files 93, 180, 209, 222-3,
225, 231

War Crimes Investigations 100-1, 107,
197, 201-2, 205, 212-3, 215-7
War Crimes Registry (Singapore) 92
War Crimes Trials (Nuremberg) 148
War Crimes Tribunal 209
War Ministry (Japan) 122, 135, 167-9,
252
Warena Airstrip 228
War Records Division (Japan) 142
War Veterans Underground (Japan) 142
Washington DC 100, 124, 147, 183,
215, 217
Watanabe, Matsuhiro, Sgt 189
Weber, Father (Executed Jesuit Priest)
126, 151, 163, 166, 178, 229, 233
Wellington (NZ) 2, 85-7, 165, 170, 262
Western Allied Powers 162
Weston, Sgt 218, 241, 246
White House 147
Wigram Air Base (NZ) 261
Wild, C.H., Col 98-9, 119-20, 122-3, 129
Williams, Apprentice, MN 41
Williams, Major 128, 130, 143-4, 149-
50, 171-3, 178, 186, 189, 190, 203-8,
216, 256
Willoughby, Charles A., Major-Gen
146, 162, 172, 180, 183-4, 190, 197-8,
209-15, 252
Woodborne Air Base (Blenheim, NZ)
261
World War II 187

Y
Yakuza Gangs 189, 196
Yamada, Sadakichi, Sgt-Major 226-7
Yamashita, Kyusuke, W/O 249
Yamashita, Tasuki, PO 247-8
Yamawaki, Major 107
Yasumura, Keisuke 225
Yat, Tay Koh 139
Yates, Corporal 231, 235
Yellow Peril 149
Yokohama 106, 198-200, 202
Yokoyama, Ichizo 104
Yoshida, Yukio 223
Yoshitake, Kunihiko, Lieut 233
Yoshizaki, Saburo 247-9
Yua, Mitsuomi, Capt 107

Z
Zen Sect 200
Zionists 172